EYEWITNESS HISTORY OF THE CIVIL WAR
War in the East

EYEWITNESS HISTORY OF THE CIVIL WAR

WAR IN THE EAST

Chancellorsville to Gettysburg, 1863

edited by
John Cannan

GALLERY BOOKS

An Imprint of W. H. Smith Publishers Inc.
112 Madison Avenue
New York City 10016

Prepared by Combined Books, Inc.
26 Summit Grove Avenue, Suite 207
Bryn Mawr, PA 19101

Produced by Wieser & Wieser, Inc.
118 East 25th Street
New York, NY 10010

Published by Gallery Books
A division of W. H. Smith Publishers, Inc.
112 Madison Avenue
New York, NY 10016

ISBN 0-8317-3083-8

CONTENTS

PREFACE TO THE SERIES

In preparing *Eyewitness to the Civil War*, the editor has made no effort to attempt a "balanced" presentation. As a consequence, many events are treated from only a Northern point of view, while others have a Southern slant, and still others are seen from two or three different perspectives. The purpose of the work is neither to achieve historical accuracy nor political balance, but to see events as they were experienced and understood by some of the people who lived through them. There will thus be redundancies, contradictions, and errors, not to mention outright falsehoods.

All of the selections appear almost exactly as they did on their original publication, save for the occasional eliding of extraneous materials. Where necessary, the editor has created titles for selections which lacked such. For the most part, he has avoided the inclusion of explanatory notes, confining himself to the insertion of occasional comments in brackets. Where explanatory notes appear in the original, they have been included only when they seemed of particular importance. In addition, the editor has refrained from modernizing the many little differences in spelling, capitalization, grammar, usage and syntax, which have developed since the Civil War. Needless to say, there has been no attempt to impose a uniformity of style. Thus, in *Eyewitness to the Civil War* the participants speak for themselves in their own voices.

Well over a century after its conclusion, the Civil War still remains the gravest crisis in the history of the Republic since the attainment of independence. It was a vast complex struggle which touched the lives of far more Americans than any other war in which the nation has fought. A conflict of momentous import, it still retains an immediate and continuing impact on the life of the nation. The story of the Civil War has been told on numerous occasions and in numerous ways. The literature is enormous, ranging from erudite scholarly tomes to dry official reports, from informative popular histories to vicious partisan tracts. All these have their value. Yet none can ever be entirely satisfactory. After all these years there exists no better way of looking at the Civil War than to see it through the eyes of those who lived through it, the thousands upon thousands for whom the war was a daily reality.

The Civil War was probably the first war in history in which most of the troops could read and write. As a result, there exists an enormous number of firsthand accounts. The range of materials is equally large, from private letters to multi-volume memoirs. These cover everything from the minutia of daily life to serious historical treatments, from amusing anecdotes to vituperative personal attacks. Nothing surpasses such original documents for developing an understanding of the events as they were perceived by the people who lived through them, for the flavor of the times, the emotions of the struggle, the force of the issues, the impact of the events. Such materials have been drawn upon several times already for the creation of a number of anthologies of firsthand accounts of the war, or of particular aspects of it. Yet the amount of material available is so vast, the stories to be told so numerous, that there still remains much material which has not received wide circulation. It was an awareness of this fact which led to the creation of the present series, *Eyewitness to the Civil War*.

CHANCELLORSVILLE

In late January of 1863, Major General Joseph Hooker inherited a demoralized and defeated Army of the Potomac from Ambrose Burnside who had led the force to disaster at Fredericksburg, Virginia, in December of the year before. In a short time, "Fighting Joe" had restored the Federal army into fighting condition, elevated the morale of his troops, and brazenly declared he would defeat Lee and take Richmond in short order. While the Yankee general could afford to make such statements of braggadocio from the safety of his encampment at Falmouth, Virginia, he found it would take more than words to beat the Confederate army even if his statements were backed up by 135,000 men. Engaging the enemy in the woods near Chancellorsville, Virginia, on 2-3 May 1863, Hooker lost his nerve and allowed the Army of the Potomac to record yet another loss at the hands of Robert E. Lee. Though the Confederates managed to win a major victory, the gallant Stonewall Jackson fell with a mortal wound. His presence was sorely missed in the battles to come.

A dejected and demoralized Army of the Potomac lies encamped at Falmouth, Virginia, after the defeat at Fredericksburg.

★★★

FREDERICK L. HITCHCOCK
Hooker Takes Command

A major in the 132nd Regiment of the Pennsylvania Volunteer Infantry, Frederick L. Hitchcock was mustered in as an adjutant of the unit only to find himself in control of a large body of troops with hardly any experience in command. Winning its baptism by fire at Antietam and participating in the action at Fredericksburg, where Hitchcock received two wounds, the regiment went on to fight its final battle at Chancellorsville. After publishing his account of battlefield experiences as installments in a local paper, Hitchcock compiled the articles into a book, War from the Inside, *from which this selection is taken.*

General Burnside was relieved from command of the army on the 26th of January, 1863, and was succeeded by Major-General Joseph Hooker. "Fighting Joe," as familiarly called, was justly popular with the army, nevertheless there was general regret at the retirement of Burnside, notwithstanding his ill success.

That there was more than the "fates" against him was felt by many, and whether under existing conditions "Fighting Joe" or any one else was likely to achieve any better success was a serious question. However, all felt that the new commander had lots of fight in him, and the old Army of the Potomac was never known to "go back" on such a man. His advent as commander was signalized by a modest order announcing the fact, and matters moved on without a ripple upon the surface. Routine work, drills, and picket duty occupied all our time. Some of our men were required to go on picket duty every other day, so many were off duty from sickness and other causes. Twenty-four hours on picket duty, with only twenty-four hours off between, was certainly very severe duty, yet the men did it without a murmur. When it is understood that this duty required being that whole time out in the most trying weather, usually either rain, sleet, slush, or mud, and constantly awake and alert against a possible attack, one can form an idea of the strain upon physical endurance it involved.

The chief event preceding the Chancellorsville movement was the grand review of the army by President Lincoln and staff. The exact date of this review I do not remember, but it occurred a short time before the movement upon Chancellorsville. Owing to the absence of Colonel Albright and the illness of Lieutenant-Colonel Shreve, the command of the regiment devolved upon me, and I had a funny experience get-

Burnside's Mud March. In January of 1862, General Ambrose Burnside attempted to flank Lee's army by having the Army of the Potomac cross the Rappahannock upstream from Fredericksburg. The maneuver ended in an embarrassing fiasco as bad weather turned roads into rivers of mud.

ting ready for it. As a sort of preliminary drill, I concluded I would put the regiment through a practice review on our drill grounds. To do this properly, I had to imagine the presence of a reviewing officer standing before our line at the proper distance of thirty to forty yards. The ceremony involved opening the ranks, which brought the officers to the front of the line, the presenting arms, and dipping the colors, which the reviewing officer, usually a general, acknowledged by lifting his hat and gracefully bowing. I had reached the point in my practice drill where the "present arms" had been executed, and the colors lowered, and had turned to the front myself to complete the ceremony by presenting sword to my imaginary general, when lo! there rose up in front of me, in the proper position, a real reviewing officer in the shape of one of the worst looking army "bums" I ever saw. He assumed the position and dignified carriage of a major-general, lifted his dirty old "cabbage-leaf" cap, and bowed up and down the line with the grace and air of a Wellington, and then he promptly skedaddled. The "boys" caught the situation instantly and were bursing with laughter. Of course I didn't notice the performance, but the effort not to notice it almost used me up. This will illustrate how the army "bummer" never let an opportunity slip for a practical joke, cost what it might. This fellow was a specimen of this genus that was ubiquitous in the army. Every regiment had one or more. They were always dirty and lousy, a sort of tramp, but always on hand at the wrong time and in the wrong place. A little indifferent sort of service could be occasionally worked out of them, but they generally skulked whenever there was business on hand, and then they were so fertile of excuses that somehow they escaped the penalty and turned up again when the "business" was over. Their one specialty was foraging. They were born foragers. What they could not steal was not to be had, and this probably accounts in a measure for their being endured. Their normal occupation was foraging and, incidentally, Sancho Panza like, looking for adventure. They knew more of our movements, and also of those of the enemy, than the commanding general of either. One of the most typical of this class that I knew as a young fellow I had known very, well before the war. He was a shining light in society, occupying a high and responsible business position. His one fault was his good-fellowship and disposition to be convivial when off duty. He enlisted among the first, when the war broke out in 1861, and I did not see him again until one day one of this genus "bummer" strayed into our camp. He stuck his head into my tent and wanted to know how "Fred Hitchcock was." I had to take a long second look to dig out from this bunch of rags and filth my one-time Beau Brummel acquaintance at home. His eyes wer bleared, and told all too surely the cause of the transformation. His brag was that he had skipped every fight since he enlisted. "It's lots more fun," he said, "to climb a tree well in the rear and see the show. It's perfectly safe, you know, and then you don't get yourself killed and planted. What is the use," he ar-

To deter desertions, a few of those caught in the act were executed before their comrades. It was a lesson that many soldiers were not quick to forget.

gued, "of getting killed and have a fine monument erected over you, when you can't see it nor make any use of it after it is done? Let the other fellows do that if they want to. I've no use for monuments." Poor fellow, his cynical ideas were his ruin. Better a thousand times had he been "planted" at the front, manfully doing his duty, than to save a worthless life and return with the record of a poltroon, despised by himself and everybody else.

This review by President Lincoln and the new commander-in-chief, General Hooker, was, from a military, spectacular point of view, the chief event of our army experience. It included the whole of the great Army of the Potomac, now numbering upward of one hundred and thirty thousand men, probably its greatest numerical strength of the whole war. Deducting picket details, there were present on this review, it is safe to say, from ninety thousand to one hundred thousand men. It was a remarkable event historically, because so far as I can learn it was the only time this great army was ever paraded in line so that it could be seen all together. In this respect it was the most magnificent military pageant ever witnessed on this continent, far exceeding in its impressive grandeur what has passed into history as the "great review," which preceded the final "muster out" at the close of the war in the city of Washington. At the latter not more than ten thousand men could have been seen at one time, probably not nearly so many, for the eye could take in only the column which filled Pennsylvania Avenue from the Capitol to the Treasury Building. Whereas, upon our review the army was first drawn up in what is known as three lines of "masses," and one glance of the eye could take in the whole army. Think of it! One hundred thousand men in one sweep of vision! If the word "Selah" in the Psalm means "stop! think! consider!" it would be particularly appropriate here.

A word now about the formation in "lines of masses." Each regiment was formed in column of divisions. To those unfamiliar with military terms, I must explain that this very common formation with large bodies of troops consists in putting two companies together as a division under the command of the senior officer, thus making of a regiment of ten companies a column of five divisions, each two-company front. This was known as "massing" the troops. When so placed in line they were called a line of "masses;" when marching, a column of "masses." It will be seen that the actual frontage of each regiment so formed was the width of two companies only, the other eight companies being formed in like manner in their rear. Now imagine four regiments so formed and placed side by side, fronting on the same line and separated from each other by say fifty feet, and you have a brigade line of masses. The actual frontage of a brigade so formed would be considerably less than that of a single regiment on dress parade. Now take three such brigades, separated from each other by say fifty feet, and you have a division line of masses. Three divisions made up an army corps. The army was formed in three lines of masses, of two corps each, on the large open plain opposite Fredericksburg, to the south and east of where the railroad crossed the river. Each of these lines of masses contained from seventy to eighty regiments of infantry, besides the artillery, which was paraded on the several lines of different intervals. I do not remember seeing any cavalry, and my impression is that this branch of the service was not represented. Some idea may be formed of the magnificence of this spectacle when I state that each of these lines of masses was more than a mile in length, and the depth of the three lines from front to rear, including the spaces between, was not less than four hundred yards, or about one-fifth of a mile. Each of the regiments displayed its two stands of silk colors, one the blue flag representing the State from which it came, the other the national colors. There were here and there a brace of these flags, very conspicuous in their brilliant newness, indicating a fresh accession to the army, but most of them were tattered and torn by shot and shell, whilst a closer look revealed the less conspicuous but more deadly slits and punctures of the minie-balls.

Ravenous Northern troops draw hearty rations. Hooker endeared himself to his men by improving the supply system and quality of food given to the common soldier.

A Yankee idles away his time as the Army of the Potomac rests at Falmouth after the exhausting Mud March.

Now place yourself on the right of their army paraded for review and look down the long lines. Try to count the standards as the favoring wind lifts their sacred folds and caressingly shows you their battle scars. You will need to look very closely, lest those miniature penants, far away, whose staffs appear no larger than parlor matches protruding above lines of men, whose forms in the distance have long since merged into a mere bluish gray line, escape your eye. Your numbering will crowd the five hundred mark ere you finish, and you should remember that each of these units represented a thousand men when in the vigor and enthusiasm of patriotic manhood they bravely marched to the front. Only a fifth of them left? you say. And the others? Ah! the battle, the hospital, the prison-pen, the h-ll of war, must be the answer.

How can words describe the scene? This is that magnificent old battered Army of the Potomac. Look upon it; you shall never behold its like again. There have been and may yet be many armies greater in numbers, and possibly, in all the paraphernalia of war, more showy. There can never be another Army of the Potomac, with such a history. As I gazed up and down those massive lines of living men, felt that I was one of them, and saw those battle-scarred flags kissed by the loving breeze, my blood tingled to my very finger-tips, my hair seemed almost to raise straight up, and I said a thousand Confederacies can't whip us. And here I think I grasped the main purpose of this review. It was not simply to give the President a sight of his "strong right arm," as he fondly called the Army of the Potomac, nor General Hooker, its new commander, an opportunity to see his men and them a chance to see their new chief,—though both of these were included,—but it was to give the army a square look at its mighty self, see how large and how strong it really was, that every man might thereby get the same enthusiasm and inspiration that I did, and know that it simply could not be beaten. The enemy, it is not strange to say, were intensely interested spectators of this whole scene, for the review was held in full view of the whole of their army. No place could have been chosen that would better have accommodated their enjoyment of the picture, if such it was, than that open plain, exactly in their front. And we could see them swarming over Marye's Heights and the lines to the south of it, intently gazing upon us. A scene more resplendent with military pageantry and the soul-stirring assessories of war they will never see again. But did it stir their blood? Yes; but with bitterness only, for they must have seen that the task before them of successfully resisting the onslaughts of this army was impossible. Here was disclosed, undoubtedly, another purpose of this grand review, viz., to let the enemy see with their own eyes how powerful the army was with which they had to contend.

A remarkable feature of this review was the marvellous celerity of its formation. The various corps and subdivisions of the army were started on the march for the reviewing ground so as to reach it at about the same time. It should be remembered that most of them were encamped from four to eight miles away. Aides-de-camp with markers by the score were already in position on the plain when the troops arrived, so that there was almost no delay in getting into position. As our column debouched upon the field, there seemed an inextricable mass of marching columns as far as the eye could see. Could order ever be gotten out of it? Yet, presto! the right of the line fell into position, a series of blue blocks, and then on down to the far left, block after block, came upon the line with unerring order and precision, as though it were a long curling whiplash straightening itself out to the tension of a giant hand. And so with each of the other two lines. All were formed simultaneously. Here was not only perfection of military evolution, but the poetry of rhythmic movement. The three lines were all formed within twenty minutes, ready for the reviewing officers.

Almost immediately the blare of the trumpets announced the approach of the latter, and the tall form of the President was seen, accompanied by a large retinue, galloping down the first line. Our division was formed, as I recollect, in the first line, about three hundred yards from the right. The President was mounted on a large, handsome horse, and as he drew near I saw that immediately on his right rode his son, Robert Lincoln, then a bright-looking lad of fourteen to fifteen years, and little "Tad" Lincoln, the idol of his father, was on his left. The latter could not have been more than seven or eight years old. He was mounted on a large horse, and his little feet seemed to stick almost straight out from the saddle. He was round and pudgy, and his jolly little body bobbed up and down like a ball under the stiff canter of his horse. I wondered how he maintained his seat, but he was really a better horseman than his father, for just before reaching our regiment there was a little summer stream ravine, probably a couple of yards wide, that had to be jumped. The horses took it all right, but the President landed on the other side with a terrific jounce, being almost unseated. The boys went over flying, little "Tad" in high glee, like a monkey on a mustang.

Of course, a might cheer greeted the President as he galloped down the long line. There was something indescribably weird about that huzzah from the throats of these thousands of men, first full, sonorous, and thrilling, and then as it rolled down that attenuated line gradually fading into a minor strain until it was lost in the distance, only to reappear as the cav-

The Commander-in-Chief joins "Fighting Joe" Hooker in a review of the Army of the Potomac before it returns to action against the Confederate Army of Northern Virginia.

alcade returned in front of the second line, first the faintest note of a violin, then rapidly swelling into the full volume, to again die away and for the third time reappear and die away as the third line was reviewed. The President was followed by a large staff dressed in full uniform, which contrasted strongly with his own severely plain black. He wore a high silk hat and a plain frock coat. His face wore that peculiar sombre expression we see in all his photographs, but it lighted up into a half-smile as he occasionally lifted his hat in acknowledgment of the cheering of the men.

About one hundred yards in rear of the President's staff came the new commanding general, "Fighting Joe." He was dressed in the full uniform of a major-general, and was accompanied by his chief of staff, Seth Williams—he who had held this position under every commander of the Army of the Potomac thus far—and a large and brilliant staff. There must have been fully twenty officers of various ranks, from his chief of staff, a general, down through all grades to a lieutenant, in this corps of staff officers. It was the first time I had seen General Hooker to know him. His personal appearance did not belie his reputation. He had a singularly strong, handsome face, sat his superb horse like a king, broad-shouldered and elegantly proportioned in form, with a large, fine head, well covered with rather long hair, now as white as the driven snow and flowing in the wind as he galloped down the line, chapeau in hand; he was a striking and picturesque figure. It was evident the head of the army had lost nothing in personal appearance by its recent change. The same cheering marked the appearance of "Fighting Joe" which had greeted the President, as he and staff galloped down and up and down through the three long lines.

Both reviewing cavalcades moved at a brisk gallop, and occupied only about twenty minutes covering the three miles of lines; and then the President and staff took position, for the marching review, some distance in front and about midway of the lines. Instantly the scene was transformed. The first line wheeled into column by brigades successively and headed by General Hooker and staff, moved rapidly forward. There were but few bands, and the drum crops had been consolidated into division corps. On passing the President, General Hooker took position by his side and remained throughout the remainder of the ceremony. The troops marched in columns of masses, in the same formation they had stood in line; that is, in column of two companies front and only six yards between divisions. This made a very compact mass of troops, quite unusual in reviews, but was necessary in order to avoid the great length of time that in the usual formation would have been required for the passing of this vast body of men. Yet in this close formation the balance of the day was nearly consumed in marching past the President.

It must have been a trying ordeal to him, as he had to lift his hat as each stand of colors successively dipped in passing. Immediately on passing the President, the several brigades were wheeled out of the column and ordered to quarters. I remember that we

After taking the helm of the Army of the Potomac, Hooker retrieved the morale of the defeated legion and restored it into fighting condition after the woeful mismanagement of his predecessor.

returned to our camp, over a mile distant, dismissed the men, and then several of us officers rode back to see the continuation of the pageant. When we got back the second line was only well on its way, which meant that only about half the army had passed in review. We could see from fifteen to twenty thousand men in column—that is to say, about one army corps—at a time. The quick, vigorous step, in rhythmical cadence to the music, the fife and drum, the massive swing, as though every man was actually a part of every other man; the glistening of bayonets like a long ribbon of polished steel, interspersed with the stirring effects of those historic flags, in countless numbers, made a picture impressive beyond the power of description. A picture of the ages. How glad I am to have looked upon it. I could not remain to see the end. When finally I was compelled to leave the third line was marching. I can still see that soul-thrilling column, that massive swing, those flaunting colors, the sheen of burnished steel! Majestic! Incomparable! Glorious!!!

★★★

DARIUS N. COUCH

The Chancellorsville Campaign

After entering the war as a colonel of the 7th Massachusetts Volunteer Regiment, Darius Couch had a close association with General George Briton McClellan that won him the rank of Brigadier General and soon after a divisional command. Having proved his solid fighting ability in McClellan's Peninsular Campaign, Couch rose to the rank of major general wielding a division in the Antietam Campaign and the II Corps at Fredericksburg and Chancellorsville. After the latter battle, he asked to be relieved from the Army of the Potomac, only to be reduced to the command of Pennsylvania militia at Gettysburg and a division out West towards the end of the war. Taken from Battles and Leaders of the Civil War, *his article describes the Federal command during the battle of Chancellorsville.*

In the latter part of January, 1863, the Army of the Potomac under Burnside was still occupying its old camps on the left bank of the Rappannock, opposite Fredericksburg. After the failures under Burnside it was evident that the army must have a new commander. For some days there had been a rumor that Hooker had been fixed upon for the place, and on the 26th of January it was confirmed. This appointment, undoubtedly, gave very general satisfaction to the army, except perhaps to a few, mostly superior officers, who had grown up with it, and had had abundant opportunities to study Hooker's military character; these believed that Mr. Lincoln had committed a grave error in his selection. The army, from its former reverses, had become quite disheartened and almost sulky; but the quick, vigorous measures now adopted and carried out with a firm hand had a magical effect in toning up where there had been demoralization and inspiring confidence where there had been mistrust. Few changes were made in the heads of the general staff departments, but for his chief-of-staff Hooker applied for Brigadier-General Charles P. Stone, who through some untoward influence at Washington, was not given to him. This was a mistake of the war dignitaries, although the officer finally appointed to the office, Major-General Daniel Butterfield, proved himself very efficient. Burnside's system of dividing the army into three grand divisions was set aside and the novelty was introduced of giving to each army corps a distinct badge, and idea which was very popular with officers and men.

Some few days after Mr. Lincoln's visit to the army in April [see p.119] I was again thrown with the President, and it happened in this wise. My pickets along the river were not only on speaking terms with those

Major General Darius Couch, commander of the II Corps at Chancellorsville.

of the enemy on the other side of the river, but covertly carried on quite a trade in exchanging coffee for tobacco, etc. This morning it was hallooed over to our side: "You have taken Charleston," which news was sent to headquarters. Mr. Lincoln hearing of it wished me to come up and talk the matter over. I went and was ushered into a side tent, occupied only by himself and Hooker. My entrance apparently interrupted a weighty conversation, for both were looking grave. The President's manner was kindly, while the general, usually so courteous, forgot to be conventionally polite. The Charleston rumor having been briefly discussed, Mr. Lincoln remarked that it was time for him to leave. As he stepped toward the general, who had risen from his seat, as well as myself, he said: "I want to impress upon you two gentlemen in your next fight,"—and turning to me he completed the sentence,—"put in all of your men"—in the long run a good military maxim.

The weather growing favorable for military operations, on April 12th were commenced those suggestive preliminaries to all great battles, clearing out the hospitals, inspecting arms, looking after ammunition, shoeing animals, issuing provisions, and making every preparation necessary to an advance. The next day, the 13th, Stoneman was put in motion at the head of ten thousand finely equipped and well organized cavalry to ascend the Rappahannock and swinging around to attack the Confederate cavalry wherever it might be found and "Fight! fight! fight!" At the end of two days' march Stoneman found the river so swollen by heavy rains that he was constrained to hold up, upon which Hooker suspended his advance until the

27th. This unexpected delay of the cavalry seemingly deranged Hooker's original plan of campaign. He had hoped that Stoneman would have been able to place his horsemen on the railroad between Fredericksburg and Richmond, by which Lee received his supplies, and make a wreck of the whole structure, compelling that general to evacuate his stronghold at Fredericksburg and vicinity and fall back toward Richmond.

I estimate the grand total of Hooker's seven corps at about 113,000 men ready for duty, although the date from which the conclusion is arrived at are not strictly official. This estimate does not include the cavalry corps of not less than 11,000 duty men, nor the reserve artillery, the whole number of guns in the army being 400. Lee's strength in and around Fredericksburg was placed at between 55,000 and 60,000 not including cavalry. It is not known if Hooker's information concerning the Confederate force was reliable, but Peck, operating in front of Norfolk, notified him that two of Lee's divisions under Longstreet were on the south side of the James. The hour was, therefore, auspicious for Hooker to assume the offensive, and he seized it with a boldness which argued well for his fitness to command. The aim was to transfer his army to the south side of the river, where it would have a manoeuvring footing not confronted by intrenched

A crowd of Yankees rest before the next big fight of their military careers, Chancellorsville.

Federal supply wagons advance towards the Rappahannock with pontoons for Hooker's crossing of the river.

positions. On the 27th of April the Eleventh and Twelfth corps were set in motion for Kelly's Ford, twenty-five miles up the Rappahannock, where they concentrated on the evening of the 28th the Fifth, by reason of its shorter marching distance, moving on the 28th. The object of the expedition was unknown to the corps commanders until communicated to them after their arrival at the ford by the commanding general in person. The Eleventh Corps crossed the Rappahannock, followed in the morning by the Twelfth and Fifth corps—the two former striking for Germanna Ford, a crossing of the Rapidan, the latter for Ely's Ford, lower down the same stream. Both columns, successfully effecting crossings with little opposition from the enemy's pickets, arrived that evening, April 30th, at the point of concentration, Chancellorsville. It had been a brilliantly conceived and executed movement.

In order to confound Lee, orders were issued to assemble the Sixth, Third, and First corps under Sedgwick at Franklin's Crossing and Pollock's Mill, some three miles below Fredericksburg, on the left, before daylight of the morning of the 29th, and throw two bridges across and hold them. This was done under a severe fire of sharp-shooters. The Second Corps, two

divisions, marched on the 28th for Banks's Ford, four miles to the right; the other division, Gibbon's, occupying Falmouth, near the river-bank, was directed to remain in its tents, as they were in full view of the enemy, who would readily observe their withdrawal. On the 29th the two divisions of the Second Corps reached United States Ford, held by the enemy; but the advance of the right wing down the river uncovered it, whereupon a bridge of pontoons was thrown across and the corps reached Chancellorsville the same night as the Fifth, Eleventh, and Twelfth. The same day, the 30th, Sedgwick was instructed to place a corps across the river and make a demonstration upon the enemy's right, below Fredericksburg, and the Third Corps received orders to join the right wing at Chancellorsville, where the commanding general arrived the same evening, establishing his headquarters at the Chancellor House, which, with the adjacent grounds, is Chancellorsville. All of the army lying there that night were in exuberant spirits at the success of their general in getting "on the other side" without fighting for a position. As I rode into Chancellorsville that night the general hilarity pervading the camps was particularly noticeable; the soldiers, while chopping wood and lighting fires, were singing merry songs and indulging in peppery camp jokes.

The position at Chancellorsville not only took in reverse the entire system of the enemy's river defense, but there were roads leading from it directly to his line of communication. But in order to gain the advantages now in the commanding general's grasp he had divided his army into two wings, and the enemy, no ordinary enemy, lay between them. The line of communication connecting the wings was by way of United States Ford and twenty miles long. It was of vital importance that the line be shortened in order to place the wings within easy support of each other. The possession of Banks's Ford, foreshadowed in the instructions given to Slocum, would accomplish all that at present could be wished.

There were three roads over which the right wing could move upon Fredericksburg: the Orange turnpike, from the west, passed through Chancellorsville, and was the most direct; the United States Ford road, crossing the former at Chancellorsville, became the Plank road, bent to the left and united with the turnpike five miles or so from Chancellorsville; the third road fell back from Chancellorsville toward the Rappahannock, passed along by Banks's Ford, six miles distant, and continued to Fredericksburg. That wing was ready for the advance at an early hour in the morning of May 1st, but somehow things dragged; the order defining the movement, instead of being issued the previous night, was not received by the corps commanders, at least by me, until hours after light. Meade was finally pushed out on the left over the Banks's Ford and turnpike roads, Slocum and Howard on the right along the Plank road, the left to be near Banks's Ford by 2 P.M., the right at the junction of its line of movement with the turnpike at 12 M. No opposition was met, excepting that the division marching over the turnpike came upon the enemy two or three miles out, when the sound of their guns was heard at Chancellorsville, and General Hooker ordered me to take Hancock's division and proceed to the support of those engaged. After marching a mile and a half or so I came upon Sykes, who commanded, engaged at the time in drawing back his advance to the position he then occupied. Shortly after Hancock's troops had got into a line in front, an order was received from the commanding general "to withdraw both divisions to Chancellorsville." Turning to the officers around me, Hancock, Sykes, Warren, and others, I told them what the order was, upon which they all agreed with me that the ground should not be

abandoned, because of the open country in front and the commanding position. An aide, Major J. B. Burt, dispatched to General Hooker to this effect, came back in half an hour with positive orders to return. Nothing was to be done but carry out the command, though Warren suggested that I should disobey, and then he rode back to see the general. In the meantime Slocum, on the Plank road to my right, had been ordered in, and the enemy's advance was between that road and my right flank. Sykes was first to move back, then followed by Hancock's regiments over the same road. When all but two of the latter had withdrawn, a third order came to me, brought by one of the general's staff: "Hold on until 5 o'clock." It was then

Despite snipers from the opposite side of the river, Hooker's engineers proceed to lay a pontoon bridge across the Rappahannock.

perhaps 2 P.M. Disgusted at the general's vacillation and vexed at receiving an order of such tenor, I replied with warmth unbecoming in a subordinate: "Tell General Hooker he is too late, the enemy are already on my right and rear. I am in full retreat."

The position thus abandoned was high ground, more or less open in front, over which an army might move and artillery be used advantageously; moreover, were it left in the hands of an enemy, his batteries, established on its crest and slopes, would command the position at Chancellorsville. Everything on the whole front was ordered in. General Hooker knew that Lee was apprised of his presence on the south side of the river, and must have expected that his enemy would be at least on the lookout for an advance upon Fredericksburg. But it was of the utmost importance that Banks's Ford should fall into our hands, therefore the enemy ought to have been pressed until their strength or weakness was developed; it would then have been time enough to run away.

Mott's Run, with a considerable brushy ravine, cuts the turnpike three-fourths of a mile east of chan-

cellorsville. Two of Hancock's regiments, under Colonel Nelson A. Miles, subsequently the Indian fighter, were directed to occupy the ravine. Continuing my way through the woods toward Chancellorsville, I came upon some of the Fifth Corps under arms. Inquiring for their commanding officer, I told him that in fifteen minutes he would be attacked. Before finishing the sentence a volley of musketry was fired into us from the direction of the Plank road. This was the beginning of the battle of Chancellorsville. Troops were hurried into position, but the observer required no wizard to tell him, as they marched past, that the high expectations which had animated them only a few hours ago had given place to disappointment. Proceeding to the Chancellor House, I narrated my operations in front to Hooker, which were seemingly satisfactory, as he said: "It is all right, Couch, I have got Lee just where I want him; he must fight me on my own ground." The retrograde movement had prepared me for something of the kind, but to hear from his own lips that the advantages gained by the successful marches of his lieutenants were to culminate in fighting a defensive battle in that nest of thickets

was too much, and I retired from his presence with the belief that my commanding general was a whipped man. The army was directed to intrench itself. At 2 A.M. the corps commanders reported to General Hooker that their positions could be held; at least so said Couch, Slocum, and Howard.

Until after dark on May 1st the enemy confined his demonstrations to finding out the position of our left with his skirmishers. Then he got some guns upon the high ground which we had abandoned as before mentioned, and cannonaded the left of our line. There were not many casualties, but that day a shell severely wounded the adjutant-general of the Second Corps, now General F. A. Walker. Chancellorsville was a strategic point to an offensive or retreating army, as roads diverged from it into every part of Virginia; but for a defensive position it was bad, particularly for such an army as Hooker had under him, which prided itself upon its artillery, which was perhaps equal to any in the world. There were no commanding positions for artillery, and but little open country to operate over; in fact, the advantages of ground for this arm were mainly with the attacking party.

During the 29th and 30th the enemy lay at Fredericksburg observing Sedgwick's demonstrations on the left, entirely unconscious of Hooker's successful crossing of the right wing, until midday of the latter date, but that night Lee formed his plan of operations for checking the farther advance of the force which had not only turned the left flank of his river defenses but was threatening his line of communication with Richmond as well as the rear of his center at Fredericksburg. Stonewall Jackson, who was watching Sedgwick, received instructions to withdraw his corps, march to the left, across the front of Hooker's intrenched position, until its right flank was attained, and assault with his column of 22,000 men, while his commanding general would, with what force he could spare, guard the approached to Fredericksburg.

Federals of Brigadier General David A. Russell's brigade cross the Rappahannock in an assault on the Confederates at Fredericksburg during the Chancellorsville Campaign.

Joseph "Fighting Joe" Hooker. After the defeat at Fredericksburg, all hopes for victory rested on Hooker.

On the morning of May 2d our line had become strong enough to resist a front attack unless made in great force; the enemy had also been hard at work on his front, particularly that section of it between the Plank road and turnpike. Sedgwick, the previous night, had been ordered to send the First Corp (Reynolds's) to Chancellorsville. At 7 A.M. a sharp cannonade was opened on our left, followed by infantry demonstrations of no particular earnestness. Two hours later the enemy were observed moving a mile or so to the south and front of the center, and later the same column was reported to the commander of the Eleventh Corps by General Devens, whose division was on the extreme right flank. At 9:30 A.M. a circular directed to Generals Slocum and Howard called attention to this movement and to the weakness of their flanks.

At 11 A.M. our left was furiously cannonaded by their artillery, established on the heights in front of Mott's Run, followed by sharp infantry firing on the fronts of the Second and Twelfth corps. As time flew along and no attack came from the enemy seen moving in front, Hooker conceived that Lee was retreating toward Gordonsville. There was color for this view, as the main road from Fredericksburg to that point diverged from the Plank road two miles to the left of Chancellorsville, and passed along his front at about the same distance. Hooker therefore jumped at the conclusion that the enemy's army was moving into the center of Virginia. But instead of the hostile column being on the Gordonsville road in retreat, it was Stonewall's corps moving on an interior neighborhood road, about one mile distant, and in search of our right flank and rear. At 2 P.M. I went into the Chancellor House, when General Hooker greeted me with the exclamation: "Lee is in full retreat toward Gordonsville, and I have sent out Sickles to capture his artillery." I thought, without speaking it: "If your conception is correct, it is very strange that only the Third Corps should be sent in pursuit." Sickles received orders at 1 P.M. to take two divisions, move to his front and attack, which he did, capturing some hundreds of prisoners. The country on the front being mostly wooded enabled the enemy to conceal his movements and at the same time hold Sickles in check with a rear-guard, which made such a show of strength that reënforcements were called for and furnished. In the meantime Jackson did not for a moment swerve from his purpose, but steadily moved forward to accomplish what he had undertaken.

It was about 5:30 in the evening when the head of Jackson's column found itself on the right and rear of the army, which on that flank consisted of the Eleventh Corps, the extreme right brigade receiving its first intimation of danger from a volley of musketry fired into their rear, followed up so impetuously that no efficient stand could be made by the brigades of the corps that successively attempted to resist the enemy's charge. When General Hooker found out what that terrific roar on his right flank meant he quickly mounted and flew across the open space to meet the onset, passing on his way stampeded pack-mules, officers' horses, caissons, with men and horses running for their lives. Gathering up such troops as were nearest to the scene of action, Berry's division from the Third Corps, some from the Twelfth, Hays's brigade of the Second, and a portion of the Eleventh, an effectual stand was made, Pleasonton, who was returning from the front, where he had been operating with Sickles (at the time Jackson attacked),taking in the state of things, rapidly moved his two regiments of cavalry and a battery to the head and right flank of the enemy's advance columns, when, making a charge and bringing up his own guns, with others of the Eleventh and Third Corps, He was enabled to punish them severely.

Pickets had been thrown out on Howard's flank, but not well to the right and rear. I suspect that the prime reason for the surprise was that the superior officers of the right corps had been put off their guard by adopting the conjecture of Hooker, "Lee's army is in full retreat to Gordonsville," as well as by expecting the enemy to attack precisely where ample preparations had been made to receive him. It can be emphatically stated that no corps in the army, surprised as the Eleventh was at this time, could have held its ground under similar circumstances.

At half past two that afternoon the Second Corps' lines were assaulted by artillery and infantry. Just previous to Jackson's attack on the right a desperate effort was made by Lee's people to carry the left at Mott's Run, but the men who held it were there to stay. Hooker, desiring to know the enemy's strength in front of the Twelfth Corps, advanced Slocum into the thicket, but that officer found the hostile line too

well defended for him to penetrate it and was forced to recall the attacking party. When night put an end to the fighting of both combatants, Hooker was obliged to form a new line for his right flank perpendicular to the old one and barely half a mile to the right of Chancellorsville. Sickles was retired, with the two columns, from his advanced position in the afternoon to near where Pleasonton had had his encounter, before mentioned, some distance to the left of the new line of our right flank and close up to the enemy. The situation was thought to be a very critical one by General Hooker, who had simply a strong body in front of the enemy, but without supports, at least near enough to be used for that purpose. At the same time it was a menace to Jackson's right wing or flank. Before midnight some of the latter's enterprising men pushed forward and actually cut off Sickles's line of communication. When this news was carried to Hooker it caused him great alarm, and preparations were at once made to withdraw the whole front, leaving General Sickles to his fate; but that officer showed himself able to take care of his rear, for he ordered after a little while a column of attack, and communication was restored at the point of the bayonet.

The situation of Jackson's corps on the moorning of May 3d was a desperate one, its front and right flank being in the presence of not far from 25,000 men, with the left flank subject to an assault of 30,000, the corps of Meade and Reynolds, by advancing them to the right, where the thicket did not present an insurmountable obstacle. It only required that

Unable to withstand Stonewall Jackson's powerful flanking attack, members of the XI Corps flee from the battle as their comrades attempt to stem the enemy tide.

Hooker should brace himself up to take a reasonable, common-sense view of the state of things, when the success gained by Jackson would have been turned into an overwhelming defeat. But Hooker became very despondent. I think that his being outgeneraled by Lee had a good deal to do with his depression. After the right flank had been established on the morning of the 3d by Sickles getting back into position our line was more compact, with favorable positions for artillery, and the reserves were well in hand. Meade had been drawn in from the left and Reynolds had arrived with the First Corps. The engineers had been directed on the previous night to lay out a new line, its front a half mile in rear of Chancellorsville, with the flanks thrown back,—the right to the Rapidan, a little above its junction with the Rappahannock, the left resting on the latter river. The Eleventh Corps, or at least that portion which formed line of battle, was withdrawn from the front and sent to the rear to reorganize and get its scattered parts together, leaving the following troops in front: one division of the Second Corps on the left from Mott's Run to Chancellorsville, the Twelfth Corps holding the center and right flank, aided by the Third Corps and one division of the Second Corps (French's), on the same flank; the whole number in front, according to my estimate, being 37,000 men. The First and Fifth corps in reserve numbered 30,000, and, placing the number of reliable men in the Eleventh Corps at 5000, it will be seen that the reserves nearly equaled those in line of battle in front.

After the day's mishaps Hooker judged that the enemy could not have spared so large a force to move around his front without depleting the defenses of Fredericksburg. Accordingly, at 9 P.M., an imperative order was sent to the commander of the left wing to cross the river at Fredericksburg, march upon Chancellorsville, and be in the vicinity of the commanding general at daylight. But Sedgwick was already across the river and three miles below Fredericksburg. It was 11 P.M., May 2d, when he got the order, and twelve or fourteen miles had to be marched over by daylight. The night was moonlight, but any officer who has had experience in making night marches with infantry will understand the vexatious delays occurring even when the road is clear; but when, in addition, there is any enemy in front, with a line of fortified heights to assault, the problem which Sedgwick had to solve will be pronounced impossible of solution. However, that officer set his column in motion by flank, leaving one division that lay opposite the enemy, who were in force to his left. The marching column, being continually harassed by skirmishers, did not arrive at Fredericksburg until daylight. The first assault upon the heights behind the town failed. Attempts to carry them by flank movements met with no success. Finally a second storming party was organized, and the series of works were taken literally at the point of the bayonet, though at heavy loss. It was then 11 A.M. The column immediately started for Chancellorsville, being more or less obstructed by the enemy until its arrival near Salem Heights, 5 or 6 miles out, where seven brigades under Early, six of which had been

Yankee reinforcements head past Hooker's headquarters on their way to the growing conflagration of musketry, cannon fire, and bloodshed on the Union front.

driven from the defenses of Fredericksburg, made a stand in conjunction with supports sent from Lee's army before Chancellorsville. This was about the middle of the afternoon, when Sedgwick in force attacked the enemy. Though at first successful, he was subsequently compelled to withdraw those in advance and look to his own safety by throwing his own flanks so as to cover Banks's Ford, the friendly proximity of which eventually saved this wing from utter annihilation.

At about 5 A.M., May 3d, fighting was begun at Chancellorsville, when the Third (Sickles's) Corps began to retire to the left of our proper right flank, and all of that flank soon became fiercely engaged, while the battle ran along the whole line. The enemy's guns on the heights to our left, as well as at every point on the line where they could be established, were vigorously used, while a full division threw itself on Miles at Mott's Run. On the right flank our guns were well handled, those of the Twelfth Corps being conspicuous, and the opposing lines of infantry operating in the thicket had almost hand-to-hand conflicts, capturing and recapturing prisoners. The enemy appeared to know what he was about, for pressing the Third Corps vigorously he forced it back, when he joined or rather touched the left of Lee's main body, making their line continuous from left to right. Another advantage gained by this success was the possession of an open field, from which guns covered the ground up to the Chancellor House. Upon the south porch of that mansion General Hooker stood leaning against one of its pillars, observing the fighting, looking anxious and much careworn. After the fighting had commenced I doubt if any orders were given by him to the commanders on the field, unless, perhaps, "to retire when out of ammunition." None were received by me, nor were there any inquiries as to how the battle was going along my front. On the right flank, where the fighting was desperate, the engaged troops were

Joseph Hooker's headquarters during the battle, the Chancellor Mansion, after being devastated by Confederate batteries during the Battle of Chancellorsville.

governed by the corps and division leaders. If the ear of the commanding general was, as he afterward stated, strained to catch the sound of Sedgwick's guns, it could not have heard them in the continuous uproar that filled the air around him; but as Sedgwick, who was known as a fighting officer, had not appeared at the time set—daylight—nor for some hours after, it was conclusive evidence that he had met with strong opposition, showing that all of Lee's army was not at Chancellorsville, so that the moment was favorable for Hooker to try his opponent's strength with every available man. Moreover, the left wing might at that very time be in jeopardy, therefore he was bound by every patriotic motive to strike hard for its relief. If he had remembered Mr. Lincoln's injunction ("Gentlemen, in your next fight put in all of your men"), the face of the day would have been changed and the field won for the Union arms.

Not far from 8:30 A.M. the headquarters pennants of the Third and Twelfth corps suddenly appeared from the right in the open field of Chancellorsville; then the Third began to fall back, it was reported, for want of ammunition, followed by that portion of the Twelfth fighting on the same flank, and the division of the Second Corps on its right. It is not known whether any efforts were made to supply the much needed ammunition to the Third as well as the Twelfth Corps, whose ammunition was nearly used up when it retired. My impression is that the heads of the ordnance, as well as of other important departments, were not taken into the field during this campaign, which was most unfortunate, as the commanding general had enough on his mind without charging it with details.

The open field seized by Jackson's old corps after the Third Corps drew off was shortly dotted with guns that made splendid practice through an opening in the wood upon the Chancellor House, and everything else, for that matter, in the neighborhood. Hooker was still at his place on the porch, with nothing between him and Lee's army but Geary's division of the Twelfth and Hancock's division and a battery of the Second Corps. But Geary's right was now turned, and that flank was steadily being pressed back along his intrenched line to the junction of the Plank road and the turnpike, when a cannon-shot struck the pillar against which Hooker was leaning and knocked him down. A report flew around that he was killed. I was at the time but a few yards to his left, and dismounting, ran to the porch. The shattered pillar was there, but I could not find him or any one else. Hurrying through the house, finding no one, my search was continued through the back yard. All the time I was thinking, "If he is killed, what shall I do with this disjointed army?" Passing through the yard I came upon him, to my great joy, mounted, and with his staff also in their saddles. Briefly congratulating him on his escape—it was no time to blubber or use soft expressions—I went about my own business. This was the last I saw of my commanding general in front. The time, I reckon, was from 9:15 to 9:30 A.M., I think nearer the former than the latter. He probably left the field soon after his hurt, but he neither notified me of his going nor did he give any orders to me whatever. Having some little time before this seen that the last stand would be about the Chancellor House, I had sent to the rear for some of the Second Corps batteries, which had been ordered there by the commanding general, but word came back that they were so jammed in with other carriages that it was impossible to extricate them. General Meade, hearing of my wants, kindly sent forward the 5th Maine battery belonging to his corps. It was posted in rear of the Chancellor House, where the United States Ford road enters the thicket. With such precision did the artillery of Jackson's old corps play upon this battery that all of the officers and most of the non-commissioned officers and men were killed or wounded. The gallant Kirby, whose guns could not be brought up, was mortally wounded in the same battery of which I had for the time placed him in command, and my horse was killed under me while I was trying to get some men to train a gun on the flank of the force then pushing Geary's division. The enemy, having 30 pieces in position on our right, now advanced some of his guns to within 500 or 600 yards of the Chancellor House, where there were only four of Pettit's Second Corps guns to oppose them, making a target of that building and taking the right of Hancock's division in reverse, a portion of which had been withdrawn from its intrenchments and thrown back to the left to meet the enemy should he succeed in forcing Mott's Run. This flank was stoutly held by Colonel Miles, who, by the bye, had been carried off the field, shot through the body. Lee by this time knew well enough, if he had not known before, that the game was sure to fall into his hands, and accordingly plied every gun and rifle that could be brought to bear on us. Still everything was firmly held excepting Geary's right, which was slowly falling to pieces, for the enemy had his flank and there was no help for it. Riding to Geary's left, I found him there dismounted, with sword swinging over his head, walking up and down, exposed to a severe infantry fire, when he said: "My division can't hold its place; what shall I do?" To which I replied: "I don't know, but do as we are doing; fight it out."

It was not then too late to save the day. Fifty pieces of artillery or even forty, brought up and run in front and to the right of the Chancellor House, would have driven the enemy out of the thicket, then forcing back Geary's right, and would have neutralized the thirty guns to the right which were pounding us so hard. But it is a waste of words to write what might have been done. Hooker had made up his mind to abandon the field, otherwise he would not have allowed the Third and part of the Twelfth Corps to leave their ground for want of ammunition. A few minutes after my interview with Geary a staff-officer from General Hooker rode up and requested my presence with that general. Turning to General Hancock, near by, I told him to take care of things and rode to the rear. The Chancellor House was then burning, having been fired in several places by the enemy's shells.

At the farther side of an open field, half a mile in the rear of Chancellorsville, I came upon a few tents (three or four) pitched, around which, mostly dismounted, were a large number of staff-officers. General Meade was also present, and perhaps other generals. General Hooker was lying down I think in a soldier's tent by himself. Raising himself a little as I entered, he said: "Couch, I turn the command of the army over to you. You will withdraw it and place it in the position designated on this map," as he pointed to a line traced on a field-sketch. This was perhaps three-quarters of an hour after his hurt. He seemed rather dull, but possessed of his mental faculties. I do not think that one of those officers outside of the tent knew what orders I was to receive, for on stepping out, which I did immediately on getting my instructions, I met Meade close by, looking inquiringly as if he expected that finally he would receive the order for which he had waited all that long morning "to go in." Colonel N. H. Davis broke out: "We shall have some fighting now." These incidents are mentioned to show the temper of that knot of officers. No time was to be lost, as only Hancock's division now held Lee's army. Dispatching Major John B. Burt, with orders for the front to retire, I rode back to the thicket, accompanied by Meade, and was soon joined by Sickles, and after a little while by Hooker, but he did not interfere with my dispositions. Hancock had a close shave to withdraw in safety, his line being three-fourths of a mile long, with an exultant enemy as close in as they dared, or wished, or chose to be, firing and watching. But everything was brought off, except five hundred men of the Second Corps who, through the negligence of a lieutenant charged by Hancock with the responsibility of retiring the force at Mott's Run, were taken

prisoners. However, under the circumstances, the division was retired in better shape than one could have anticipated. General Sickles assisted in getting men to draw off the guns of the Maine battery before spoken of. General Meade wished me to hold the strip of thicket in rear of Chancellorsville, some six hundred yards in front of our new line of defense. My reply was: "I shall not leave men in this thicket to be shelled out by Lee's artillery. Its possession won't give us any strength. Yonder [pointing to the rear] is the line where the fighting is to be done." Hooker heard the conversation, but made no remarks. Considerable bodies of troops of different corps that lay in the brush to the right were brought within the lines, and the battle of Chancellorsville was ended. My pocket diary, May 3d, has the following: "Sickles opened at 5 A.M. Orders sent by me at 10 for the front to retire; at 12 M. in my new position"; the latter sentence meaning that at that hour my corps was in position on the new or second line of defense.

As to the charge that the battle was lost because the general was intoxicated, I have always stated that he probably abstained from the use of arden spirits when it would have been far better for him to have continued in his usual habit in that respect. The shock from being violently thrown to the ground, together with the physical exhaustion resulting from loss of sleep and the anxiety of mind incident to the last six days of the campaign, would tell on any man. The enemy did not press us on the second line, Lee simply varying the monotony of watching us by an occasional cannonade from the left, a part of his army having been sent to Salem Church to resist Sedgwick. Sedgwick had difficulty in maintaining his ground, but held his own by hard fighting until after midnight, May 4th–5th, when he recrossed at Banks's Ford.

Some of the most anomalous occurrences of the war took place in this campaign. On the night of May 2d the commanding general, with 80,000 men in his wing of the army, directed Sedgwick, with 22,000 to march to his relief. While that officer was doing this on the 3d, and when it would be expected that every effort would be made by the right wing to do its part, only one-half of it was fought (or rather half-fought, for its ammunition was not replenished), and then the whole wing was withdrawn to a place where it could not be hurt, leaving Sedgwick to take care of himself.

At 12 o'clock on the night of the 4th–5th General Hooker assembled his corps commanders in council. Meade, Sickles, Howard, Reynolds, and myself were present; General Slocum, on account of the long distance from his post, did not arrive until after the meeting was broken up. Hooker stated that his instructions compelled him to cover Washington, not to jeopardize the army, etc. It was seen by the most casual observer that he had made up his mind to retreat. We were left by ourselves to consult, upon which Sickles made an elaborate argument, sustaining the views of the commanding general. Meade was in favor of fighting, stating that he doubted if we could get off our guns. Howard was in favor of fighting, qualifying his views by the remark that our present situation was due to the bad conduct of his corps, or words to that effect. Reynolds, who was lying on the ground very much fatigued was in favor of an advance. I had similar views to those of Meade as to getting off the guns, but said I "would favor an advance if I could designate the point of attack." Upon collecting the suffrages, Meade, Reynolds, and Howard voted squarely for an advance, Sickles and myself squarely no; upon which Hooker informed the council that he should take upon himself the responsibility of retiring the army to the other side of the river. As I stepped out of the tent Reynolds, just behind me, broke out, "What was the use of calling us together at this time of night when he intended to retreat anyhow?"

On the morning of May 5th, corps commanders were ordered to cut roads, where it was necessary, leading from their positions to the United States Ford. During the afternoon there was a very heavy rainfall. In the meantime Hooker had in person crossed the river, but, as he gave orders for the various corps to march at such and such times during the night, I am not aware that any of his corps generals knew of his departure. Near midnight I got a note from Meade informing me that General Hooker was on the other side of the river, which had risen over the bridges, and that communications was cut off from him. I immediately rode over to Hooker's headquarters and found that I was in command of the army, if it had any commander. General Hunt, of the artillery, had brought the information as to the condition of the bridges, and from the reports there seemed to be a danger of losing them entirely. After a short conference with Meade I told him that the recrossing would be suspended, and that "we would stay where we were and fight it out," returning to my tent with the intention of enjoying what I had not had since the night of the 30th ultimo—a good sleep; but at 2 A.M., communication having been reëstablished, I received a sharp message from Hooker, to order the recrossing of the army as he had directed and everything was safely transferrred to the north bank of the Rappahannock.

In looking for the causes of the loss of Chancellorsville, the primary ones were that Hooker expected Lee to fall back without risking battle. Finding himself mistaken he assumed the defensive, and was outgeneraled and became demoralized by the superior tactical boldness of the enemy.

Joseph Hooker (second from right in front row) poses with his staff before the fateful Chancellorsville Campaign. Hooker made numerous statements of braggadocio claiming he would bag Lee in short order. When the time came to back his words with action, Fighting Joe nearly bagged himself.

The commander of Longstreet's artillery at the battle of Gettysburg, Colonel E.P. Alexander.

★★★

E. P. ALEXANDER
Lee Triumphant

One of the most continuously valued eyewitness histories of the Civil War is Military Memoirs of a Confederate by Edward Porter Alexander. After serving stints as a signal officer and chief of ordinance in the Confederate Army of Northern Virginia, E.P. Porter went on to serve in the artillery where he rose to the rank of Brigadier General. After the war, he wrote his memoirs in a style that achieved historical accuracy and spurned the romanticism of his age. This selection on the battle of Chancellorsville was taken from his famous book.

Each commander planned to take the initiative. Hooker knew that he had double Lee's infantry, and great superiority in artillery, and he desired only to get at Lee away from breastworks. On April 13 he ordered Stoneman's cavalry upon a raid to Lee's rear, which expedition was to be the opening of his campaign. A rain-storm on the 14th, lasting 36 hours, halted the movement, after its leading brigade had forded the Rappahannock. The brigade was recalled, having to swim horses across the fast-rising river, and two weeks elapsed before the movement could be renewed. It was intended that Stoneman should destroy the railroads, which would force Lee to retreat. Stoneman should then harass and delay him as he fell back, pursued by Hooker.

Lee's proposed campaign was another invasion; this time of Pa. He could neither attack Hooker, nor even threaten his rear across the Rappahannock. But he could again sweep the Valley and cross the Potomac; and beyond, both Lee and Jackson imagined great possibilities. Three months later the opportunity offered, and Lee put it to the test; but his great lieutenant, Jackson, was no longer at the head of his 2d corps.

On April 29, Lee found himself anticipated by Hooker's having, the night before, laid pontoon bridges across the Rappahannock, below Deep Run, at the site of Franklin's crossing in Dec. Hooker had commenced his movement, on the 27th, by going with the 5th, 11th, and 12th corps to cross the Rappahannock at Kelly's Ford, above the mouth of the Rapidan, 27 miles from Fredericksburg. A picket, at this point, was driven off, a pontoon bridge laid, and the whole force, about 42,000 men, was across the river on the 29th, when the 6th corps, under Sedgwick, was crossing in front of Jackson. Hooker immediately pushed his force by two roads from Kelly's to Germanna and Ely's fords of the Rapidan—about 11 miles off, and, on arriving, the troops forded, although the water was nearly shoulder deep. The fording was kept up all night by light of large bonfires, and the next morning the march of Chancellorsville, six miles away, was resumed.

Meanwhile, two divisions of the 2d corps had moved up from Fredericksburg to United States Ford, where they laid a pontoon bridge about noon on the 30th. by 9 P.M. they had crossed and united with the 5th, 11th, and 12th corps at Chancellorsville. No resistance had been encountered anywhere, but that of picket forces. Hooker, in 84 hours, had covered about 45 miles, crossing two rivers, and had established a force of 54,000 infantry and artillery upon Lee's flank at Chancellorsville. Hooker was naturally elated at his success, and issued an order to his troops, congratulating them, and announcing that now:

the enemy must either ingloriously fly, or come out from behind his defences, and give us battle on our own ground, where certain destruction awaits him.

And, indeed, if a general may ever be justified in enumerating his poultry while the process of incubation is incomplete, this might be an occasion. He was on the left flank and rear of Lee's only strong position with a force fully equal to Lee's, while another equal force threatened Lee's right. And somewhere in Lee's rear—between him and Richmond—was Stoneman with 10,000 sabres, opposed only by two regiments of cavalry, tearing up the railroads and waiting to fall upon Lee's flank when he essayed the retreat which Hooker confidently expected to see. He had said to those about him that evening:

The rebel army is now the legitimate property of the Army of the Potomac. They may as well pack up their haversacks and make for Richmond, and I shall be after them.

But Hooker had made one mistake, and it was to cost him dearly. He had sent off, with Stoneman, his entire cavalry force, except one brigade. This proved insufficient to keep him informed of the Confederate movements, even though their efforts were supplemented by many signal officers with lookouts and field telegraphs, and by two balloons.

It was during the morning of the 30th, that Lee learned that Hooker had divided his army, and that one-half of it was already at Chancellorsville, while most of the remainder was in his front. By all the rules of war, one-half or the other should be at once attacked, and as Sedgwick's was the nearest, and Lee's whole force was already concentrated, Jackson at first proposed to attack Sedgwick. Lee, however, thought the position impregnable, and Jackson, after careful reconnoissance, came to the same conclusion. Orders were then at once prepared to march and attack Hooker before he could move from Chancellorsville.

Early with his division, Barksdale's brigade, Pendleton's artillery reserve, and the Washington artillery, in all about 10,000 men, were left to hold the lines before Fredericksburg. These covered about six miles, and the force averaged about one man to each yard, and nine guns to each mile. About midnight on the 30th, Jackson marched from Hamilton's Crossing with his three remaining divisions, under A.P. Hill, Rodes, and Colston. He was joined on the road in the morning by Lee with the remaining brigades of McLaws, and by Anderson's division, and Alexander's battalion of artillery.

Jackson's three divisions numbered about 25,000, Anderson's division about 8000, and three brigades of McLaws about 6000. Thus, Lee had in hand nearly 40,000 men, with which to attack Hooker at Chancellorsville, where Hooker now had four corps— the 3d, 5th, 11th, and 12th—and two divisions of the 2d; a total effective of about 72,000 infantry and artillery, and was intrenching himself.

Chancellorsville was situated about a mile within the limits of a tract called the Wilderness. It stretched some 12 or 14 miles westward along the Rapidan and was some 8 or 10 miles in breadth.

The original forest had been cut for charcoal many years before, and replaced by thick and tangled smaller growth. A few clearings were scattered at intervals, and a few small creeks drained it. Chancellorsville was merely a brick residence at an important junction of roads, with a considerable clearing on the west. Three roads ran toward Fredericksburg: the old Turnpike most directly; the Plank road to its right, but uniting with the Turnpike at Tabernacle Church—about halfway; the River road to the left, by a roundabout course passing near Banks Ford of the Rappahannock.

George Stoneman (center) with his subordinates. Charged with threatening Lee's supply lines during the Chancellorsville Campaign, Stoneman only managed to get his 10,000 troopers stuck in the mud and, when he finally did get in the Confederate rear, failed to cause the enemy much real concern.

Hooker's line of battle ran from Chancellorsville, about two miles northeastward to the Rappahannock, covering United States Ford. Westward it covered the Plank road for about three miles, ending in a short offset northward. Intrenchment was quickly done by cutting abattis, or an entanglement, in front, and throwing up slight parapets, or piling breastworks of logs. About 11 A.M., however, Hooker prepared to resume his advance, and ordered the 5th and 12th corps to move out on the three roads toward Fredericksburg and establish a line in the open-country beyond the Wilderness. Griffin's and Humphreys's divisions of the 5th were sent down the River road, on the left, Sykes's division down the Turnpike in the centre, and the 12th corps, under Slocum, down the Plank road on the right.

Meanwhile, Lee and Jackson disposed Anderson's division for an advance, covering both the Pike and the Plank roads. Wilcox's and Mahone's brigades, with Jordan's battery of Alexander's battalion, moved upon the former; Wright's, Perry's, and Posey's brigades, with the remainder of Alexander's battalion, on the latter. McLaws's division moved by the Pike, and Lee, with Jackson's three divisions, followed the Plank road. Thus the two armies were marching toward each other on these two roads, while on the River road two of the Federal Divisions were marching toward Banks Ford, which was at this time undefended, although some intrenchments had been erected there. The possession of Banks Ford by Hooker would shorten the distance between Chancellorsville and his left wing under Sedgwick, by several miles.

The advancing forces first came into collision on the Pike. Sharp fighting followed, Semmes's brigade coming up on the left of Mahone and bearing the brunt of it against Sykes's regulars. Sykes's orders had been, however, only to advance to the first ridge beyond the forest, and he maintained his position there, though menaced by the extension of the Confederate lines beyond his flank, until orders were received from Hooker to withdraw to the original position within the forest. Similar orders were also sent to Slocum on the Plank road, and to Griffin and Humphreys who had advanced, nearly five miles down the River road, entirely unopposed, and who were within sight of Banks Ford when the orders for the counter-march reached them. Slocum's corps had not become seriously engaged, but its skirmishers had been driven in and its right flank threatened by Wright's brigade. This advanced upon the line of an unfinished railroad, which, starting from Fredericksburg, ran through the Wilderness generally a mile or two south of the Plank road.

Up to the moment of the withdrawal of his troops, Hooker's campaign had been well planned and well managed, and its culmination was now at hand in the open field—as he had desired. He could scarcely hope for more propitious circumstances, and, by all the rules of the game, a victory was now within his grasp. His lieutenants received the order to fall back with surprise and regret. The advance, upon both the Plank

Learning the tricks of the trade from the Southern cavalier J.E.B. Stuart and his daring raids against Northern supply lines, a large cavalry force under Major General George Stoneman moves out on an attack against Lee's rear during the Chancellorsville Campaign.

road and the Pike, had cleared the forest and reached fairly good positions. An officer was sent to Hooker to explain and request permission to remain, but he returned a half-hour, with the orders repeated.

Hooker has been severely blamed for these orders, subverting all the carefully prepared plans only published to the army that morning. It is interesting to learn the cause. Reports from the balloons and signal officers had informed him of the march of a force toward Chancellorsville, estimated at two corps. Rumors had also been brought by deserters, the night before, that Hood's division had rejoined Lee, coming from Suffolk, but Hooker's information from Fortress Monroe should have shown that to be impossible. There is no sign of any hesitation upon his part until 2 P.M. At that hour he wired Butterfield, his chief of staff at Falmouth:

From character of information have suspended attack. The enemy may attack me,—I will try it. Tell Sedgwick to keep a sharp lookout, and attack if he can succeed."

This despatch makes clear Hooker's mind. He realized from the rapid manner of Lee's approach, and from the sounds of battle already heard, both on the Pike and the Plank road, that Lee meant to attack. He had confidently expected Lee to retreat without battle, and finding him, instead, so quick to take the aggressive, he lost his nerve and wished himself back on the line he had taken around Chancellorsville, where he would enjoy the great advantage of acting upon the defensive. He had seen in Dec. the enormous advantage which even slight breastworks could confer, and now he saw the chance of having his battle a

The troops of Major General George Sykes' division march out of the Wilderness to find their path obstructed by Rebel adversaries. When Hooker found his advance blocked by Lee's army, he took to the defensive and retreated his forces back into the woods.

Members of Daniel Sickles III Corps at Chancellorsville as Jackson was making his famous march against the Federal left.

defensive one behind intrenchments. It was surely the safest game to play, and Hooker is fully justified in electing to play it. No remonstrances shook his confidence in the least. He said to Couch,

It is all right, Couch, I have got Lee just where I want him. He must fight me on my own ground.

Orders were given to intrench, and work was at once begun with abundance of men and tools, and it was pushed during most of the night. Couch says,

At 2 A.M. the corps commanders reported to Gen. Hooker that their positions could be held; at least so said Couch, Slocum, and Howard.

Indeed, no better field fortification can be desired than what it was the quickest to build in the Wilderness. A wide belt of dense small growth could be soon felled in front of shallow ditches, with earth and log breastworks. Any charging line is brought to a halt by the entanglement, and held under close fire of musketry and canister, while the surrounding forest prevents the enemy from finding positions to use his own artillery.

So the corps commanders, responsible only for the front of their own lines, might truly report that their positions could be held. Yet the line, as a whole, may have a weak feature. This was the case here. Its right flank "rested in the air," and was not even covered by a curtain of cavalry.

Hooker, however, was not entirely blind to this weakness of his line. He inspected it early next morning, May 2, and ordered changes and enjoined vigilance which might have saved him from the surprise of the afternoon, had he not, like Pope in his campaign of the previous fall, failed to fathom the boldness of Lee's designs even after discovering the Confederate movements.

Lee appreciated that Hooker's withdrawal into the Wilderness was not forced, but to fortify and concentrate. He could, therefore, lose no time in finding how and where he might attack. Until nightfall the skirmishes were pushed forward everywhere, in order to locate the exact position of the enemy.

The result is briefly given in Lee's report, as follows:

> The enemy had assumed a position of great natural strength, surrounded on all sides by a dense forest, filled with a tangled undergrowth, in the midst of which breastworks of logs had been constructed, with trees felled in front so as to form and almost impenetrable abattis. His artillery swept the few narrow roads by which his position could be approached from the front, and commanded the adjacent woods.

Hooker had, indeed manoeuvred Lee out of his position without a battle. There was now nothing left but to attack the greatly superior force in the impregnable position, or to attempt a retreat already dangerously delayed. But presently there came some more cheerful news. Fitzhugh Lee, who held the extreme left of our cavalry, had also reconnoitred the enemy, and had discovered that his right flank was in the air.

The one chance left to Lee was to pass undiscovered entirely across the enemy's front and turn his right flank. The enterprise was of great difficulty and hazard. To try it and fail meant destruction. For the army, already divided, must now be further subdivided, and the largest fraction placed in a position whence retreat would be impossible. Only a very sanguine man could even hope that 15 brigades, with over 100 guns, could make a march of 14 miles around Hooker's enormous army without being discovered. The chance, too, must be taken of aggressive action by the enemy at Fredericksburg or Banks Ford, even if Hooker himself did nothing during the eight hours in which the flanking force would be out of position in a long defile through the forest.

But no risks appalled the heart of Lee, either of odds, or position, or of both combined. His supreme faith in his army was only equalled by the faith of his army in him. The decision to attack was quickly made and preparations begun. Wilcox's brigade was ordered to Banks Ford to hold the position. This precaution was well taken, for after midnight of the 1st, Hooker ordered Reynolds's corps to leave Sedgwick and join the army at Chancellorsville. Reynolds started at sunrise and marched by Banks Ford, where he expected to find a bridge. But, as has been told, Griffin's and Humphreys's divisions, after being within sight on the afternoon of the 1st, had been recalled. Wilcox, at dawn on the 2d, had occupied the trenches. So Reynolds, arriving after sunrise and seeing Confederates in possession, continued his march on the north side, and crossed at United State Ford.

Anderson's four remaining brigades, with McLaws's three, were ordered to intrench during the night. Jackson with his three divisions, his own artillery, and Alexander's battalion of Longstreet's corps, were assigned to make the march through the Wilderness and turn Hooker's right.

Lee himself would remain with McLaws's and Anderson's troops, and occupy th enemy while the long march was made. Cheering was forbidden, and stringent measures taken to keep the column closed. Fitz-Lee with his cavalry, would precede the infantry and cover the flank. Two hours after sunrise, Lee, standing by the roadside, watched the head of the column march by, and exchanged with Jackson the last few words ever to pass betwen them. Rodes's division led the column, Colston's division followed, and A. P. Hill's brought up the rear.

The sun rose on May 2 a few minutes after five, and set at 6:50 P.M. The moon was full that night. The march led by a cross-roads near the Catherine Furnace, thence southward for over a mile and then southwestward for two miles before turning west and striking the Brock road within another mile. At the cross-road, the line of march was nearest the Federal lines and was most exposed. Here the 23d Ga. regiment of Colquitt's brigade, Rodes's division, was left to cover the rear.

When the line of march reached the Brock road, it turned southward for about a mile, and then, almost doubling back upon itself, it took a woods road running a trifle west of north, nearly parallel to the Brock road itself, and coming back into it about three miles north of the point at which it was first entered. This made a route two miles longer than would have been made by turning northward when the Brock road was first reached. And as the part of the road was farthest of all from the enemy (over three miles), and in the densest woods, it would seem that two miles might have been saved, had there been time and opportunity for reconnoissance.

Where the Brock road crossed the Plank road, the column halted, while Fitz-Lee took Jackson to the front to a point whence he could see the Federal lines, with arms stacked, in bivouac behind their intrenchments, and utterly unconscious of the proximity of an enemy. Until that moment it had been uncertain exactly where Jackson would attack. But he now saw that by following the Brock road about two miles farther he would get upon the old turnpike, beyond the enemy's flank, and could take it in the rear. So the march was at once resumed to reach that position. But Paxton's brigade of Colston's division was here detached and placed with the cavalry, in observation on the Plank road, and did not rejoin its division until near midnight.

The head of the column made about two and a half miles an hour, the rear about one and a half, for in spite of all efforts the column lost distance. During the day there were three halts for rest of perhaps twenty minutes each. There were no vehicles except the artillery, ambulances, and ammunition wagons. These, marching each behind its division, made the column 10 miles in length, of which the infantry occupied over six. The head, marching at about 6 A.M., reached the deploying point on the turnpike by 4 P.M. The distance had proven greater than anticipated, and time was now of priceless value.

Meanwhile the movement, though misunderstood, had been detected by the enemy. About a mile southwest of Chancellorsville was a settlement called Hazel Grove, on a cleared ridge. From this ridge, about 8 A.M., Birney, of Sickles's corps, discovered a column of infantry, trains, and artillery passing his front. He brought up a battery and opened on the train at a range of 1600 yards, throwing it into much confusion, and compelling it to find other routes around the exposed point. Jackson sent a battery to reply and check the enemy from advancing. Sickles came to Birney's position and observed Jackson's column. His official report says:—

> This continuous column—infantry, artillery, trains, and ambulance—was observed for three hours, moving apparently in a southerly direction toward Orange C. H., on the O. & A. R. R. or Louisa C. H. on the Va. Cen. The movement indicated a retreat on Gordonsville, or an attack upon our right flank—perhaps both, for if the attack failed, the retreat would be continued. At noon I received orders to advance cautiously toward the road followed by the enemy, and attack his columns.

Sickles advanced Birney's division, which engaged an outpost on the flank and captured a regiment, the 23d GA. the two rear brigades, under Thomas and Archer, with Brown's battalion of artillery, were halted for an hour in observation, but were not engaged, and then followed on after the column. They were only able to overtake it, however, after night.

It was about 4 P.M. when the head of Jackson's column began its deployment on both sides of the Plank road, beyond Hooker's right, in the tangled forest; and it was nearly 6 P.M. when eight of the 12 brigades now in his column, had formed in two lines of battle, and one of the remaining four in a third line.

A detachment of Federals launch a valiant, but desperate counterattack on 3 May in effort to reverse the fortunes of the Army of the Potomac. However, the fate of Hooker's Chancellorsville Campaign had already been sealed.

Meanwhile Sickles, though now unopposed in front, had brought up Whipple's division of his own corps, and, having asked for reenforcements, had also received Barlow's brigade from the right flank of the 11th corps, Williams's division of the 12th corps, and three regiments of cavalry and some horse artillery under Pleasonton. Posey's brigade held the left flank of Lee's line of battle in Hooker's front, while Jackson conducted the flanking movement. Posey had a strong force of skirmishers in front, which became hotly engaged iwth the left flank of Sickles's advance, when it engaged Jackson's rear-guard. While bringing up their reenforcements, the Federal made several efforts to carry Posey's position, but were always repulsed. Sickles then planned to outflank and surround it, but he had been so slow that, before he was ready to act, Jackson had attacked, and Sickles was hastily recalled.

Otherwise there might have been a strange spectacle. Sickles might have routed Anderson at the same time that Jackson was routing Howard. For he was on Anderson's flank with over 20,000 infantry, a brigade of cavalry, and some horse artillery. He wandered off, however, to the south and west, for miles, where there was no enemy before him.

Along the front of Lee's line the six brigades present of Anderson's and McLaws's divisions, aided by their artillery, had spent the day in more or less active skirmishing and cannonading with the enemy. Where the enemy showed a disposition to advance, the Confederates were well satisfied to lie quiet and repel them, as on the left in front of Posey. But on the Confederate right the Federal skirmish-line, under Col. Miles, being strongly posted and showing no disposition to advance, it was wise to be moderately aggressive and keep the enemy in hopes of an attack. Kershaw and Semmes did this handsomely throughout the day, though the threat of Sickles's movements caused Lee to draw his troops to his left, and reduce his right to less than a full line.

About 6 P.M., the sun being then about one hour high, Jackson gave the signal to Rodes to move forward. His brigades were in the following order from left to right: Iverson, O'Neal, Doles, and Colquitt, with Ramseur's brigade 100 yards in rear of Colquitt on the right. Colston's three brigades formed in line with Ramseur, and in the following order from the left: Nichols, Jones, Warren. About half of each division was on each side of the pike, and two Napoleons of Breathed's horse artillery stood in the pike ready to follow the skirmishers. Two hundred yards behind Colston, A. P. Hill had deployed Pender on the left of the pike. Lane, McGowan, and Heth were coming in column down the pike. Archer and Thomas were following, but some miles behind. Jackson had made his play so far with fair success, and he now stood ready with over 20,000 men to surprise Howard's 13,000. He was sure of an important victory, but the fruits to be reaped from it would be limited for two reasons.

1st. Two brigades were some hours behind, for Archer, without orders, had taken them to protect the rear. 2d. There were now but two hours of daylight

left, and only in daylight can the fruits of victories be gathered. The question is suggested whether or not time had been anywhere lost unnecessarily. It would seem that 12 hours should not be needed to march 14 miles and form 20,000 men in line of battle. Briefly, it may be said, that with good broad roads, or with troops formed, ready to march at the word, and disciplined to take mud holes and obstructions without loss of distance, two hours could have been saved. But none of these conditions existed. Especially was time lost in the morning in getting the column formed.

Rodes reports it about 8 A.M. before the start was made. Further on, his report notes, "a delay was caused by an endeavor on our part to entrap some Federal cavalry." There may have been, during the morning, lack of appreciation of the value, even of the minutes, in an enterprise of the character now on foot, and an inadequate idea of the distance to be covered.

Some time was also lost in deploying Pender's brigade in the third line just before the charge was ordered. It would have saved a half-hour of great value to have ordered the charge as soon as the 2d line was formed, and allowed A. P. Hill's division to follow Rodes and Colston in column from the first, as they actually did at last. For, after advancing some distance through the tangled undergrowth, Pender's brigade was brought back to the road and placed at the head of the column for the rest of the advance.

It was nearly 6 P.M. when the signal for the advance was given by a bugle, and taken up and repeated for each brigade by bugles to the right and left through the woods. But the sounds seem to have been smothered in the forest, for the Federal reports make no mention of them. Their first intimation of anything unusual was given by wild turkeys, foxes, and deer, startled by the long lines of infantry and driven through the Federal camps. Then came shots from the Federal pickets, and then the guns on the turnpike opened and were soon followed by Confederate volleys and yells, impressing upon the enemy the fact that an overwhelming force had surprised them. Nevertheless, a gallant effort at resistance was made. The extreme right of the Federals was held by Von Gilsa's brigade of four regiments, about 1400 strong, which was formed, a half facing south and half facing west. They stood to fire three volleys, but by that time the Confederate lines were enveloping their flanks, and enfilade and reverse fire was being opened upon them. Only prompt flight could save the brigade from annihilation. After the third volley the brigade very wisely took to its heels and made its escape with a loss of 264 killed, wounded, and captured. Two guns with Von Gilsa were also captured. The next brigade to the left, McLean's, endeavored to change front. But it did not take long for the stern facts of the situation to become clear to every man of the brigade. As the canister fire of the Confederate guns was added to the enfilade fire of the Confederate infantry, this brigade also dissolved into a mass of fugitives, and two more guns, serving with them, were captured. But that they had fought well is shown by their losses, which were

The leader of the hapless XI Corps at Chancellorsville and Gettysburg, Major General Oliver Otis Howard.

692 out of about 2500. The division commander and four out of five regimental commanders were killed or wounded.

For a while, now, the fight degenerated into a foot race. Howard's original force of 13,000 had been reduced to 10,000 by the sending off of Barlow's large brigade. Of the 10,000, in a half-hour 4000 had been routed. The Confederates, recognizing the importance of pushing the pursuit, exerted themselves to the utmost. The lines broke into the double-quick wherever the ground was favorable, stopping only to fire at fugitives, or when completely out of breath. The horse artillery kept nearly abreast, and directed its fire principally at the Federal batteries which endeavored to cover the retreat. Some of these were fought gallantly, and some were overrun and captured. More might have been, and more prisoners taken, but for a blunder by Colquitt. His brigade was on the right of the front line, and its advance was least obstructed either by woods or the enemy. It could have moved most rapidly, and might have narrowed the enemy's avenue of escape.

Jackson's instructions had been explicit. Rodes's report says:—

Each brigade commander received positive instructions which were well understood. The whole line was to push ahead from the beginning, keeping the road for its guide. . . . Under no circumstances was there to be any pause in the advance.

Ramseur's brigade was ordered to move in rear of Colquitt's and to support it. Colquitt, early in the advance, halted to investigate a rumor of a body of the enemy on his right flank, which proved to be a small party of cavalry. He delayed so that neither his brigade or Ramseur's rejoined the line until late at night.

Thus two brigades, by disregard of instructions and without need, were kept entirely out of action during the whole afternoon. So it happened that five of Jackson's 15 brigades (Thomas, Archer, Paxton, Colquitt and Ramseur) were missing from his line of battle during the whole afternoon, and, as A. P. Hill's four remaining brigades were not deployed until after dark, only six brigades were in the attack and pursuit of the 11th corps: to wit, Rodes, Doles, and Iverson of Rodes's division, and Jones, Warren, and Nichols of Colston's division. The great advantage of the Confederates lay in their being able to bring the centre of their line of battle against the flank of the enemy's line. This overwhelmed the two right brigades in a very short while, as we have seen, and the line pushed rapidly on, hoping to overwhelm the succeeding brigades likewise, one at a time.

The next division was Schurz's of two brigades, in line of battle along the Plank road, with two batteries which took positions and fired on the approaching Confederates. Schurz endeavored to form at right angles to their approach, but the mass of fugitives with wagons, ambulances, beef cattle, etc., entirely overwhelmed some of his regiments, and only two or three isolated ones were able to march in good order, and, facing about, to fire from time to time at their pursuers.

Next, at Dowdall's tavern, was a line of rifle-pits at right angles to the Plank road, and already occupied by Buschbeck's brigade of Von Steinwehr's division, the last of Howard's corps—its companion brigade, Barlow's, being away with Sickles. Three or four batteries were here established upon the line, and to it were rallied numbers of fugitives. At last an organized resistance was prepared. When the Confederates approached, in very scattered shape, they met a severe fire, and the advance was checked. Had Colquitt here been on the Confederate right with his and Ramseur's brigades, an opportunity was offered for a large capture. It might have been accomplished by the force at hand with a little delay. But they were already flushed with victory and would not be denied. After a sharp fight of perhaps 20 minutes, Colston's second line merged into the first, and the two lines pushed forward everywhere. The Federal artillery foresaw the end and fled, five guns being too late and captured. Buschbeck followed in fairly good order, but preceded by a stampede of troops and trains, principally down the Plank road, though a part diverged to the left by a road to the White House, called the Bullock road.

The casualties in Schurz's division were 919. In Buschbeck's brigade were 483. The total loss of Howard's corps was: killed, 217; wounded, 1221; missing, 974; total, 2412; only about 20 per cent of the corps.

It was a very trifling loss, compared with what it might have been had all of Jackson's troops been upon the field, and had his orders been strictly observed.

The casualties of the Confederates are not known, their returns consolidating all separate actions together.

Much undeserved obloquy was heaped upon the 11th corps for their enforced retreat. No troops could have acted differently. All of their fighting was of one brigade at a time against six. With the capture of the Buschbeck position, the fighting of the day practically ceased. The Confederate troops were at the limit of exhaustion and disorganization. Daylight was fading fast, and commands badly intermingled. The pursuit was kept up, however, for some distance, although the enemy was no longer in sight. A few hundred yards beyond the Buschbeck position, the Plank road entered a large body of forest, closing on both sides of the road for nearly a mile before the open Chancellorsville plateau is reached. At the entrance of the wood a single Federal gun, with a small escort, was formed as a rearguard, and followed the retreat to Chancellorsville without seeing any pursuers.

A notable case of acoustic shadows occurred during this action. Sickles, some two and a half miles away, heard nothing of the attack upon Howard until word was brought him, which he at first refused to believe. At 6:30 P.M., Hooker sat on the veranda of the Chancellorsville house in entire confidence that Lee was retreating to Gordonsville and that Sickles was "among his trains." Faint sounds of distant cannonading were at first supposed to come from Sickles. Presently, an aid looking down the road with his glass suddenly shouted, "My God! here they come." All

Brigadier General Hiram G. Berry, killed while leading his division in the first day of combat at Chancellorsville.

sprang to their horses and, riding down the road, met, in a half-mile, the fugitive rabble of Howard's corps, and learned that Jackson, with half of Lee's army, had routed the Federal flank. Had there been some hours of daylight, Hooker's position would have been critical. For Lee and Jackson were now less than two miles apart, and between them were of infantry less than two divisions; Geary's of the 12th corps in front of Lee, and two brigades of Berry's of the 3d, near the path of Jackson.

But darkness puts an embargo upon offensive operations in a wooded country. Troops may be marched during the night, where there is no opposition, but the experiences of this occasion will illustrate the difficulty of fighting, even when the moon is at its best. The night restored to the Federals nearly all the advantages lost during the day. Hooker acted promptly and judiciously. Urgent recalls were sent for Sickles and his entire force. His advance had gone two miles to the front and was preparing to bivouac, when orders overtook it. It did not reach the field until after 10 P.M.

The force first available against Jackson was the artillery of the 12th corps, for which a fine position was offered along the western brow of the Chancellorsville plateau, south of the Plank road. This position was known as Fairview, and it now became the key-point of the battle. In front of it the open ground extended about 600 yards to the edge of the forest. A small stream, between moderate banks at the foot of

Ambrose Powell Hill. A major general commanding a division at Chancellorsville, Hill was advanced to the position of Lieutenant General with the III Corps of the Army of Northern Virginia at his disposal by the time of Gettysburg.

the plateau, offered shelter for a strong line of infantry in front of the guns. Here, within an hour, was established a powerful battery of 34 guns, and during the night all were protected by parapets. The position was essentially like the Confederate position at Marye's Hill before Fredericksburg, but on a larger scale. The forest in front offered no single position for a Confederate gun.

Only from one point could it be assailed by artillery. Across the stream in front, about 1000 yards obliquely to the left, was the small settlement called Hazel Grove, occupying some high open fields, from which, as has been told, Birney had that morning discovered Jackson's march. Hazel Grove offered excellent positions for attacking the Fairview lines, but Hazel Grove was itself within the Federal lines, and, about sundown, was occupied by a few cavalry with some artillery of the 3d corps, and some miscellaneous trains.

The only Federal infantry near at hand when the fugitives reached Chancellorsville were Carr's and Revere's brigades of Berry's division of the 3d corps. These brigades were formed in line of battle in the forest north of the Plank road, with their left resting on the guns at Fairview. Here they promptly set to work to intrench themselves in the forest across the Plank road, and to cut an abattis in front. They were soon reenforced by Hays's brigade of French's division

Dowdell's Tavern, the site where Major General Oliver O. Howard had set up his headquarters as Jackson was planning to descend upon his exposed forces.

of the 2d corps, and later by Mott's, the remaining brigade of Berry's division, which had been guarding bridges at United States Ford.

Meanwhile, as darkness fell, the Confederate pursuit died out upon entering the forest beyond the open lands about Dowdall's tavern. The cessation was not voluntary on Jackson's part, but it was necessary that Rodes's and Colston's divisions should be re-formed, and that Hill's division should take the lead. It had followed the pursuit, marching in column, and was in good order and comparatively fresh. The other divisions were broken, mingled, and exhausted, and several brigades were far behind. During the long pause in the advance, while Hill's brigades filed into the woods to the right and left, and the disorganized brigades were withdrawn to re-form, Jackson impatiently supervised and urged forward the movements. It is possible that he proposed to push his attack down the Bullock road which, a short distance ahead, diverged to the left, toward the river, instead of following the Plank road to Chancellorsville, as he had said to Hill: "Press them, Hill! Press them! Cut them off from United States Ford." It would, however, have been an error to make such a diversion, for the attack would have met an overwhelming force. Its only hope of success was to reunite with Lee at Chancellorsville with the least delay. Meanwhile, partaking of the impatience of Jackson, his chief of artillery, Col. Crutchfield, pushed some guns forward on the Plank road, and opened a random fire down it toward Chancellorsville, now less than a mile away.

It was an unwise move, for it provoked a terrific response from the 34 guns now in position upon Fairview plateau. The Plank road was now crowded with

troops and artillery in column, and the woods near it were full of the reorganizing brigades. Under such a fire, even in the dim light of the rising moon, great confusion soon resulted, and although casualities were few, it became necessary to discontinue our fire before order could be restored and the formation of the line of battle be resumed.

Lane's N.C. brigade was at the head of Hill's division. One regiment, the 33d, was deployed and sent some 200 yards ahead as skirmishers, and the other four formed line of battle with the centre on the Plank road in the following order from left to right: 28th, 18th, 37th, 7th. The Bullock road here diverged to the left, toward United States Ford, but the enemy was evidently close in front, and Jackson said to Lane, "Push right ahead, Lane. Right ahead."

While the formation was still in progress, Jackson, followed by several staff-officers and couriers, rode slowly forward upon an old road, called the Mountain road, which left the Bullock to its left near the Plank road, and ran parallel to the latter, about 80 yards distant, toward Chancellorsville.

Up this road the party advanced for 100 or 200 yards, but not passing the 33d N.C. skirmish-line. They then halted and listened for a while to the axes of the Federals, cutting abattis in the forest ahead. Beyond the Plank road, the Federal troops who had been off with Sickles were now returning, and were slowly working their way to reoccupy some breastworks which had been built the night before in the forest south of the Plank road. Between their skirmishers and those of the 33d N.C. on their side of the

These powerful cannons supported Sedgwick's columns as they moved forth to attack Jubal Early's Southern soldiers who occupied the heights overlooking the town on 3 May, 1863.

Plank road, there suddenly began some firing. The fire spread rapidly in both directions, along the picket-lines, and was presently taken up by Federal regiments and lines of battle in the rear. Jackson, at the head of his party, was slowly retracing his way back to his line of battle, when this volley firing began. Maj. Barry, on the left of the 18th N.C., seeing through the trees by the moonlight a group of horsemen moving toward his line, ordered his left wing to fire. Two of the party were killed, and Jackson received three balls; one in the right hand, one through the left wrist and hand, and one shattering the left arm between shoulder and elbow.

The reins were dropped, and the horse, turning from the fire, ran into overhanging limbs which nearly unhorsed him; but, recovering the rein, he guided into the Plank road where Capt. Wilbourn of his staff helped him off. Meanwhile, the enemy had advanced guns to their skirmish-line, and presently began to sweep the Plank road with shell and canister. A litter was brought and Jackson placed in it, but a bearer was shot, and Jackson fell heavily on his wounded side. With great difficulty he was finally gotten to an ambulance, which already held his chief of artillery, Col. Crutchfield, with a shattered leg.

During the night Jackson's left arm was amputated, and the next day he was taken in an ambulance via Spottsylvania, to a small house called Chandler's, near Guinea Station. For a few days his recovery was expected, but pneumonia supervened, and he died on May 10. In his last moments his mind wandered, and he was again upon the battle-field giving orders to his troops: "Order A. P. Hill to prepare for action. Pass the infantry to the front. Tell Maj. Hawks—" There was a pause for some moments, and then, calmly, the last words, "Let us pass over the river, and rest under the shade of the trees."

Jackson's fall left A. P. Hill in command, but Hill was himself soon disabled by a fragment of shell, and sent for Stuart. Rodes ranked Stuart, but the latter was not only best known to the army, but was of great popularity, and Rodes cheerfully acquiesced. His whole career, until his death at Winchester, Sept. 19, '64, was brilliant, and justifies the belief that he would have proven a competent commander, but, as will be seen, Stuart's conduct, upon this occasion, was notably fine. A little before dark, Stuart, with Jackson's consent, had taken his cavalry and a regiment of infantry and started to attack the camps and trains of the enemy near Ely's Ford. He had reached their vicinity and was forming for the assault, when one of Jackson's staff brought the message of recall. He ordered the command to fire three volleys into the nearest camp and then to withdraw, while he rode rapidly back—about five miles—and took command between 10 and 11 P.M.

There was but one course to take—to make during the night such preparation as was possible, and, at dawn, to renew the attack and endeavor to break through the enemy's line and unite with Lee at Chancellorsville. The wounding of Crutchfield had left me the senior artillery officer present, and I was sent for,

The great Thomas J. "Stonewall" Jackson. An unsurpassed tactician and fighter, his tragic death was a serious blow to the Confederacy.

and directed to reconnoitre, and to post before dawn as many guns as could be used. I spent the night in reconnoissance and, beside the Plank road, could find but one outlet through the forest, a cleared vista some 200 yards long and 25 wide, through a dense pine thicket, opening upon a cleared plateau held by the enemy. This plateau afterward proved to be the Hazel Grove position, and I concentrated near it several batteries.

One of Jackson's engineers was sent by a long detour and found Lee before daylight and explained to him Stuart's position and plans, that he might, during the action, extend his left and seek a connection with our right. During the night, the brigades in rear rejoined, and the three divisions were formed for the attack in the morning, with Hill's division in front, Colston's in a second line, and Rodes's in a third.

Two brigades on Hill's right were placed obliquely to the rear, to present a front toward that flank.

When Hooker found that the Confederate attack had come to a standstill in front of the Fairview line, with Sickles near Hazel Grove upon its right flank, he ordered Sickles to move forward by the moonlight, and attack. Birney's division, in two lines with supporting columns, about midnight, advanced from Hazel Grove upon the forest south of the Plank road and in front of the Fairview position. The left wing of this force grazed the skirmishers of McGowan and

struck the right flank of Lane's brigade, of which two and a half regiments became sharply engaged. But the whole Federal advance glanced off, as it were, and, changing its direction, it turned toward the Federal line in front of Fairview, where it approached the position of Knipe's and Ruger's brigades of Williams's division of the 12th corps.

Hearing their noisy approach, and believing them to be Confederates, the Fairview guns and infantry opened fire upon the woods, while the approaching lines were still so distant that they were unable to locate their assailants, and supposed the fire to come from the Confederate line. And now for a long time, for one or perhaps two hours, the Confederates listened to a succession of furious combats in the forest in their front, accompanied by heavy shelling of the woods, volleys of musketry, and a great deal of cheering. Our pickets and skirmish-lines were forced sometimes to lie down or seek protection of trees from random bullets, but we had no other part in it. It extended northward sometimes even across the Plank road. And the official reports of many Federal officers give glowing accounts of the repulse of desperate Confederate attacks, and even of the capture of Confederate guns. These stories were founded on the finding of some Federal guns, which had been abandoned in one of the stampedes of the afternoon.

Col. Hamlin's book says:

Where the grand plans of the Chancellorsville were hatched and a General indulged in his infamous sexual improprieties: "Fighting Joe" Hooker's quarters at Falmouth.

Lee, the mastermind behind the demise of many a Federal general's career.

Some of the reports of this midnight encounter are missing, and their publication will throw much light on the details. On the Federal side it was undoubtedly a mixed-up mess, and some of the regiments complain of being fired into from the front and from both flanks. . . . At all events, after reading the reports of Gen. Sickles at the time, and his statement a year afterward to Congress . . . the brilliant array of gallant troops in the moonlight . . . the bold attack . . . the quick return of one of the columns to be stopped by the bayonets of the 63d Pa. . . . the advance of the other column deflecting to the right, until it met Gen. Slocum in person . . . certainly there is occasion for a slight smile on the part of the reader. And this smile may be lengthened on reading the story of Gen. De Trobriand, who was a participator, or the account left by Col. Underwood of the 23d Mass., who returned from the depths of the wilderness in time to witness and describe the ludicrous scene.

Hooker had little cause for apprehension after darkness had come to his relief, yet the shock to his overconfidence had been so severe that his only new dispositions were defensive. Yet he had over 60,000 fresh troops present, while Lee had on the east but about 16,000 and on the west about 24,000.

His first care was to order the intrenchment of an interior line, upon which he could fall back in case Stuart forced his way through to a junction with Lee. A short line was quickly selected, of great natural strength, behind Hunting Run on the west, and behind Mineral Spring Run on the east, with both flanks resting on the river and covering his bridges. This line will be more fully described and referred to later. It took in the White House, some three fourths of a mile in the rear of Chancellorsville, and was probably the strongest field intrenchment ever built in Va. Next, Hooker sent orders to Sedgwick at 9 P.M., as follows:

The major-general, commanding, directs that

you cross the Rappahannock at Fredericksburg on receipt of this order, and at once take up your line of march on the Chancellorsville road until you connect with him, and will attack and destroy any force you may fall in with on your road.

"You will leave all your trains behind, except pack trains of your ammunition, and march to be in the vicinity of the general at daylight. You will probably fall upon the rear of the forces commanded by Gen. Lee, and between you and the major-general, commanding, he expects to use him up. Send word to Gen. Gibbon to take possession of Fredericksburg. Be sure not to fail.

These orders were good, and would have insured victory, had they been carried out. And Hooker took a further precaution, most desirable whenever important orders are issued. He despatched a competent staff-officer, Gen. Warren, his chief engineer, to supervise their execution. Unfortunately for him, however, under the conditions it proved impossible to execute the orders within the time set, as will be told later. Here it is only necessary to note that Sedgwick was never able to get near Chancellorsville.

Even as the field stood, with or without the arrival of Sedgwick, the battle was still Hooker's, had he fought where he stood. But about dawn he made the fatal mistake of recalling Sickles from the Hazel Grove position, which he was holding with Whipple's and Birney's divisions, and five batteries. There has rarely been a more gratuitous gift of a battle-field. Sickles had a good position and force enough to hold it, even without reenforcements, though ample reenforcements were available. The Federal line was longer and overlapped ours on its right, and our only opportunity to use artillery was through the narrow vista above referred to, which was scarcely sufficient for four guns, and had but a very restricted view.

Had Stuart's attack been delayed a little longer, our right flank might have marched out upon Hazel Grove plateau without firing a shot. A Federal battery, supported by two regiments, had been designated as a rear-guard, and it alone occupied the plateau when our advance was made, though the rear of the retiring column was still near.

Stuart's men, when the lines were finally formed, got from two to three hours' rest before dawn. About that time, cooked rations were brought up. Before the distribution, however, was finished, Archer's and McGowan's brigades were moved forward, from their retired positions as the right flank, to straighten the line. They soon came upon a picket-line of the enemy, and sharp firing began. Stuart, without waiting further, ordered the whole line to the attack.

Archer's brigade, about 1400 strong, in advancing through the pine thickets, drifted to the right, and gradually opened a gap between it and McGowan's brigade, emerging from the forest alone, and in front of the enemy's rear-guard. A sharp action ensued, while Archer extended his right and threatened the enemy's rear, forcing the battery to retreat. He then charged and captured 100 prisoners, and forced the abandonment of four of the guns.

He attempted to push his advance much farther,

Commander of the Army of Northern Virginia, Robert E. Lee.

but was checked by the fire of the enemy's artillery and of the rear brigade, Graham's, of Sickles's column. After two efforts, realizing that his force was too small, and leaving one of his captured guns, he fell back to Hazel Grove ridge, about 6:30 A.M. This was now being occupied rapidly by our guns. Thus, so easily that we did not at once realize its great value, we gained space for our batteries, where we soon found that we could enfilade the enemy's adjacent lines.

Meanwhile, the first assault had been made along the whole line by Hill's division. The enemy's advanced line crossed the Plank road and was held by Williams's division of the 12th corps, Berry's of the 3d corps, and Hays's brigade of the 2d corps. In rear of the front line was a second line near the edge of the forest. Across the small stream and along the edge of the elevated plateau, their artillery had been strongly intrenched during the night, making a third line. The two divisions from Hazel Grove, with their four batteries, were brought up in rear of the forces already holding the front to the west. This whole front from north to south was scarcely a mile and a quarter long. It was defended by about 25,000 men, and it was being attacked by about an equal number. The Confederates, however, had the hot end of the affair, in having to take the aggressive and advance upon breastworks protected by abattis and intrenched guns.

In his first assault, however, Hill's division, now commanded by Heth, after a terrific exchange of musketry, succeeded in driving the Federals from the whole of their front line. They followed the retreating enemy, and attacked the second line, where the resistance became more strenuous. On the extreme right, Archer's brigade had now fallen back to Hazel Grove, where it remained, supporting the guns now taking position there. This left McGowan's flank uncovered, and a Federal force attacked it, and drove it back to the captured line. This uncovered Lane's brigade, and it was also forced to fall back. On the left of the Plank road, the advance of Thomas beyond the enemy's first line met both a stronger second line and a flank attack, his left being in the air. After an hour's hard fighting, the whole line was forced back to the captured breastworks, with severe losses. It was clear that extreme efforts would be needed to drive the enemy from his position. Stuart ordered 30 additional guns to Hazel Grove, and brought forward both the second and third lines, putting in at once his last reserves. It would be useless to follow in detail the desperate fighting which now ensued and was kept up for some hours. The Federal guns on the Fairview heights were able to fire over the heads of two lines of infantry, and other batteries aided from the new position in which Hooker had now established the 1st, 2d, and 5th corps. This was so near on our left that Carroll's and McGregor's brigades of the 2d corps, with artillery, were sent forward to attack our flank, and were only repulsed after such fighting that they lost 367 men. With the aid of our second and third lines, fresh assaults were made on both sides of the Plank road, and now the enemy's second lines were carried. But his reserves were called upon, and again our lines

were driven back, and countercharges south of the road again penetrated the gap between McGowan and Archer. Paxton's brigade was brought across from the north and restored the situation at a critical moment, Paxton, however, being killed. Some of our brigades were now nearly fought out, the three divisions being often massed in one, and the men could only be moved by much example on the part of their officers. Stuart himself was conspicuous in this, and was everywhere encouraging the troops with his magnetic presence and bearing, and singing as he rode along the lines, "Old Joe Hooker, won't you come out the Wilderness." There can be no doubt that his personal conduct had great influence in sustaining the courage of the men so that when, at last, our artillery had begun to shake the Federals' lines, there was still the spirit to traverse the bloody ground for the fourth time and storm the Fairview batteries.

Guns had been brought to Hazel Grove from all the battalions on the field—Pegram's, Carter's, Jones's, McIntosh's, and Alexander's. Perhaps 50 guns in all were employed here, but less than 40 at any one time, as guns were occasionally relieved, or sent to the rear to refill. Their field of fire was extensive, being an oblique on both the enemy's artillery and infantry. Some ground having been gained on the Plank road, Cols. Jones and Carter had also been able to establish 10 rifle guns there, which enfiladed the Plank road as far as the Chancellorsville house.

About nine o'clock, the Federal artillery fire was perceptibly diminished. Many of their guns were running short of ammunition, and fresh ammunition was

Federal engineers laying a bridge across the Potomac.

not supplied. Sickles asked for it, and for reenforcements, but none were sent. It would seem that Hooker preferred to lose the Chancellorsville plateau entirely, and fall back into his new position, which was like a citadel close at hand, rather than risk fighting outside of it.

At Stuart's last charge, the Federal lines yielded with but moderate resistance. The guns in the Fairview intrenchments abandoned them, and fell back to the vicinity of the Chancellorsville house.

The guns at Hazel Grove moved forward across the valley and occupied the deserted Federal positions, here making connection with Anderson's division which Lee was extending to his left to meet them. They were soon joined by Jordan's battery of my own battalion, which had been serving with Anderson.

The enemy, driven out of their fortified lines, attempted to make a stand near the Chancellorsville house, but it was a brief one. There were no breastworks here to give shelter, and their position was now so contracted that our guns from three directions crossed their fire upon it. Hooker, in the porch of the Chancellorsville house, was put *hors de combat* for two or three hours by a piece of brick torn from a pillar by a cannon-shot. No one took command in his place, and for a while the army was without a head. Meanwhile, McLaws and Anderson had seen the enemy withdrawing from their fronts and pressed forward at the same time that Stuart's infantry crowned the plateau from the west. Some prisoners were cut off and captured on each flank, and a few guns also fell into our hands, but, as a whole, the enemy's with-

Major General John Sedgwick of the VI Corps.

Members of Sedgwick's VI Corps seize Marye's Heights at Fredericksburg. Almost six months earlier at this same location, the Army of the Potomac was slaughtered as it tried to storm the elevation.

drawal was orderly and well managed, and with less loss than might have been expected. One sad feature of the occasion was that the woods on the north of the road were set on fire by shells, and the dry leaves spread the fire rapidly, although the trees and undergrowth did not burn. Efforts were made to remove the wounded, but the rapid spread of the fire prevented, and some of the wounded of both armies were burned.

About 10 A.M., Lee, advancing with McLaws's division, met Stuart with Jackson's corps near the site of the Chancellorsville house, now only a smoking ruin, for our shells had set it on fire. It was, doubtless, a proud moment to Lee, as it was to the troops who greeted him with enthusiastic cheering.

Lee, by no means, intended the battle to end here. Both infantry and artillery were ordered to replenish ammunition and renew the assault, but there came news from the rear, which forced a change of programme. Sedgwick's corps had broken through the flimsy line in front of it, and was now moving up the Plank road. With all his audacity Lee could not venture to attack five corps intrenched in his front, while Sedgwick came up in his rear.

The story of events at Chancellorsville must now pause, as the action there paused, while that is told of Sedgwick's venture against Lee's rear.

Hooker had sent urgent orders the night before to Sedgwick to come to his help, and a staff-officer, Warren, to supervise their execution. But Sedgwick, though already on the south side of the river, which Hooker did not seem to know, was three miles below Fredericksburg, near the scene of Franklin's crossing in Dec. He had been under orders to advance toward Richmond on the Bowling Green road, and had disposed his troops accordingly.

To advance up the Plank road, it was necessary to march to Fredericksburg and force the Confederate lines on Marye's Hill. These lines were held from Taylor's Hill to the Howison house, about three miles, by only two brigades, Barksdale's and Hays's, with a small amount of artillery. The regiments were strung out in single rank, the men sometimes yards apart, and with wide intervals at many places between regiments. On Marye's Hill, two regiments, the 18th and 21st Miss., with six guns of the Washington Arty. and two under Lt. Brown of Alexander's Bat., were distributed from the Plank road to Hazel Creek, about a half-mile.

Sedgwick had marched at midnight with a good moon, but his progress was slow, for the Confederate pickets annoyed it. By daylight he was in Fredericksburg, and his batteries from both banks of the river and from the edge of the town opened on the Confederates. Sedgwick had been informed by Hooker that the Confederate force left at Fredericksburg was very small, and, without delay, he sent forward four regiments from Wheaton's and Shaler's brigades to charge the works in front of Marye's Hill. It was sending a boy on a man's errand. The Confederate infantry reserved its fire until the enemy were within 40 yards, when they opened and quickly drove them back. A second assault was made, but with similar

result. Sedgwick was now convinced that a heavy force confronted him, and he waited for Gibbon's division of the 2d corps. This had just crossed from Falmouth, and it made an effort upon the extreme Confederate left. It proved futile on account of the canal along the front at that part of the field, which was defended by three regiments of Hays's brigade fo Early's division, hurried there by Early on seeing the enemy's preparations.

Soon afterward, Wilcox's brigade came to the scene from Banks Ford, where it had been in observation on the 2d. At dawn on the 3d, Wilcox noted that the enemy's pickets on the north side were wearing haversacks, and correctly guessed that the forces opposite were leaving for Chancellorsville. He was preparing to march in the same direction, when a messenger brought word of the advance of Gibbon's division. Thereupon leaving a picket of 50 men and two guns in observation at Banks Ford, Wilcox marched to Taylor's Hill.

About 10 A.M., Gibbon having reported that an attack on our extreme left was impracticable, and Howe's division, making no progress east of Hazel Run, Sedgwick had no recourse but to renew his attack upon Marye's Hill by main force. He accordingly prepared a much stonger assault than that of the morning. Newton's division, supported by Burnham's brigade, was to attack Marye's Hill, while Howe's division assaulted Lee's Hill beyond Hazel Run.

This force numbered about 14,000 men, with an abundant artillery. Across Hazel Creek were seven guns of Cutt's and Cabell's battalions, and the two remaining regiments of Barksdale's brigade and one LA. of Hays's brigade.

About 11 A.M., both Newton and Howe renewed the assault. Newton advanced rapidly through the fire of the few Confederate guns, but recoiled soon after the infantry opened, although Barksdale's line was so thin that it scarcely averaged a man to five feet of parapet. Some of the Federal regiments, however, suffered severely, and a number of killed and wounded were left near the Confederate line.

This, by a strange piece of good nature on the part of one of our best officers, proved our undoing. When Newton's line was beaten back, the firing on both sides nearly ceased, and some Federal officer sent forward a flag of truce. No Federal report mentions this incident. The flag was probably sent by only a brigade commander, for the fighting, by Howe's division, across Hazel Run, was kept up without cessation. Col. Griffin of the 18th Miss. received the flag. The officer bearing it asked to be allowed to remove his dead and wounded in Griffin's front. Without referring to his brigade commander, Griffin granted the request, and, still more thoughtlessly, allowed his own men to show themselves while the wounded were being delivered. The enemy, to their great surprise, discovered what a small force was in their front.

They lost little time in taking advantage of the information. The action was reopened, and now a charge was made with a rush, and the enemy swarmed over our works. The Mississippians had no chance to

The remnants of battle at the infamous stonewall of Marye's Heights at Fredericksburg. After three desperate attempts on 3 May 1862, the 25,000 men of Sedgwick's VI Corps managed to wrest this position from the possession of a Confederate force less than half their numbers under Major General Jubal Early.

escape, but fought with butts of guns and bayonets, and were mostly captured, with the loss of about 100 killed and wounded. The casualties in Newton's division and Burnham's brigade, in the whole battle, were about 1200, of which probably 900 fell in this affair. All of the guns on the hill were captured, Brown's section last of all, firing until surrounded.

Meanwhile, Howe's division had a full mile to traverse before Reaching the Confederate lines. Instead of a charge, their progress was a slow advance under cover of heavy artillery fire. Before they reached the Confederate line, Newton's division had made its second charge and was in possession of Marye's Hill. Thereupon, Early, who was in command, ordered the withdrawal of his whole division, and the formation of a new line of battle across the Telegraph road, about two miles in the rear. Here he concentrated Gordon's,

Hoke's, and Smith's brigades, with the remnants of Barksdale's. Hays's brigade had been cut off with Wilcox, and these two brigades were in position to delay Sedgwick in advancing upon the Plank road toward Chancellorsville. But Hays, under orders from Early, crossed the Plank road before Sedgwick had made any advance. Wilcox then took position with four guns across the Plank road, and delayed the enemy's advance as much as possible, while he fell back slowly to Salem Church, where he had been notified that McLaws would meet him with reenforcements. He reached this point about 3 P.M., meeting there Wofford's, Semmes's, Kershaw's, and Mahone's brigades, under McLaws. The five brigades rapidly formed a single line of battle across the Plank road. Wilcox's brigade held the centre, with the 14th and 11th Ala. on the left of the Plank road, and the 10th and 8th on the right. The 9th Ala. was in reserve a short distance in rear of the 10th. Four guns were posted across the Plank road, and a company of infantry was put in Salem Church, and one in a schoolhouse a short distance in front. Kershaw's brigade was on the right of Wilcox, and Wofford on right of Kershaw; Semmes's brigade was on Wilcox's left, and Mahone's brigade was on the left of Semmes.

In front of the line of battle stretched a fringe of dense young wood, some 200 yards wide, and beyond that, for perhaps a half-mile, were open fields, which extended with a few interruptions on each side of the Plank road back to Fredericksburg, about four miles. Sedgwick had been delayed over four hours in traversing that distance.

About 4:30 P.M., Sedgwick established a battery 1000 yards in front of Wilcox, and opened fire. The Confederate artillery was nearly out of ammunition, and after a few rounds it was withdrawn. Encouraged by this, the Federals now sent forward Brooks's division, formed across the road in two lines, with Newton's division in the same formation upon Brooks's right.

Now ensued one of the most brilliant and important of the minor affairs of the war. McLaws had reached the field and assumed the command, but credit is also due to Wilcox, who had delayed many times his number for several hours, and gained time for reenforcements to arrive.

The story of the battle may be told very briefly. North of the road, opposite the 14th and 11th Ala., was Torbert's Jersey brigade under Brown, in a double line. On the south, opposite the 8th, 9th, and 10th Ala., was Bartlett's brigade, one of the best in the Federal army, which boasted that it had never been repulsed, and had never failed to hold any position it was ordered to occupy.

The strength of the Confederate position consisted in the thick undergrowth which completely hid their lines, lying down on the crest of a slight ridge in rear of the woods. These were held by skirmishers during the enemy's approach across the open. When the artillery was withdrawn, it left a gap of about 50 yards between the 11th Ala., on the left of the road and the 10th on the right. Bartlett's brigade advanced gallantly through the severe skirmish fire, fought through the strip of woods, drove the company from the church, and cut off the one in the schoolhouse. Pushing on and overlapping the left of the 10th Ala., they enfiladed it, broke its line, and drove it back in confusion. The 8th Ala., under Lt.-Col. Herbert, on the right of the 10th, however, did not break, but threw back its three left companies, and brought an enfilade fire on the enemy's further advance. The 9th Ala., being in reserve a little in rear of the 10th, rose from the ground, and, giving the enemy a volley, charged them and drove them back.

Brown's brigade, on the opposite side of the road, had a wider body of woods to cross, and had not advanced as far as Bartlett. But when Bartlett was driven back, Wilcox's whole brigade joined in the counter-stroke. Bartlett's first line was followed so

Members of the VI Corps capturing a Confederate battery near Fredericksburg.

Rescuing wounded from a funeral pyre of burning brush.

rapidly that the prisoners in the schoolhouse were liberated, and the rush of the fugitives and the quick pursuit overwhelmed the second line, giving it no chance to make a stand.

Across the Plank road, Semmes's two right regiments, the 10th and 51st Ga., joined the 14th and 11th Ala., and these four regiments, meeting the Jersey brigade in the woods, drove it back in such a direction that the fugitives from each side of the Plank road converged upon the road. The Confederates in pursuit said that they had never had such crowds to fire upon. The pursuit was dangerously prolonged, but fortunately the enemy contented himself by checking it, and the Confederates then slowly withdrew. Long-range firing, however, was kept up until night.

Bartlett's brigade reported a loss in this attack of 580 officers and men out of less than 1500 men. Brown's brigade reported a loss of 511.

Wilcox's brigade lost 75 killed, 372 wounded, and 48 missing, a total of 495. The losses of Semmes's brigade are included with the campaign losses. One of its regiments, however, the 10th Ga., reports for this day: 21 killed, 102 wounded, and 5 missing, a total of 128 out of 230 present. In the morning at Chancellorsville, this regiment had received the surrender of the 27th Conn., which had been on picket and was cut off by the capture of Chancellorsville. During this charge it also captured 100 prisoners. While this action was going on, Early had formed line of battle to resist an advance of the enemy upon the Telgraph road, and was bringing up his extreme right from Hamilton's Crossing. It was about night when his whole division was concentrated.

The enemy was holding Gibbon's entire division idle in Fredericksburg, guarding the pontoon bridges to Falmouth. Had Gibbon moved up on Sedgwick's flank to Banks Ford, his division would have counted for something in the next day's affairs. His force was just what Segwick needed to enable him to hold his ground.

Returning now to Chancellorsville, we have to note a movement which involved an unfortunate Confederate delay on the next day—a delay which enabled Sedgwick's corps to escape scot-free from a position which should have cost him all his artillery

On 13 December 1862, the city of Fredericksburg was devastated by the battle that raged there between the Burnside's Army of the Potomac and Lee's Army of Northern Virginia. Several months later on 3 May, war and devastation would return to the city.

and half his men. The River road, from Chancellorsville to Fredericksburg via Banks Ford, was left unoccupied when Hooker took refuge in his fortified lines on the morning of the 3d. Anderson, with his three remaining brigades,—Wright's, Perry's and Posey's,—was sent at 4 P.M. to watch that road, and threaten the enemy upon that flank. Two hours after sunrise on the 4th, Heth arrived with three brigades to relieve Anderson, who was now ordered to proceed to Salem Church, about six miles, and report to McLaws, which he did about noon. This sending Anderson to reënforce McLaws might have been done the afternoon before. He would then have been on hand at the earliest hour for the joint attack upon Sedgwick, on the 4th, which is now to be described.

The events of the morning of the 4th had been as follows: No communication had been received by Sedgewick from Hooker, and he was still under orders to come to Chancellorsville. But at an early hour, movements of Early's troops were discovered in his rear, and, instead of advancing, Segwick had deployed Howe's division perpendicular to the Plank road facing to his rear, and stretching to the river above Banks

Sedgwick's opponent at Marye's Heights, Jubal Early.

Ford, where pontoon bridges had been laid the afternoon before. Sedgwick's scouts had reported that "a column of the enemy, 15,000 strong, coming from the direction of Richmond, had occupied the heights of Fredericksburg, cutting him off from the town." He at once abandoned all idea of taking the aggressive, and only wished himself safely across the river. But he did not dare to attempt a crossing, except under cover of night. His lines were too long, and were weak in plan, as they faced in three directions,—east, south, and west. But he dared not venture a change, for fear of precipitating an attack. When at last he received a despatch from Hooker, its noncommital advice was not encouraging. It said:

> Everything snug here. We contracted the lines a little and repulsed the last assault with ease. Gen. Hooker wishes them to attack him tomorrow, if they will. He does not desire you to attack them again in force, unless he attacks him at the same time. He says you are too far away for him to direct. Look well to the safety of your corps, and keep up communication with Gen. Benham at Banks Ford and Fredericksburg. You can go to either place if you think it best to cross. Banks Ford would bring you in supporting distance of the main body, and would be better than falling back to Fredericksburg.

A little later Hooker sent another message, urging Sedgwick, if possible, to hold a position on the south bank, to which Sedgwick replied:

> The enemy threatens me strongly on two fronts. My position is bad for such attack. It was assumed for attack, not for defence. It is not improbable that the bridges at Banks Ford may be sacrificed. Can you help me strongly if I am attacked?

No answer to his inquiry appears, and Sedgwick stood on the defensive, awaiting nightfall. Meanwhile, early in the morning, Early's division, with Barksdale's brigade, had moved down upon Marye's Hill, which they found held by a picket force only, and easily occupied. An advance was attempted into Fredericksburg, but it was found with barricades across the streets held by one of Gibbon's brigades, supported by two other brigades and a number of guns on the north bank. Early then sent to communicate with McLaws and endeavor to arrange a joint attack upon Sedgwick, but received information that Anderson's division was coming, and was himself sent for to meet Lee.

Before leaving Chancellorsville that morning, Lee had examined Hooker's lines with the view of assaulting at once, but their strength made it imprudent to do so while Sedgwick was still south of the river. So he next set out to dispose of Sedgwick, that he might then concentrate his whole force to attack Hooker.

Probably no man ever commanded an army and, at the same time, so entirely commanded himself, as Lee. This morning was almost the only occasion on which I ever saw him out of humor. It was when waiting the arrival of Anderson, with his three brigades from the River road, after being relieved by Heth. Anderson was in no way to blame for the delay, but he should have been relieved the afternoon before, which would have let him move during the night.

Some delay was inevitable, as Sedgwick's peculiar rectangular formation was not readily understood. It was about three miles in extent, and occupied high ground, with a wide, open valley in its front, forcing a development of our line of nearly six miles to cover its three fronts. An entire day would have been none too much to devote to the attack, if the fruits of victory were to be reaped. Although Lee urged all possible speed, it was 6 P.M. when the advance commenced. Sunset was at seven. Darkness fell before the lines could be gotten into close action. In the dusk, two of Early's brigades, Hoke's and Hays's, fired into each other by mistake, and were thrown into confusion. Both had to be withdrawn and re-formed. The enemy was, however, forced back to the vicinity of Banks Ford, and had there then been daylight to bring up our batteries, there might have been large captures. Upon McLaws's front, ranges were marked by daylight for firing upon Banks Ford and some guns were kept firing all night. But all that was possible amounted only to annoyance. It was again illustrated that afternoon attacks seldom reap any fruits of victory.

It was with great elation on the morning of the 5th, that our guns fired the two last shots across the Rappahannock at Sedgwick's retreating columns. But orders, soon received from headquarters, indicated that our commander was not yet satisfied. Early's division and Barksdale's brigade were directed to remain in observation at Banks Ford and Fredericksburg,—which has also been evacuated by Gibbon's division during the previous night,—while all the rest of the army was ordered to return to the front of Hooker's lines near Chancellorsville, which Lee intended to assault on the morrow with his whole force.

What was known of the enemy's position gave as-

The 9th Massachusetts Battery racing for room on the road with a wagon train.

In a scene of horrific butchery near Marye's Heights, caissons and horses lie scattered about after being torn apart by a missile fired from the Federal heavy artillery on the opposite side of the Rappahannock River.

surance that the task would be the heaviest which we had ever undertaken. Hooker now had his entire army concentrated, and, allowing for his losses, must have had fully 90,000 men to defend about five miles of breastworks. These he had had 48 hours to prepare, with all the advantages for defence which the Wilderness offered. Lee would scarcely be able to bring into action 35,000 under all the disadvantages imposed by the Wilderness upon the offensive and by two streams which on the southeast and northwest covered three-fourths of the enemy's front. Behind these streams both flanks rested securely upon the river. The attack would have to be made everywhere squarely in front, and our artillery would be unable to render any efficient help. When, upon the 6th, we found the lines deserted and the enemy gone, our engineers were amazed at the strength and completeness of the enemy's intrenchments. Impenetrable abattis covered the entire front, and the crest everywhere carried head-logs under which the men could fire as through loopholes. In rear, separate structures were provided for officers, with protected outlooks, whence they could see and direct without exposure.

The 29th Pennsylvania of Kane's Brigade of the XII Corps weathering enemy artillery fire at Chancellorsville.

Four of Hooker's corps had suffered casualties averaging 20 per cent, but three, the 1st, 2d, and 5th, had scarcely been engaged. It must be conceded that Lee never in his life took a more audacious resolve than when he determined to assault Hooker's intrenchments. And it is the highest possible compliment to the army commanded by Lee to say that there were two persons concerned who believed that, in spite of all the odds, it would have been victorious. These two persons were Gens. Lee and Hooker. For Hooker was already hurrying his preparations to retreat during the coming night. Clearly, this decision was the mistake of his life.

During the afternoon of the 5th, there came on one of the remarkable storms which on many occasions closely followed severe engagements. The rainfall was unusually heavy and continued long after dark, converting roads into quagmires, rivulets into torrents, and causing great discomfort to man and beast. But its occurrence was advantageous to the Confederates, as it prevented their pressing upon the enemy's impregnable line, and it hurried the efforts of the Federals to cross the river, as rapidly rising waters overflowed the approaches to their bridges. Before the rain, I had found positions for several guns close upon the river-bank, partly around a bend below the Federal left, giving an oblique fire upon some of their batteries. During the night we constructed pits, and, at early dawn, were putting the guns in them, when we were suddenly fired upon by guns square upon our own flank and across the river. A lieutenant had his ankle smashed, some horses were killed, and some dismounted limber chests were exploded, before all could be gotten under cover in the pits. From these we could make no reply, as they faced Hooker's lines, and we could only lie close and wait for more daylight. This revealed that the enemy had abandoned his works during the night and recrossed the river. To retaliate I brought up seven other guns, under cover of a wood, and engaged the enemy for a half-hour, inflicting "some loss in killed and wounded," as reported by Gen. Hunt, with no further loss to ourselves, but the wheel of a gun. Finding by then that the battle was over and no enemy left on our side of the river, the guns were gradually withdrawn and camps were sought in another severe rain-storm, which came up about 5 P.M. and lasted far into the night.*

The battle made by Stuart on the 3d, has rarely been surpassed, measured either by the strength of the lines carried or by the casualties suffered in so brief a period. In Colston's division four brigades lost eight brigade commanders, three killed and five disabled. Three out of six of the division staff fell. In Pender's brigade of Heth's division, six out of ten field-officers were killed or wounded. Our brigades rarely came to the field 2000 strong, and casualties of 600 to a brigade were rarely reached even in battles prolonged over a day. Here within six hours, five of the 15 brigades lost over 600 in killed and wounded each: Lane's N.C. brigade losing 786; Colston's N.C. and Va. losing 726; Pender's N.C., 693.

The battle of Chickamauga is generally called the bloodiest of modern battles. The losses given by Livemore are 22 per cent in the Federal army and 25 per cent in the Confederate, in two days' fighting. Jackson's three divisions had a paper strength of 26,661, and their losses were 7158, about 27 per cent. They were, doubtless, over 30 per cent of the force actually engaged. The losses in the 3d and 12th Federal corps, which composed the principal part of our opponents, were less, as they fought behind breastworks. Their strength on paper was 32,171. Their losses were 4703, being about 15 per cent of the paper strength and probably 18 per cent of the actual.

Had Gen. Lee been present on the left, during the Sunday morning attack, and seen Stuart's energy and efficiency in handling his reserves, inspiring the men by his contagious spirit, and in the cooperation of artillery, with the infantry, he might have rewarded Stuart on the spot by promoting him to the now vacant command of Jackson's corps. Ewell, who did succeed Jackson, was always loved and admired, but he was not always equal to his opportunities, as we shall see at Gettysburg. Stuart's qualities were just what were needed, for he was young, he was not maimed, and he had boldness, persistence, and magnetism in very high degree. Lee once said that he would have won Gettysburg, had he had Jackson with him. Who so worthy to succeed Jackson as the man who had successfully replaced him on his last and greatest field?

---

* A reminiscence of that night is the finding of our camp in the heaviest of the rain and blackest of the darkness by a lost ambulance carrying a Virginian colonel, whose leg had been amputated on the field. He was taken out and fed, slept on the crowded floor of our tent, and next morning was started for a hospital in fine spirits in spite of his maimed condition.

A common maneuver for the Army of the Potomac: a retreat in the wake of a military defeat bordering on disaster.

★★★

D. AUGUSTUS DICKERT

Routing the Yankees

The Battle of Chancellorsville proved to be one of Lee's most stunning victories of the war as well as a testament to his audacity and tactical brilliance. Heavily outnumbered by Hooker in the depths of the Wilderness, Lee divided his forces and sent Jackson's corps against the Federal right on a flank attack to roll up the enemy line while the rest of the Confederate force occupied the attention of Hooker's front. The next day, Lee vigor- *ously engaged the Army of the Potomac convincing its commander to withdraw across the Rappahannock River even though most of his troops had not yet been engaged. A captain in the 3rd South Carolina Regiment of Brigadier General Joseph B. Kershaw's Brigade, D. Augustus Dickert was in the ranks at the time of this bloody confrontation and wrote an account of the battle in his* History of Kershaw's Brigade.

On the morning of April 29th the soldiers were aroused from their slumbers by the beating of the long roll. What an ominous sound is the long roll to the soldier wrapped in his blanket and enjoying the sweets of sleep. It is like a fire bell at night. It denotes battle. It tells the soldier the enemy is moving: it means haste and active preparation. A battle is imminent. The soldiers thus roused, as if from their long sleep since Fredericksburg, feel in a touchous mood.

The frightful senses of Fredericksburg and Mayree's Hill rise up before them as a spectre. Soldiers rush out of their tents, asking questions and making suppositions. Others are busily engaged folding blankets, tearing down tents, and making preparations to move: companies formed into regiments and regiments into brigades. The distant boom of cannon beyond the Rappahannock tells us that the enemy is to cross the river again and try conclusions with the soldiers of

Despite the loss of Stonewall Jackson in a tragic accident on the night of 2 May, the Confederates renewed the offensive the next day, eventually forcing the Union to retreat in ignominious defeat.

Lee. All expected a bloody engagements for the Federal Army had been greatly recruited under excellent discipline, and headed by Fighting Joe Hooker. He was one of the best officers in that army, and he himself had boasted that his was the "finest army that had ever been organized upon the planet." It numbered one hundred and thirty-one thousand men of all arms, while Lee had barely sixty thousand. We moved rapidly in the direction of Fredericksburg. I never saw Kershaw look so well. Riding his iron-gray at the head of his columns, one could not but be impressed with his soldierly appearance. He seemed a veritable knight of old. Leading his brigade above the city he took position in the old entrenchments.

Before reaching the battle line, the enemy had already placed pontoons near the old place of landing, crossed over a portion of their army, and was now picketing on the south side of the river. One company from each regiment was thrown out as sharp shooters or skirmishers under Captain Goggans, of the Seventh, and deployed in the valley below, where we could watch the enemy. My company was of the number. Nothing was done during the day but a continual change of positions. We remained on the skirmish line during the night without fire or without any relief, expecting an advance next morning, or to be relieved at least. The sun was obscured by the densest fog the following morning I almost ever witnessed. When it cleared up, about 10 o'clock, what

was our astonishment?—to find no enemy in our front, nor friends in our rear. There were, however, some Federals opposite and below the city, but they belonged to another division. We could hear occasional cannonading some miles up the Rappahannock. By some staff officers passing, we ascertained that Hooker had withdrawn during the night in our front, recrossed the river at Ely's and Raccoon fords, or some of the fords opposite the Wilderness. This was on Friday, May the first. After a consultation with the officers of our detachment, it was agreed to evacuate our position and join our regiments wherever we could find them. We had no rations, and this was one of the incentives to move. But had the men been supplied with provisions, and the matter left to them alone, I doubt very much whether they would have chosen to leave the ground now occupied, as we were in comparative safety and no enemy in sight, while to join our commands would add largely to the chances of getting in battle. I am sorry to say a majority of the officers were of that opinion, too. Some brought to bear one of Napoleon's maxims I had heard when a boy, "When a soldier is in doubt where to go, always go to the place you hear the heaviest firing," and we could indistinctly hear occasional booming of cannon high up the river, indicating that a part of the army at least was in that direction.

So we moved back and over the breastworks, on to the plank road leading to Orange Court House. Mak-

Members of the Teutonic XI Corps who were nicknamed the "flying Dutchmen" for their penchant to retreat.

ing our way, keeping together as a battalion, up that road in the direction of the Wilderness, near noon we could hear the deep bay of cannon, now distant and indistinct, then again more rapidly and quite distinguishable, showing plainly that Lee was having a running fight. Later in the day we passed dead horses and a few dead and wounded soldiers. On every hand were indications of the effects of shot and shell. Trees were shattered along the road side, fences torn down and rude breastworks made here and there, the evidence of heavy skirmishing in our front. Lee was pressing the advance guard that had crossed at one of the lower fords back on the main army, crossing then at fords opposite and above the Chancellor's House. Near sundown the firing was conspicuously heavy, especially the artillery. The men of most of the companies evinced a desire to frequently rest, and in every way delay our march as much as possible. Some of the officers, too, joined with the men and offered objections to rushing headlong into battle without orders. I knew that our brigade was somewhere in our front, and from the firing I was thoroughly convinced a battle was imminent, and in that case our duty called us to our command. Not through any cowardice, however, did the men hesitate, for all this fiction written about men's eagerness for battle, their ungovernable desire to throw themselves upon the enemy, their great love of hearing the bursting of shells over their heads, the whizzing of minnie balls through their ranks is all very well for romance and on paper, but a soldier left free to himself, unless he seeks notoriety or honors, will not often rush voluntarily into battle, and if he can escape it honorably, he will do it nine times out of ten. There are times, however, when officers, whose keen sense of duty and honorable appreciation of the position they occupy, will lead their commands into battle unauthorized, when they see the necessity, but a private who owes no obedience nor allegiance only to his superiors, and has no responsibility, seldom ever goes voluntarily into battle; if so, once is enough.

Under these circumstances, as the sun was near setting, we learned from some wounded soldier that Kershaw was moving in line of battle to the left of the plank road. Another Captain and myself deserted our companions and made our way to our regiments with our companies. As we came upon it, it was just moving out from a thicket into an open field under a heavy skirmish fire and a fierce fire from a battery in our front. We marched at a double-quick to rejoin the regiment, and the proudest moments of my life, and the sweetest words to hear, was as the other portion of the regiment saw us coming they gave a cheer of welcome and shouted, "Hurrah! for the Dutch; the Dutch has come; make way to the left for the Dutch," and such terms of gladness and welcome, that I thought, even while the "Dutch" and its youthful commander were but a mere speck of the great army, still some had missed us, and I was glad to feel the touch of their elbow on the right and left when a battle was in progress.

Companies in the army, like school boys, almost all have "nick-names." Mine was called the "Dutch"

from the fact of its having been raised in that section of the country between Saluda River and the Broad, known as "Dutch Fork." A century or more before, this country, just above Columbia and in the fork of the two rivers, was settled by German refugees, hence the name "Dutch Fork."

After joining the regiment, we only advanced a little further and halted for the night, sleeping with guns in arms, lest a night attack might find the troops illy prepared were the guns in stack. We were so near the enemy that fires were not allowed, and none permitted to speak above a whisper. Two men from each company were detailed to go to the rear and cook rations. It is not an easy task for two men, who had been marching and fighting all day, to be up all night cooking three meals each for thirty or forth men, having to gather their own fuel, and often going half mile for water. A whole day's ration is always cooked at one time on marches, as night is the only time for cooking. The decrees of an order for a detail are inexorable. A soldier must take it as it comes, for none ever know but what the next duties may be even worse than the present. As a general rule, soldiers rarely ever grumble at any detail on the eve of an engagement, for sometimes it excuses them from a battle, and the old experienced veteran never refuses that.

At daylight a battery some two hundred yards in our front opened a furious fire upon us, the shells coming uncomfortably near our heads. If there were an infantry between the battery and our troops, they must have laid low to escape the shots over their heads. But after a few rounds they limbered up and scampered away. We moved slowly along with heavy skirmishing in our front all the morning of the second. When near the Chancellor's House, we formed line of battle in a kind of semi-circle, our right resting on the river and extending over the plank road, Kershaw being some distance to the left of this road, the Fifteenth Regiment occupying the right. Here we remained for the remainder of the day. We heard the word coming up the line, "No cheering, no cheering." In a few moments General Lee came riding along the

Some of the many Confederate soldiers who time and again managed to frustrate the plans of Abe Lincoln and his subordinates.

lines, going to the left. He had with him quite a number of his staff and one or two couriers. He looked straight to the front and thoughtful, noticing none of the soldiers who rushed to the line to see him pass. He no doubt was then forming the masterful move, and one, too, in opposition to all rules or order of military science or strategy, "the division of his army in the face of the enemy," a movement that has caused many armies, before, destruction and the downfall of its commander. But nothing succeeds like success. The great disparity in numbers was so great that Lee could only watch and hope for some mistake or blunder of his adversary, or by some extraordinary strategic manoeuvre on his own part, gain the advantage by which his opponent would be ruined. Hooker had one hundred and thirty thousand men, while Lee had only sixty thousand. With this number it seemed an easy task for Hooker to threaten Lee at Fredericksburg, then fall upon him with his entire force at Chancellorsville and crush him before Lee could extricate himself from the meshes that were surrounding him, and retreat to Richmond. The dense Wilderness seemed providential for the movement upon which Lee has now determined to stake the fate of his army and the fortunes of the Confederacy. Its heavy, thick undergrowth entirely obstructed the view and hid the movements to be made. Jackson, with Rhodes, Colston's, and A. P. Hill's Divisions, were to make a detour around the enemy's right, march by dull roads and bridle paths through the tangled forest and fall upon the enemy's rear, while McLaws, Anderson's and Early's Divisions were to hold him in check in front. Pickett's Division had, before this time, been sent to Wilmington, N.C.,

while Ransom's Division, with Barksdale's Mississippi Brigade, of McLaws' Division, were to keep watch of the enemy at Fredericksburg. The Federal General, Stoneman, with his cavalry, was then on his famous but disastrous raid to Richmond. Jackson commenced his march early in the morning, and kept it up all day, turning back towards the rear of the enemy when sufficiently distant that his movement could not be detected. By marching eighteen or twenty miles he was then within three miles of his starting point. But Hooker's Army stood between him and Lee. Near night Jackson struck the enemy a terrific blow, near the plank road, just opposite to where we lay, and the cannonading was simply deafening. The shots fired from some of the rifled guns of Jackson passed far overhead of the enemy and fell in our rear. Hooker, bewildered and lost in the meshes of the Wilderness, had formed his divisions in line of battle in echelon, and moved out from the river. Great gaps would intervene between the division in front and the one in rear. Little did he think an enemy was marching rapidly for his rear, another watching every movement in front, and those enemies, Jackson and Lee,

Major General Howard appeals to his troops to rally in the face of Jackson's attack.

"The great chieftain" of the Confederacy, Thomas Jonathan "Stonewall" Jackson.

unknown to Hooker, his flank stood exposed and the distance between the columns gave an ordinary enemy an advantage seldom offered by an astute General, but to such an enemy as Jackson it was more than he had hoped or even dared to expect. As he sat watching the broken columns of the enemy struggling through the dense undergrowth, the favorable moment came. Seizing it with promptness and daring, so characteristic of the man, he, like Napoleon at Austerlitz, when he saw the Russians passing by his front with their flanks exposed, rushed upon them like a wild beast upon its prey, turning the exposed column back upon its rear. Colston, commanding Jackson's old Division, led the attack, followed by A. P. Hill. Rhodes then fell like an avalanche upon the unexpectant and now thoroughly disorganized divisions of the retreating enemy. Volley after volley was poured into the seething mass of advancing and receding columns. Not much use could be made of artillery at close range, so that arm of the service was mainly occupied in shelling their trains and the woods in rear. Until late in the night did the battle rage in all its fury. Darkness only added to its intensity, and the fire was kept up until a shot through mistake lay the great Chieftain, Stonewall Jackson, low. General A. P. Hill now took command of the corps, and every preparation was made for the desperate onslaught of to-morrow. By some strange intuition peculiar to the soldier, and his ability to gather news, the word that Jackson had fallen burst through the camp like an explosion, and cast a gloom of sorrow over all.

As our brother South Carolinians, of McGowan's Brigade, were on the opposite side of us, and in the heat of the fray, while we remained idle, I take the liberty of quoting from "Caldwell's History" of that brigade a description of the terrible scenes being enacted on that memorable night in the Wilderness in which Jackson fell:

"Now it is night. The moon a day or two past full, rose in cloudless sky and lighted our way. We were fronted, and then advanced on the right of the road into a thick growth of pines. Soon a firing of small arms sprang up before us, and directly afterwards the enemy's artillery opened furiously, bearing upon us. The scene was terrible. Volley after volley of musketry was poured by the Confederate line in front of us upon the enemy. The enemy replied with equal rapidity; cheer, wild and fierce, rang over the whole woods; officers shouted at the top of their voices, to make themselves heard; cannon roar and shells burst continuously. We knew nothing, could see nothing, hedged in by the matted mass of trees. Night engagements are always dreadful, but this was the worse I ever knew. To see your danger is bad enough, but to hear shells whizzing and bursting over you, to hear shrapnell and iron fragments slapping the trees and cracking off limbs, and not know from whence death comes to you, trying beyond all things. And here it looked so incongruous—below raged, thunder, shout, shriek, slaughter—above soft, silent, smiling moonlight peace!"

The next morning A. P. Hill was moving early, but was himself wounded, and General Jeb. Stuart, of the cavalry, took command. The fighting of Jackson's Corps to-day surpassed that of the night before, and after overcoming almost insurmountable obstacles, they succeeded in dislodging Hooker from his well fortified position.

Kershaw remained in his line of battle, keeping up a constant fire with his skirmishers. An advance upon the Chancellor's House was momentarily expected. The long delay between the commencement of Jackson's movement until we heard the thunder of his guns immediately in our front and in rear of the enemy, was taken up in conjecturing, "what move was next." All felt that it was to be no retreat, and as we failed to advance, the mystery of our inactivity was more confounding. Early next morning, however, the battle began in earnest. Hooker had occupied the night in straightening out his lines and establishing a basis of battle, with the hope of retrieving the blunder of the day before. Stuart (or rather A. P. Hill, until wounded,) began pressing him from the very start. We could hear the wild yells of our troops as line after line of Hooker's were reformed, to be brushed away by the heroism of the Southern troops. Our skirmishers began their desultory firing of the day before. The battle seemed to near us as it progressed, and the opening around Chancellor's House appeared to be alive with the enemy's artillery. About two o'clock our lines were ordered forward, and we made our way through the tangled morass, in direction of our skirmish line. Here one of the bravest men in our regiment was killed, private John Davis, of the "Quitman Rifles." He was reckless beyond all reason. He loved danger for danger's sake. Stepping behind a tree to load (he was on skirmish line) he would pass out from this cover in plain view, take deliberate aim, and fire. Again and again he was entreated and urged by his comrades to shield himself, but in vain. A bullet from the enemy's sharp-shooters killed him instantly.

A singular and touching incident of this family is here recorded. David had an only brother, who was equally as brave as John and younger, James, the two being the only children of an aged but wealthy couple, of Newberry County. After the death of John, his mother exerted herself and hired a substitute for her baby boy, and came on in a week after the battle for the body of her oldest son and to take James home with her, as the only hope and solace of the declining years of this aged father and mother. Much against his will and wishes, but by mother's entreaties and friends' solicitations, the young man consented to accompany his mother home. But fate seemed to follow them here and play them false, for in less than two weeks this brave, bright, and promising boy lay dead from a malignant disease.

As our brigade was moving through the thicket in the interval between our main line and the skirmishers, and under a heavy fire, we came upon a lone stranger sitting quietly upon a log. At first he was thought an enemy, who in the denseness of the undergrowth had passed our lines on a tour of observation. He was closely questioned, and it turned out to be Rev. Boushell, a methodist minister belonging to one of McGowan's South Carolina regiments, who became lost from his command in the great flank movement of Jackson (McGowan's Brigade belonged to Jackson's Corps), and said he came down "to see how the battle was going and to lend aid and comfort to any wounded soldier should he chance to find one in need of his services."

The batteries in our front were now raking the matted brush all around and overhead, and their infantry soon became aware of our presence, and they, too, began pouring volleys into our advancing column. The ranks became confused, for in this wilderness we could not see twenty paces in front. Still we moved forward with such order as was under the conditions permissible. When near the turn-pike road General Kershaw gave the command to "charge. The Fifteenth raised the yell; then the Third dashed forward; the Seventh was somewhat late on account of the almost impassable condition of the ground, but still it and the Third Battalion, with the Second on the left, made a made rush for the public road, and entered it soon after the Fifteenth and Third. A perfect sea of fire was in our faces from the many cannon parked around the Chancellor House and graping in all directions but the rear. Lee on the one side and Stuart on the other had closed upon the enemy, their wings joining just in front of the house. Some of the

pieces of the enemy's artillery were not more than fifty yards in our front, and the discharges seemed to blaze fire in our very ranks. Infantry, too, was there massed all over the yard, and in rear of this one vast, mingling, moving body of humanity, dead horses lay in all directions, while the dead and wounded soldiers lay heaped and strewn with the living. But a few volleys from our troops in the road soon silenced all opposition from the infantry, while cannoneers were hitching up their horses to fly away. Some were trying to drag away their caissons and light pieces by hand, while thousands of "blue coats," with and without arms, were running for cover to the rear. In less than twenty minutes the firing ceased in our front, and men were ordered to prepare breastworks. Our soldiers, like the beaver, by this time had become accustomed to burrow in the ground as soon as a "halt" was made. A shovel and a spade were carried at all times by each company to guard against emergencies. The bursting of a shell near my company caused a fragment to strike one of my own men on the shoulder. He claimed to be desperately wounded, and wished to go to the hospital. I examined him hastily to see if I could give him any assistance. He claimed his shoulder was broken. Just then the order was given to "commence to fortify." "G.," the wounded man, was the first to grasp the shovel, and threw dirt with an energy that caused my Orderly Sergeant, a brave and faithful soldier, but who never allowed the comic side of any transaction to pass him, to say: "Captain,

The Federal line holding Jackson's troops at the Plank Road.

look at the 'wild pigeon;' see how he scratches dirt." All soldiers carried a "nick-name," a name given by some physical disability or some error he had made, or from any circumstance in his life out of the usual order. Hardly had we taken possession of the turnpike road and began fortifying, than the sound of shells down the river was heard, and we were hurriedly marched down the road. McLaws' and Anderson's Divisions were double-quicked down the turnpike road and away from the battle to meet Sedgwick, who had crossed the Rappahannock at Fredericksburg, stormed Mayree's Height's, routed and captured the most of Barksdale's Mississippi Brigade, and was making his way rapidly upon Lee's rear.

This Battle of Chancellorsville certainly had its

many sides, with its rapid marching, changing of positions, and generalship of the highest order. On the day before Jackson had gone around the right flank of Hooker and fell upon his rear, while to-day we had the novel spectacle of Sedgwick in the rear of Lee and Stuart in rear of Hooker. No one can foretell the result of the battle, had Hooker held his position until Sedgwick came up. But Lee's great mind ran quick and fast. He knew the country and was well posted by his scouts of every move and turn of the enemy on the chess-board of battle. Anderson, with his division, being on our right, led the advance down the road to meet Sedgwick. We passed great parks of wagons (ordnance and commissary) on either side of the road. Here and there were the field infirmaries where their

A group of Confederate officers pose for a photograph. Though the South won a major victory at Chancellorsville, it lost the services of some fine commanders among them: Brigadier General Elisha F. "Bull" Paxton, Colonels Thomas J. Purdie and James M. Perrin and of course Stonewall Jackson.

wounded were being attended to and where all the surplus baggage had been stacked before the battle.

On reaching Zoar Church, some five miles in rear, we encountered Sedgwick's advance line of skirmishers, and a heavy fusilade began. Anderson formed line of battle on extreme right, and on right of plank road, with the purpose of sweeping round on the enemy's left. McLaws formed on left of the corps, his extreme left reaching out toward the river and across the road; Kershaw being immediately on the right of the road, with the Second resting on it, then the Fifteenth, the Third Battalion, the Eighth, the Third, and the Seventh on the right. On the left of the road leading to Fredericksburg was a large open field extending to the bluff near the river; on the right was a dense thicket of pines and undergrowth. In this we had to form. The Seventh experienced some trouble in getting into line, and many camp rumours were afloat a few days afterwards of an uncomplimentary nature of the Seventh's action. But this was all false, for no more gallant regiment nor better officered, both in courage and ability, was in the Confederate service than the "bloody Seventh." But it was the unfavorable nature of the ground, the difficulties experienced in

forming a line, and the crowding and lapping of the men that caused the confusion.

Soon after our line of battle was formed and Kershaw awaiting orders from McLaws to advance, a line of support came up in our rear, and mistaking us for the enemy, commenced firing upon us. Handkerchiefs went up, calls of "friends," "friends," but still the firing continued. One Colonel seeing the danger—the enemy just in front, and our friends firing on us in the rear—call out, "Who will volunteer to carry our colors back to our friends in rear?" Up sprang the handsome and gallant young Sergeant, Copeland, of the "Clinton Divers," (one of the most magnificent and finest looking companies in his service, having at its enlistment forty men over six feet tall), and said, "Colonel, send me." Grasping the colors in his hand, he carried them, waving and jesticulating in a friendly manner, until he convinced the troops that they were friends in their front.

While thus waiting for Anderson to swing around the left of the enemy, a desperate charge was made upon us. The cannonading was exceedingly heavy and accurate. Great trees all around fell, snapped in twain by the shell and solid shot, and many men were killed

Hooker's headquarters during the events of 2 May, the Chancellor House.

Members of Jackson's Corps carrying Howard's defensive works in their surprise attack on the Federal right.

The XI Corps stampedes in panic when the enemy launched an attack that caught the unsuspecting Federals by complete surprise.

and wounded by the falling timber. Trees, a foot in diameter, snapped in two like pipe stems, and fell upon the men. It was growing dark before Anderson could get in position, and during that time the troops never experienced a heavier shelling. It was enough to make the stoutest hearts quake. One of my very bravest men, one who had never failed before, called to me as I passed, "Captain, if I am not here when the roll is called, you may know where I am. I don't believe I can stand this." But he did, and like the man he was, withstood it. Another, a young recruit, and under his first fire, almost became insane, jumping upon me and begging "for God's sake" let him go to the rear. I could not stand this piteous appeal, and knowing he could not be of any service to us in that condition,

told him "to go." It is needless to say he obeyed my orders. Dr. Evans, our surgeon, told me afterwards that he came to his quarters and remained three days, perfectly crazy. At last the order came after night to advance. In a semicircle we swept through the thicket; turning, we came into the road, and over it into the opening in front. The enemy was pushed back into the breastworks on the bluff at the river. These breastworks had been built by our troops during the Fredericksburg battle, and afterwards to guard and protect Raccoon and Ely's fords, just in rear. As night was upon us, and the enemy huddled before us at the ford, we were halted and lay on the field all night. This was the ending of the battle of Chancellorsville.

Next morning the sun was perfectly hidden by a heavy fog, so much so that one could not see a man twenty yards distant. Skirmishers were thrown out and our advance made to the river, but nothing was found on this side of the river but the wounded and the discarded rifles and munitions of war. The wounded lay in all directions, calling for help and heaping curses upon their friends, who had abandoned them in their distress. Guns, tent flies, and cartridge boxes were packed up by the wagon loads. Hooker's Army was thoroughly beaten, disheartened, and disorganized. Met and defeated at every turn and move, they were only too glad to place themselves across the river and under the protection of their siege guns on Stafford's Heights. Hooker's looses were never correctly given, but roughly computed at twenty-five thousand, while those of Lee's were ten thousand two hundred and eighty-one. But the Confederates counted it a dear victory in the loss of the intrepid but silent Stonewall Jackson. There was a magic in his name that gave enthusiasm and confidence to the whole army. To the enemy his name was a terror and himself an apparition. He had frightened and beaten Banks out of the Shennandoah Valley, had routed Fremont, and so entangled and out-generaled Seigle that he was glad to put the Potomac between himself and this silent, mysterious, and indefatigable chieftain, who often prayed before battle and fought with a Bible in one hand and a sword in the other. He came like a whirlwind upon the flank of McClellan at Mechanicsville, and began those series of battles and victories that terminated with the "Lit-

Some of the 6,000 Yankees captured during the battle of Chancellorsville.

On facing page, some of the 1700 Confederates captured in the heat of battle head to the Federal rear. Though no doubt concerned about their fate, these Rebels found the time to taunt Yankee captors over the most recent defeat of the Army of the Potomac.

tle Giant" being hemmed in at Drury's Bluff and Malvern Hill. While Pope, the "Braggart," was sweeping the fields before him in Northern Virginia, and whose boast was he "saw only the enemy's back," and his "headquarters were in the saddle," Jackson appeared before him like a lion in his path. He swings around Pope's right, over the mountains, back through Thoroughfare Gap: he sweeps through the country like a comet through space, and falls on Pope's rear on the plains of Manassas, and sent him flying across the Potomac like McDowell was beaten two years before. While pursuing the enemy across the river and into Maryland, he turns suddenly, recrosses the river, and stands before Harper's Ferry, and captures that stronghold with scarcely a struggle. All this was enough to give him the sobriquet of the "Silent Man," the man of "mystery," and it is not too much to say that Jackson to the South was worth ten thousand soliders, while the terror of his name wrought consternation in the ranks of the enemy.

★★★

W. F. RANDOLPH

Jackson's Mortal Wound

Though the Confederates had managed to win a great victory at Chancellorsville, the seeds of defeat were sown when Stonewall Jackson was mortally wounded when he was accidentally fired upon by some of his own men while reconnoitering the battlefield on the evening of 2 May 1863. Historians still ponder what effect Jackson's presence at Gettysburg might have had on that battle and the entire war. Jackson died from his wound on 10 May. A member of Jackson's body guard, Captain W.F. Randolph was present at Jackson's fatal shooting. His account originally appeared in the Greeneville News Times *and later in the* Southern Society Historical Papers.

Stonewall Jackson in a photograph taken two weeks before he fell with the wound that would eventually kill him.

It is not the purpose of the writer of this article to give a detailed account of the memorable battle of Chancellorsville, which has been so often described by pens more felicitous than mine, but only to give some few incidents of the first two days leading up to the terrible catastrophe, which was the closing scene of one of the most brilliant and successful movements in the history of any war.

The writer was, during these two days, attached to the person of General Jackson, and only left his side occasionally as the bearer of orders to his division commanders.

During the winter of '62 and '63, the Army of Northern Virginia was encamped near and around Fredericksburg, and the writer was in command of a company of cavalry and attached to the headquarters of General Stonewall Jackson, then located near Hamilton's Crossing, about three miles below the town.

The battle of Fredericksburg, which took place the 13th of December, resulted in the defeat of Burnside, and his retreat across the river ended all active operations for the winter. So we settled down in quiet observation, awaiting with anxious expectation the advance of General Hooker, whose artillery crowned the heights of the other side of the river, where the white tents of the Federal army could be seen here dotting the same hills.

The spring was well advanced, the country all around us was covered with verdure, and the roads had become dry and hard, when we were awakened from our long holiday by the welcome announcement that the Federal commander's long-expected advance had at last commenced, and that a portion of his army had crossed the Rapidan at Gorman's Ford, and were marching upon Fredericksburg. General Lee at once put his whole army in motion, with Jackson's corps in the front, leaving one division, under General Early, to prevent the enemy from crossing at Fredericksburg and attacking his rear.

It will be remembered that two of the best divisions of Longstreet's corps had been detached and sent to Southeastern Virginia, leaving General Lee with scarcely fifty thousand infantry with which to meet that well-equipped and splendidly-appointed army of Hooker's, consisting of more than one hundred thousand men. After an arduous and exciting march, without rest, the army, frequently advancing in line of battle, was expecting every moment to meet the enemy. The advance column, consisting of a portion of Hill's division, halted about sunset within less than a mile of the Chancellorsville house, in the vicinity of which the enemy was evidently concentrated, awaiting our attack. But the impenetrable nature of the thickets, which separated us, prevented any further advance in that direction, and the whole army was forced to bivouac for the night. At this point a road, which was then known as the Bun road, intersected about at right angles the plank road, along which we had been moving, and here, with no other protection than the spreading arms of an immense oak, and without camp equippage of any kind, the two generals-- Lee and Jackson—slept for the night, myself and a few of my troops lying within a few feet of them.

Jackson's favorite steed, Little Sorrel, a few days after his masters death. The horse was eventually given to Jackson's wife and lived to the grand old age of 30, dying in 1886.

I was awakened next morning by a light touch on my shoulder, and on jumping up had the mortification to find that the sun had already risen and General Lee had gone. General Jackson, who was just mounting his horse, turned to me with a kindly word and smile, telling me to follow as soon as possible, and dashed off at a furious gallop down the Mine Run road, along which his troops had been rapidly marching since daylight. I did not succeed in overtaking the General again for several hours, and when at last I came up with him, he was far in advance of his columns, standing talking to General Fitzhugh Lee in the old turnpike road, at a point about five miles distant from Chancellorsville, having made a circuit of fifteen miles, thus putting the whole Federal army between himself and General Lee, and the two divisions of Longstreet's corps which were with him. As the several divisions of the corps came up they were formed in line of battle, and about 4 o'clock in the evening everything was in readiness for the attack.

While Fitzhugh was talking to the General a half-dozen troopers rode up, bringing with them a Yankee lieutenant, whom they had just captured. Lee turned to the officer and asked him smilingly what would Hooker think if old Stonewall were to suddenly fall upon his rear. "Ah," said the Federal officer, "Hooker has both Jackson and your great Lee in the hollow of his hand, and it is only a matter of a very short time when your whole army will be bagged." Jackson's lips closed in a grim smile, but he said nothing, and Lee and his troopers rode away, laughing, leaving us alone.

The General turned to me and asked how far behind was the advance of his army. I replied that the leading division ought to be up in an hour. We both dismounted, Jackson seating himself on a log by the road, studying a map, which he spread out before him. After tying our horses I took my seat not far from him, and, being somewhat fatigued from the long ride, I fell asleep. Waking with a start, I turned and saw the General kneeling, with his arms resting on the log, in earnest prayer. I was profoundly impressed, and a feeling of great security came over me. Surely this great soldier, who held such close and constant communion with his Maker, must certainly succeed in whatever he undertook!

Presently the General, who was still seated on the log, called me to his side, and ordered me to ride down the turnpike as far as possible in the direction of the enemy, and ascertain if any of his pickets were stationed in the direction facing our advance, and to gather any other information it was possible to obtain.

Taking one man with me, I mounted my horse and galloped rapidly down the road until I came within sight of the camp fires of the enemy. Dismounting, I tied my horse in a thicket near the road, advanced cautiously, expecting every moment to come in contact with some outlying picket, but met no enemy until I came to an opening in the woods, overlooking a large field, where I saw a sight most amazing and unexpected. No less than a vast force of Federals in every conceivable state of disorder, without any formation; several batteries of artillery unlimbered; hundreds gathered around the camp fires cooking, some lying sunning themselves in the bright May sunshine, as apparently unconscious of danger as if they had been encamped around the environs of Washington city—no sentinels, no pickets, no line of battle anywhere. My heart bounded with exultation, and I could have shouted for joy. "Verily," I said to myself, "the God of battles has this day delivered these people into our hands." But I had time only for a brief glance. Hurrying to where I had tied my horse, I mounted and rode with all possible speed back to where I had left the General. I made my report. Not a word escaped his lips. He raised his eyes to heaven, and his lips seemed to murmur a prayer, and then turning to General Hill said, "Order the whole line to advance, General Hill; but slowly, with great caution, and without noise."

And so the movement commenced slowly, silently, with no sound save the occasional cracking of a stick beneath the feet of the men; those long grey lines stretching far into the gloom of the forest, pressed on; twenty-five thousand veterans of many a hard fought field, who had never moved save in the path of victory; on and on in the gathering evening, the sinking sun casting long shadows behind them, the frightened birds twittering and chirping as they flew from tree to

The site where Confederate hopes were dashed. It was here that Lee's most famous lieutenant, Stonewall Jackson, fell with a mortal wound accidentally inflicted by his own troops.

tree, and an occasional bark of a squirrel as he looked out, startled at the unwonted scene, were the only sounds that interrupted the stillness, solemn and oppressive; a strange calm preceding a storm, the light of which has rarely been chronicled in the annals of war.

When our line of battle debouched from the dense wood which effectually concealed the advance, it came immediately upon the Federal encampment and directly in the rear of their whole line. The first intimation the enemy had of our approach was the characteristic Confederate yell, which rolled along the line, and rung out clear and loud above the thunderous clash of musketry and re-echoed through the forest, which had until than been as silent as the grave. Never was surprise so complete, never was a victory more easily won. As our lines swept like an avalanche over the Federal camps, they were overwhelmed and outnumbered at every point, resistance was paralyzed, and the panic which ensued is indescribable. On the part of the enemy it was not a retreat, but the wildest flight—a race for life.

At one time during the evening a young officer, wild with enthusiasm, dashed up to the General, crying: "General, they are running too fast for us; we can't come up with them." "They never run too fast for me, sir," was the immediate response. And thus onward rushed pursuers and pursued down the road toward Chancellorsville. Now and then Jackson would press his horse to a gallop and dash to the front, and whenever he appeared the troops would break ranks and rush around him with the wildest cheers I ever heard from human throats. When night closed upon the scene the victory seemed to be complete. The infantry of the enemy had disappeared from our immediate front, falling back under cover of several batteries of artillery, which, halting upon every eminence, poured a furious fire of shot and shell down the road upon our advancing columns. In order to avoid this furious fire as much as possible, our men were formed in columns and made to march up the edges of the dense wood, and parallel with the road. This they were able to do by the aid of the moon, which shone very brightly, rendering all objects in our immediate vicinity clearly distinct. About this time General A. P. Hill rode up, and Jackson and himself had a conference of some length. I did not hear all that was said, but both were deeply absorbed, for shells from the battery of the enemy were bursting all around us and ploughing up the ground under our horses' feet without either of them taking the slightest notice of the little incident. As for myself, I cared but little either, as I was then impressed with the idea that the bullet had not been moulded which was to kill our General. The firing soon ceased and Hill rode away.

At this juncture the General had no officer with him, except Lieutenant Keith Boswell, an officer belonging to his signal corps, and myself, together with a dozen of my own men, who were riding behind. A Confederate brigade was marching slowly in column on the left of the road and close to the woods, Keith Boswell was riding on the right of the General, and

myself on the left, between him and our lines. The General turned to me and asked: "Whose brigade is that?" "I don't know, sir," I replied, "but will find out in a moment." I at once rode up to our line and asked the first officer I met whose brigade it was. He replied: "Lane's North Carolina." I rode back to Jackson, giving him the reply. "Go and tell the officer in command," he said, "to halt his brigade." I rode up to the same officer, gave the command, and told him that it came from General Jackson in person. The order was passed along the line, and the whole brigade halted at once, making a half-wheel to the right, facing the road, and rested upon their arms. We continued our movement in the same order, walking our horses very slowly towards the front of the brigade. Suddenly the General asked: "Captain, is there a road near our present position leading to the Rappahannock?" I replied that not far from where we stood there was a road which led into the woods in the direction of the Rappahannock river.

"This road must be found, then, at once," he said. He had hardly uttered these words when a few scattering random shots were heard in the woods to our right. The men in line on our left, excited apparently by this fire, commenced firing across the road into the woods beyond, not in regular volleys, but in a desultory way, without order, here and there along the line.

General Jackson turned to me and said: "Order those men to stop that fire, and tell the officers not to allow another shot fired without orders."

I rode up and down the line and gave the order to both men and officers, telling them also that they were endangering the lives of General Jackson and his escort, but in vain. Those immediately in my front would cease as I gave the order, but the firing would break out above or below me, and instead of decreasing the shots increased in frequency, I rode back to Jackson and said: "General, it is impossible to stop these men. I think we had best pass through their line and get into the woods behind them." "Very well said," was the reply. So, making a half whirl to the left, thus presenting a front of, say, sixty yards, our little company commenced the movement to pass through the line, and thus put ourselves beyond the range of the fire.

A few more seconds would have placed us in safety, for we were not over three yards from the line, but as we turned, looking up and down as far as my eye could reach, I saw that long line of shining bayonets rise and concentrate upon us. I felt what was coming, and driving spurs into my horse's flanks, a powerful animal and full of spirit, he rose high in the air, and as we passed over the line the thunder crash from hundreds of rifles burst in full in our very faces. I looked back as my horse made the leap, and everything had gone down like leaves before the blast of a hurricane. The only living thing besides myself that passed through that stream of fire was Boswell's black stallion, my attention being called to him by the rattle of a chain-halter that swung loose from his neck, as he passed out of sight in the darkness of the wood. But his saddle was empty. Boswell, too, an old comrade of many a perilous scout, had gone down with all the rest before that inexcusable and unwarranted fire. My own horse was wounded in several places, my clothes and saddle were perforated with bullets, yet I escaped without a wound, the only living man to tell the fearful story.

As soon as I could control my horse, rendered frantic by his wounds, I rode among our men, who were falling back into the woods, and from behind the trees were still continuing that reckless and insane fire, and urging them to form their line and come back to the road, telling them that they had fired not upon the enemy, but upon General Jackson and his escort.

Then sick at heart I dashed back to the road, and there the saddest tragedy of the war was revealed in its fullest horror.

I saw the General's horse, which I recognized at once, standing close to the edge of the road, with his head bent low, and a stream of blood running from a wound in his neck. Jumping from my horse I hastened to the spot and saw the General himself lying in the edge of the woods. He seemed to be dead, and I wished all the bullets had passed through my own body rather than such a happening as this. I threw myself on the ground by his side and raise his head and shoulders on my arm. He groaned heavily.

"Are you much hurt, General?" I asked, as soon as I could find voice and utterance.

"Wild fire, that sir; wild fire," he replied, in his usual rapid way. This was all he said. I found that his left arm was shattered by a bullet just below the elbow, and his right hand was lacerated by a minie ball that passed through the palm. Not a living soul was in sight then, but in a few moments A. P. Hill rode up, and then Lieutenant Smith, one of his aids. General Hill ordered me to mount my horse and bring an ambulance as quickly as possible. "But don't tell the men that it is General Jackson who is wounded," he said. I soon found two of the ambulance corps with a stretcher, and ordered them to the front, saying that a wounded officer needed their services. Then I rode further on to find an ambulance. Before coming up with one I met Sandy Pendleton, Jackson's adjutant-general, and told him what had occurred, and he ordered me to go and find General J. E. B. Stuart and tell him to come up at once.

"Where shall I find him?" I asked.

"Somewhere near the Rappahannock," he replied, "not more than four or five miles away."

I rode off through the woods in the direction of the river, and by a piece of good luck soon struck a well-defined road, which seemed to lead in the right direction. After riding along that road for a few miles I had the good fortune to meet General Stuart himself with a small escort of cavalry. I stated that General Jackson had been badly wounded, and that Pendleton had ordered me to tell him to come to the army at once. Without making any comment, he dashed off at full speed. I tried to follow, but by this time my horse was much weakened by the loss of blood, and began to stagger under me. I was obliged to dismount, and

Jackson's grave site at Lexington Virginia. His amputated arm was interred elsewhere.

found that he was shot through both thighs, and slightly wounded in several other places, so I was forced to walk, leading the wounded animal slowly behind me.

This ended my connection with the tragic incident of this most memorable night. I did not reach headquarters until 2 o'clock that night. I saw Dr. McGuire, and, asking him about the General's condition, he told me that his arm had been amputated below the elbow, his wounded hand had been dressed, and that he was resting quietly. The wounds were serious and very painful, he said, but not necessarily fatal, and there seemed to be no reason why he should not recover.

If asked why and how such a fire could have occurred, I can only answer that it was then and is still a mystery, wholly unaccountable and without provocation or warrant. We had been for some time walking our horses along the road in close proximity to this very brigade from which the fire came. The moon, which was not far from full, poured a flood of light upon the wide, open turnpike. Jackson and his escort were plainly visible from every point of view, and the General himself must have been recognized by any one who had ever seen him before. There was no reason for mistaking us for an enemy, and when turning to pass through our line to avoid the scattering random fire which was sending bullets around and about us, I did not for a minute dream that there was a possibility of the guns of our men being directed upon us. An accident inexplicable, unlooked for, and impossible to foresee, deprived the army of its greatest general at a time when his services were indispensable. If Jackson had lived that night he would without doubt have marched his columns along the very road upon which I met Stuart, thus throwing his entire force in the rear of Hooker's army, his left resting upon the Rappahannock, cutting off the enemy's communications and forming around his flanks a net of steel from which he could never have extricated himself.

Broken, dispirited, panic-stricken, his right wing routed and doubled back upon his center, tangled in a wilderness without room to employ his immense force. His very numbers working to its disadvantage, hemmed in on every side, with Jackson's victorious corps in his rear and Lee in his front, strange as it may seem, Hooker's immense army of 100,000 men, would have been forced to surrender, and the war would have ended with a clap of thunder. The whole North would have been laid open, and Lee's victorious army, augmented by thousands of enthusiastic volunteers. Washington and Baltimore would have been occupied and all of Maryland aroused.

This young and virile Confederacy, sprung all at once armed and equipped a very Cyclops from the brain of Minerva, would have taken its place high up among the family of nations.

That blast in the wilderness put an end to the almost assured result, and the hope of a great southern empire became only a dream.

Was it Providence, or fate? Who can tell?

★★★

FREDERICK L. HITCHCOCK

Misadventures in the Wilderness

A nine months regiment mustered into service in August 1862, the 132nd Pennsylvania fought its last battle at Chancellorsville. Serving with the Third Brigade of French's division in the II Corps, the 132nd was heavily engaged on the Federal Center.

On April 28 our corps broke camp and joined the column northward. The winter's rest had brought some accessions to our ranks from the sick and wounded, though the severe picket duty and the excessively damp weather had given us a large sick list. We had, to start with, upward of three hundred and seventy-five men, to which was added some twenty-five or thirty from the sick list, who came up to us on the march. It is a curious fact that many men left sick in camp, unable to march with the regiment leave, will get themselves together after the former has been gone a few hours and pull out to overtake it. I saw men crying like children because the surgeon had forbidden them going with the regiment. The loneliness and homesickness, or whatever you please to call it, after the regiment has gone are too much for them. They simply cannot endure it, and so they strike out and follow. They will start by easy marches, and they generally improve in health from the moment they start. Courage and nerve are both summoned for the effort, and the result is that at the end of the second or third day they rejoin the regiment and report for duty. This does not mean that they were not really sick, but that will power and exercise have beaten the disease. I have heard many a sick man say he would rather die than be left behind.

We marched about six miles the first day, much of our route being through a wooded country, some of it so wet and spongy that corduroy roads had to be built for the wagons and artillery. The army can, as a rule, move as rapidly as it can move its artillery and supply trains, and no faster. Of course, for short distances and special expeditions, where circumstances require, both cavalry and infantry move very rapidly, ignoring the wagon trains and artillery; but on a general campaign this is impossible, and so where the ground is bad these must be helped along. In a wooded country the usual method is by corduroy road. Extra details are made to assist the pioneer corps, who cut down young saplings three to six inches in diameter and about six feet in length and lay them side by side on the ground, which is roughly levelled to receive them. They do not make a handsome road to speed over, but they bear up the artillery and army schooners, and that is all that is wanted of them.

The second day we crossed the Rappahannock at United States ford on a pontoon bridge. There had been a sharp skirmish here when the first troops crossed a couple of days before, and a battery of artillery was still in position guarding the crossing. We now began to experience once more the unmistakable symptoms of approaching battle,—sharp spurts of cannonading at irregular intervals some distance to the south and west of us, with the hurry of marching troops, ambulances and stretcher corps toward the front; more or less of army debris scattered about, and the nervous bustle everywhere apparent. We reached the famous Chancellorsville House shortly after midnight. This was an old-time hostelry, situated on what was called the Culpeper plank-road. It stood with two or three smaller houses in a cleared square space containing some twenty or thirty acres, in the midst of the densest forest of trees and undergrowth I ever saw. We had marched all day on plank and corduroy roads, through this wild tanglewood forest, most of the time in a drizzling rain, and we had been much delayed by the artillery trains, and it was after midnight when we reached our destination. The distance marched must have been twelve or more miles, and our men became greatly fatigued towards the last.

It was my first experience with the regiment on the march in the field in my new position as major. As adjutant my place had been with the colonel at the head of the column. Now my duties required me to march in the rear and keep up the stragglers. After nightfall it became intensely dark, and at each rest the men would drop down just where they were and would be instantly sound asleep. Whether they dropped down into mud or not made little difference to many of them, for they were soaking wet and were so exhausted that they did not care. My troubles began when the "forward" was sounded, to arouse these seeming logs and get them on their feet once more, and started. All who were practically exhausted had drifted to the rear and were on my hands. We had a provost guard in the rear, whose duty it was to bring up every man and permit no straggling, but they were in almost as bad a plight as the rest of the regiment. To arouse these sleeping men I had occasionally to resort to a smart blow with the flat of my sword and follow it up with the most energetic orders and entreaties. An appeal to their pluck and nerve was generally sufficient, and they would summon new courage and push manfully on. My own condition was scarcely better than that of the men. I rode that night considerable distances between our halts for rest, sitting bolt upright in my saddle fast asleep. I had all day alternated with some of the men in marching whilst they rode, and was not only thoroughly tired, but wet through. The march was much more trying to us because of our unseasoned condition owing to the long winter's exemption from this exercise. Furthermore, we had been marching towards the firing, and were under the nervous strain always incident to operations in the presence of the enemy. Nothing will quicker exhaust men than the nervous tension occa-

The 110th Pennsylvania on parade at Falmouth Virginia.

sioned by the continued firing which indicates the imminence of a battle.

At daylight we were aroused and under arms again. We found we were at the head-quarters of the army. The Chancellorsville House, which had been vacated by its occupants, was used for office purposes, and much of the open space around it was occupied by the tents of General Hooker and staff and hospital tents. Of the latter there were three or four pitched so as to connect with each other, and over them was flying the yellow flag of our corps hospital. The First and Third Divisions of our Second Corps were massed in this Chancellorsville square, beside Pettit's battery. Our brigade now consisted of the Fourth New York, First Delaware, and our regiment. The first named was sent off on some guard duty, which left Colonel Albright, of our regiment, the senior officer in command of the brigade. The ominous rattle of musketry not far away became momentarily more pronounced, and ambulances and stretcher-carriers were passing back and forth to the hospitals, carrying wounded men. The dead body of a regular army captain was soon brought back from the front, where Sykes's division of regulars was sharply engaged. I do not know the name of this captain, but he was a fine-looking young officer. He had been killed by a minie-ball squarely through his forehead.

Within the tangled woodland of the Wilderness, Yankee troops anxiously await the next Confederate move. Though perhaps hoping battle could be avoided in an enemy retreat, these troops would become involved in one of the bloodiest battles of the war.

Hooker's army crosses the Rappahannock to enter the dark woodland of the Wilderness.

Yankee skirmishers put their lives on the line to feel enemy positions.

We were marching out the plank-road as they brought this body in. Passing out of the clearing, the woods and undergrowth each side the road was so dense that we could not see into it a half-dozen steps. We had gone possibly a quarter of a mile when we were overtaken by a staff-officer, who in whispers ordered us to turn back, regardless of orders from the front, and get back to the Chancellorsville House as rapidly as possible, and to do so absolutely noiselessly; that a heavy force of rebels were in the woods on both sides of us, and we were in great danger of being cut to pieces and captured. We obeyed, and he rapidly worked his way to the front of the brigade and succeeded very quickly in getting us all safely out. We formed line near the Chancellorsville House and were resting on our arms when I noticed another brigade going down that same road from which we had just been so hurriedly gotten out. The circumstance was so strange that I inquired what brigade it was, and learned that it was Colonel (afterwards Governor) James A. Beaver's brigade of Hancock's division of our corps. They had been gone but a short time when the rebels opened upon them from both sides of the road, and they were very roughly handled. Colonel Beaver was soon brought back, supposed mortally wounded. I saw him as he was brought to the rear. It was said he was shot through the body. Afterwards, whilst he was governor, I mentioned the circumstance to him, and asked how he succeeded in fighting off the last enemy at that time. He said he then fully believed his wound was mortal. The bullet had struck him nearly midway of his body and appeared to have passed through and out of his back, and he was bleeding freely. He was brought to the hospital, where the corps surgeon—his own family physician at home—found him, and with an expression of countenance indicating the gravest fear proceeded to examine his wound. Suddenly, with a sign of relief, he exclaimed: "Colonel, you are all right; the ball has struck a rib and followed it around and out." It was one of the hundreds of remarkable freaks performed by those ugly minie-balls during the war. Why that brigade should have been allowed to march into the ambuscade, from which we had so narrowly escaped, I could not understand. It was one of the early *faux pas* of that unfortunate comedy, rather tragedy of errors,—battle.

In view of the events of the next two days, it will be interesting to recall the somewhat windy order published to the army by General Hooker on the morning of the 1st of May, the date of the first day's battle, on which the events narrated in the last chapter occurred. This is the order:

Despite being hard pressed, the Federals of Hooker's center fight on against an aggressive though numerically inferior enemy.

It is with heartfelt satisfaction the commanding general announces to the army that the operations of the last three days have determined that our enemy must either ingloriously fly or come out from behind his defences and give us battle on our own ground, when certain destruction awaits him.

My recollection recalls a phrase in this order reading something like this: "We have got the enemy where God Almighty can't save him, and he must either ingloriously," etc. I have been surprised not to find it in the records, and my memory is not alone in this respect, for a lieutenant-colonel of Portland, Me., in his account of this battle alludes to Hooker's blasphemous order.

The purpose of this order was to encourage the men and inspire them with the enthusiasm of forthcoming victory. But when we consider that the portion of the army operating around Chancellorsville was at that very moment apparently as thoroughly caged up in a wilderness of almost impenetrable undergrowth, which made it impossible to move troops, and into which one could not see a dozen feet, as though they were actually behind iron bars, it will be seen how little ground there was for encouragement. I can think of no better comparison of the situation than to liken it to a fleet of ships enveloped in a dense fog endeavoring to operate against another having the advantage of the open.

It will be remembered that when this movement commenced the Army of the Potomac numbered from one hundred and twenty thousand to one hundred and thirty thousand men, about double the opposing rebel force. Hooker divided this army, taking with him four corps, numbering probably seventy thousand men, to operate from Chancellorsville towards Fredericksburg, and leaving three corps, about fifty thousand men, under Sedgwick, to move upon the latter place from below. The purpose was to get Lee's army between these two forces and crush him. All historians of this battle agree that up to a certain point Hooker's strategy was most admirable. General Pleasanton, who commanded our cavalry forces in that action, says that up to a certain point the movement on Chancellorsville was one of the most brilliant in the annals of war. He put that point at the close of Thursday, April 30. He had made a full reconnoissance of all that country and had informed General Hooker of the nature of the ground, that for a depth of from four to five miles it was all unbroken tan-

The rear guard of the Army of the Potomac bids farewell to their campground at Falmouth to take on the Army of Northern Virginia once again.

glewood of the densest undergrowth, in which it was impossible to manoeuvre an army or to know anything of the movements of the enemy; that beyond this wilderness the country was open and well adapted to military movements, and he had taken occasion to urge upon him the importance of moving forward at once, so as to meet the enemy in open ground, but his information and advice, he tells us, fell upon leaden ears.

Lee had, up to this time, no information of the movement upon Chancellorsville, having been wholly occupied with Sedgwick at Fredericksburg. The former was therefore a complete surprise to him. The "golden moment," according to Pleasanton, to move forward and carry the battle out into the open, where the army could have been handled and would have had a chance, was on that day, as instantly the movement was disclosed, the enemy, being familiar with every foot of the country, would detach a sufficient force to operate in the open, and along the edge of the wilderness could keep us practically bottled up there and beat us in detail; and that is precisely what seems to have been done. The inexplicable question is "Why did fighting "Joe Hooker," with seventy thousand as good troops as ever fired a gun, sit down in the middle of that tanglewood forest and allow Lee to make a monkey of him while Sedgwick was doing such magnificent work below? Two distinguished participants in all these events holding high commands, namely, General Alfred Pleasanton, quoted above, and General Doubleday, commanding First Division, First Army Corps, have written articles upon this battle, agreeing on the feasibility and brilliancy of the movement, but by inference and things unsaid have practically left the same question suspended in the air. It is possible the correct answer should not now be given.

To return to our own doings, on that Friday, 1st of May, our division was drawn up in line of battle in front of the Chancellorsville House, and we were permitted to rest on our arms. This meant that any moment we might be expected to move forward. The battle was now on in earnest. Heavy firing was heard some miles below us, which was Sedgwick's work at Fredericksburg. Nearer by there was cannonading and more or less severe musketry firing. Ambulances and stretcher-carriers were constantly coming back from the front with wounded soldiers, taking them to the field hospital, which was just in our rear, and we could see the growing piles of amputated legs and arms which were thrown outside with as little care as if they were so many pieces of wood. We were evidently waiting for something, nobody seemed to know what. Everything appeared to be "at heads." Our corps and division commanders, Couch, Hancock, and French, with their staffs, were in close proximity to the troops, and all seemed to be in a condition of nervous uncertainty. What might be progressing in those black woods in front, was the question. A nearer volley of musketry would start everybody up, and we would stand arms in hand, as if expecting the unseen enemy to burst through the woods upon us. Then the firing would slacken and we would drop down again for a time.

In the mean time shells were screeching over us continually, and an occasional bullet would whiz uncomfortably near. The nervous strain under such conditions may be imagined. This state of affairs continued all through Friday night and most of Saturday. Of course, sleep was out of the question for any of our officers. On Thursday and Friday nights the men got snatches of sleep, lying on their arms, between the times all were aroused against some fresh alarm.

On Saturday some beef cattle were driven up and slaughtered in the open square in front of our lines, and the details were progressing with the work of preparing the meat for issue when the storm of disaster of Saturday afternoon burst upon us and their

With the Federal right collapsing, the II and III Corps attempt to save the rest of Hooker's army from total disaster by fending off Jackson's powerful attack.

Cavalry commander Alfred J. Pleasonton leads Federal artillery in attempting to halt Jackson's powerful drive on the Union right.

work was rudely interrupted. We had anxious pre-monitions of this impending storm for some hours. Captain Pettit, who commanded the famous battery of that name, which was posted immediately in our rear, had spent much of his time in the forenoon of Saturday high up in a tall tree which stood just in front of the Chancellorsville House and close to our line, with his field glass reconnoitring. Several time he had come down with information that heavy bodies of the enemy were massing for a blow upon our front and where he believed they would strike. This information, we were told, he imparted to Hooker's chief of staff, and begged permission to open at long range with his rifled guns, but no attention was paid to him. I saw him up the tree and heard some of his ejaculating, which indicated that he was almost wild with apprehension of what was coming. Once on coming down he remarked to General Hancock that we would "catch h—l in less than an hour." The latter seemed to be thoroughly alive to the situation and exceedingly anxious, as were Couch and French, to do something to prepare for what was coming, yet nothing more was done until suddenly the firing, which had been growing in volume and intensity and gradually drawing nearer, developed in a storm of musketry of terrific fury immediately in our right front, apparently not more than three hundred yards away.

We could not see a thing. What there might be between us and it, or whether it was the onslaught of the enemy or the firing of our troops, we knew not.

But we had not long to wait. Soon stragglers, few in numbers, began to appear, emerging form the woods into our clearing, and then more of them, these run-ning, and then almost at once an avalanche of panic-stricken, flying men without arms, without knap-sacks, many bareheaded, swearing, cursing, a wild, frenzied mob tearing to the rear. Instantly they began to appear, General Couch, commanding our corps, took in the situation and deployed two divisions to catch and hold the fugitives. Part of the Third Corps was also deployed on our left. We were ordered to charge bayonets and permit no man to pass through our ranks. We soon had a seething, howling mob of Dutchmen twenty to thirty feet in depth in front of our line, holding them back on the points of our bayonets, and still they came. Every officer of our division, with drawn sword and pistol, was required to use all possible endeavor to hold them, and threaten-ing to shoot the first man who refused to stand as ordered. General French and staff were galloping up and down our division line assisting in this work.

In the mean time another line of battle was rapidly thrown in between these fugitives and the woods to stay the expected advance of the enemy. This was the famous break of the Eleventh Corps, starting with Blenker's division and finally extending through the whole corps, some fifteen thousand men. It seemed as though the whole army was being stampeded. We soon had a vast throng of these fugitives dammed up in our front, a terrible menace to the integrity of our own line as well as of all in our rear. We were powerless to do anything should the enemy break through, and were in great danger of being ourselves swept away and disintegrated by this frantic mob. All this time the air was filled with shrieking shells from our own batteries as well as those of the enemy, doing, however, little damage beyond adding to the terror of the situation. The noise was deafening. Pandemonium seemed to reign supreme in our front. Our line, as well as that of the Third Corps on our left, was holding firm as a rock. I noticed a general officer, I thought it was General Sickles, was very conspicuous in the vigor of his efforts to hold the line. A couple of fugitives had broken through his line and were rapidly going to the rear. I heard him order them to halt and turn back. One of them turned and cast a look at him, but paid no further attention to his order. He repeated the order in stentorian tones, this time with his pistol levelled, but it was not obeyed, and he fired, dropping the first man dead in his tracks. He again ordered the other man to halt, and it was sullenly obeyed. These

men seemed to be almost stupid, deaf to orders or entreaty in their frenzy.

An incident in our own front will illustrate. I noticed some extra commotion near our colors and rushed to see the cause. I found an officer with drawn sword threatening to run the color-sergeant through if he was not allowed to pass. He was a colonel and evidently a German. My orders to him to desist were answered with a curse, and I had to thrust my pistol into his face, with an energetic threat to blow his head off if he made one more move, before he seemed to come to his senses. I then appealed to him to see what an example he as an officer was setting, and demanded that he should get to work and help to stem the fight of his men rather than assist in their demoralization. To his credit be it said, he at once regained his better self, and thenceforth did splendid work up and down amongst these German fugitives, and later on when they were moved to the rear, he rendered very material assistance. I did not learn who he was,

With Lee and his legion of Southerners beating back the Army of the Potomac on 2 May, troops of Major General John F. Reynolds' I Corps advance into the growing inferno in the Wilderness to reinforce Hooker.

but he was a splendid-looking officer and spoke both English and German fluently.

One may ask why those men would have lost their heads so completely. To answer the question intelligently, one needs to put oneself into their place. The facts as we were told at the time were: That the Eleventh Corps, which contained two divisions of German troops, under Schurz and Blenker (I think Steinwehr commanded the latter division of this action), was posted on the right of Hooker's line in the woods, some distance in front and to the right of the Chancellorsville House. That at the time Stonewall Jackson made his famous attack, above referred to, he caught one of those divisions "napping"—off their guard. They had stacked their guns and knapsacks, and were back some twenty yards, making their evening coffee when suddenly the rebel skirmishers burst through the brush upon them, followed immediately by the main line, and before they realized it were between these troops and their guns. Consternation reigned supreme in an instant and a helter-skelter fight followed. Jackson followed up this advantage with his usual impetuosity, and although the other divisions of the Eleventh made an effort to hold their ground, this big hole in the line was fatal to them and all were quickly swept away. Of course, the division and brigade commanders were responsible for that unpardonable carelessness. No valid excuse can be made for such criminal want of watchfulness, especially for troops occupying a front line, and which

had heard, or should have heard, as we a half mile farther in the rear had, all the premonitions of the coming storm. But it was an incident showing the utter folly of the attempt to maintain a line of battle in the midst of a dense undergrowth, through which nothing could be seen. It is exceedingly doubtful whether they could have held their line against Jackson's onset under those conditions had they been on the alert, for he would have been on and over them almost before they could have seen him. To resist such an onset needs time to deliver a steady volley and then be ready with the bayonet.

It was towards six o'clock in the evening when this flying mob struck our lines, and darkness had fallen before we were rid of them and something like order had been restored. In the mean time it certainly seemed as if everything was going to pieces. I got a little idea of what a panic-stricken army means. The fearful thing about it was, we knew it was terribly contagious, and that with all the uncertainties in that black wilderness from which this mob came and the pandemonium in progress all about us, it might seize our own troops and we be swept away to certain destruction in spite of all our efforts. It is said death rides on horseback with a fleeing army. Nothing can be more horrible. Hence a panic must be stopped, cost what it may. Night undoubtedly came to our rescue with this one.

One of the most heroic deeds I saw done to help stem the fleeing tide of men and restore courage was

Hooker's final line of defence at Chancellorsville.

not the work of a battery, nor a charge of cavalry, but the charge of a band of music! The band of the Fourteenth Connecticut went right out into that open space between our new line and the rebels, with shot and shell crashing all about them, and played "The Star-Spangled Banner," the "Red, White, and Blue," and "Yankee Doodle," and repeated them for fully twenty minutes. They never played better. Did that require nerve? It was undoubtedly the first and only band concert ever given under such conditions. Never was American grit more finely illustrated. Its effect upon the men was magical. Imagine the strains of our grand national hymn, "The Star-Spangled Banner" suddenly bursting upon your ears out of that horrible pandemonium of panic-born yells, mingled with the roaring of musketry and the crashing of artillery. To what may it be likened? The carol of birds in the midst of the blackest thunder-storm? No simile can be adequate. Its strains were clear and thrilling for a moment, then smothered by that fearful din, an instant later sounding bold and clear again, as if it would fearlessly emphasize the refrain, "Our flag is still there."

★★★

ROBERT P. DOUGLAS

Behind Confederate Lines

Robert Douglas was a private in Company E of the 155th Pennsylvania and suffered the misfortune of being captured by the enemy after he was left behind by his army to care for wounded soldiers that could not be removed from the field in the Federal retreat from Chancellors- ville. Later paroled and exchanged, Douglas survived the war to embark on a fruitful career as manager of the Eliza Furnace Works in Pittsburgh. This article titled "In the Enemy's Lines After Chancellorsville" appeared in the history of his regiment, Under the Maltese Cross.

The writer's experience after the battle of Chancellorsville was a most unusual one. About the time the Fifth Corps crossed the Rappahannock at Kelly's Ford, Jacob Landsburger, of Company F, and the writer were detailed, by order of our Regimental Surgeon, Dr. Reed, acting surgeon in charge of the Second Division, Fifth Corps field hospital, for duty at that hospital. We were considered very fortunate in getting this detail, as we were relieved of our arms and the burden of our knapsacks, which were thrown into the ambulances and not seen again. Landsburger and the writer, after reporting, remained on duty with the Division hospital corps until the night of May 5th, when we were left, with other Union soldiers, to guard some of the wounded of both armies in an old saw-mill on the road from Chancellorsville to the United States Ford. The corps had been withdrawn across the Rappahannock, and we knew we were then outside our lines. In this field hospital, thus abandoned, there was a wounded Confederate Captain, two Lieutenants and twenty or more of their enlisted men, also wounded, and a few of our own wounded, unable to be moved. Orders came from headquarters of the Fifth Corps to allow none of the enemy's wounded to overhear, or to obtain any news from us of Hooker's retreat.

All that night we heard the retreating columns of our army marching back to the Rappahannock. We would have been only too glad to have gone along, but our strict orders were to remain at our posts, and as good soldiers we remained in obedience to those orders. The little squad of abandoned guards, thus left at the saw-mill, were in for developments, which soon came. At one o'clock in the morning of the 6th of May, Dr. Reed, surgeon in charge of the United States forces, sent an orderly to the guards and nurses just before the retreat, with orders to destroy all medical stores, to cut the leather medicine bags, and to break up all the medicine chests, to prevent them from falling into the enemy's hands. These stores would have been a great boon to them at any time, and especially at this time when they had thousands of their wounded requiring attention. We carried out our orders to the letter.

When our wounded were taken within our lines, after a delay of two weeks following the retreat of Hooker's army, a flag of truce arrangement was made by Generals Hooker and Lee, by which all the Union wounded, aggregating several thousand left within the Confederate lines, should be paroled and removed to Hooker's hospital on the north side of the Rappahannock near the United States Ford. The guards and nurses naturally expected to go back with them, but in this they were sorely disappointed. When the Fifth Corps ambulance trains under a flag of truce came out, Corporal John M. Lancaster, of Company E, was in charge of the detail. Dr. Reed, our Regimental Surgeon, a non-combatant, under orders, withdrew with this detail. Several trips were made by the ambulance trains of the Fifth corps from the north side of the Rappahannock, by way of the United States Ford. The distance was about five miles, and required time and care to transport so many sufferers back within the Union lines. There were about one hundred of our men originally detailed in all the squads besides ourselves; many from the Sixty-second Pennsylvania, the One Hundred and Fortieth New York, and some of the Sixty-third Pennsylvania, of the Third Corps, their duties being the same as Landsburger's and the writer's viz., to nurse and care for our wounded. These nurses were subsequently not permitted by the Confederates under the terms of the flag of truce to return to their regiments after the removal of our wounded, except those who were not fit to be removed. The

Confederates had taken charge of their own wounded at the saw-mill hospital and elsewhere the day following Hooker's retreat. All the Union details of nurses and guards immediately after the retreat of our army were made prisoners of war.

The first knowledge of and introduction to the enemy occurred on the 6th of May, about eight o'clock in the morning. We saw some cavalry approaching wearing the Union uniform. The writer remarked to Comrade Landsburger, "We are all right yet. Here comes our cavalry." A cavalryman rode up to us and drawing a huge navy revolver, with great bravado and many foul oaths, boisterously threatened to shoot us. None of the Union soldiers in the details of guards and nurses was armed, so we, being in the same condition, could offer no resistance. We expostulated with our captor, showing him we were unarmed, being non-combatants on detail in charge of Confederate wounded as well as of our own, that had not been able to be removed under a flag of truce regularly agreed on by the commanders of both armies. It was a very exciting experience, and nerve-racking in the extreme to look into the chambers of a huge "Colt," which our blood-thirsty captor held so close to the writer's head that he could plainly see the bullets in the cylinder. When the remainder of the Confederate scouts came up, we were declared prisoners by the commanding officer, and at once marched to the rear of Lee's army, where the officer in whose charge we were given, immediately placed us

Map of the Gettysburg Campaign.

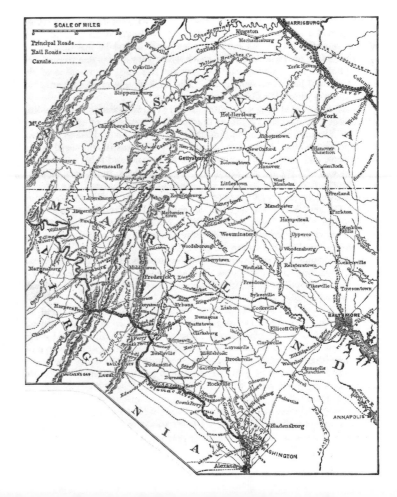

in a Confederate hospital to take care of many wounded Union prisoners.

On our march from the saw-mill to the rear, we passed over the battlefield, and our little party saw many horrible scenes. Many of the dead of both armies lay unburied where they fell, with their clothing burned from their bodies by the fire which swept over the field after the battle on Sunday afternoon, May 3rd.

Around the trees where there were patches of grass, many wounded of both armies had crawled and died. The writer noticed that the trousers of many of these dead soldiers had been burned to the knees and that the woolen material had not burned further than where the bodies had been lying among the dried leaves. The fresh grass would not ignite, and the fire in the clothing had gone out. The dried leaves and brush had been set on fire by the explosive shells used by each army. All such wood fires spread rapidly and many wounded and dying had met a horrible end. These grewsome and terrible sights convey an apt illustration of General Sherman's celebrated epigram—"War is hell."

The writer noticed particularly, an oak tree that had been hit three times during the battle by cannon balls from the Union artillery, each shot cutting off a section of the tree, and it had been literally cut down at the stump by bullets. This stump was not far from where General Jackson was killed.

On this same march, as prisoners, we passed an old tobacco house where there were still many of our wounded mostly belonging to Howard's (Eleventh) Corps. There the writer gave away the last cracker he had to a wounded Union soldier, suffering the pangs of hunger and pain. The condition of all the wounded in this hospital was terrible in the extreme.

Outside of the tobacco shed lay five dead Union soldiers, stripped of every stitch of their clothing. These horrors were all observed on the Eleventh Corps' line. These five dead bodies were utterly neglected and unburied three days. The writer gave them a decent burial.

After a halt here by our little band of prisoners for ten days we were marched to a point near Gordonsville, Va., and were halted at a farm house in which there were about seventy-five Union wounded in the recent battle, who were, of course, prisoners. With a comrade of the Sixty-second Pennsylvania, the writer was left by the officer in charge of the prisoners, to care for these wounded. There was no lint and no medicines of any kind on hand and nothing from which we could make bandages. Many of these sufferings ones were in even worse condition than those at the tobacco house we had just left. In a word, it was frightful. Many, thus neglected, died of blood poisoning. We cleaned the sores of those still alive by using plenty of cold water, going from one sufferer to another day and night. This was long before the day of

Convalescents attempt to heal their wounds in a Federal hospital.

Probably every Yankee fighting man feared ending up here, the infamous Libby Prison in Richmond.

Federal hospital in the field.

antiseptic surgery, but it was there, the best and only treatment possible.

Jackson's old corps, now commanded by General J. E. B. Stuart, was encamped close by, and one day, while off duty, the writer took a stroll through their camps. While watching the Confederate bakers making bread, one of their soldiers said, "Yank, aren't you afraid to be here, sah, by yourself?" To which the writer replied, "No, sir, I am unarmed, and a prisoner in charge of our wounded." "Yes, sah," he replied, "but you might be taken for a spy." Realizing at once the risks being taken, the writer began to move off for the hospital when the same man said, "Yank, you see those boys over there? Those uns are North Carolina troops. They didn't want to fight for the South, sah, but we placed them in the front, sah, at Chancellorsville, and they had to fight."

A few days after this conversation, one of these same North Carolina soldiers came to the hospital of the Union prisoners and begged the guards to arrange for him to be sent through the Confederate lines with the Union wounded, which was expected to be ordered at any time. He declared he was tired fighting and had had enough of it. This man came every day to the hospital for nearly a week. One of the Union wounded—a Berdan sharpshooter—died. The North Carolina visitor was told that if he would help bury the body, we would let him have the deceased's uniform, and he could take his name and in that manner get through the lines with the convalescent Union wounded. He donned the Union uniform and worked with us in the hospital for another week before the Union wounded and their guards were to start for exchange and parole at Annapolis, Md. When the day came, the entire party was marched to United States Ford on the Rappahannock River, under escort of a squad of Confederate cavalry, where the North Carolina "Johnny" metamorphosed into a Berdan sharpshooter of the Union army, stood right at my left when the Union wounded crossed. Captain Kyd Douglass, Adjutant-General of Jackson's Corps, recorded the names of the party and gave out the paroles both to the returning guard and the nurses. The North Carolina deserter passed without detection, and crossed with the wounded, and we never saw him again.

My comrade of the Sixty-second Pennsylvania and myself were very glad when our North Carolina friend passed safely through into our lines. We greatly feared that he might prove traitor and inform the Confederate office in charge of our party of our connivance in his escape, in which event our lives would not have been greatly prolonged.

The wounded turned over to the Union army here were the last of the prisoners captured at Chancellorsville, all of whom were wounded, numbering about five thousand and upwards in that battle. The detachment of guards and nurses and prisoners were treated as a distinct body separate and aside from the wounded. The Confederates at the United States Ford, when the exchange was made, seemed to have doubts as to he military status of our party, and of our right to be treated as non-combatants under the flag of truce which the Confederates evidently construed as applying only to the wounded prisoners. We were much surprised and disappointed, therefore, after all the wounded were transferred with the Union lines, when we were informed that our little party were still prisoners of war. We were marched to Richmond and put in Libby prison, where we remained four days without rations. In the meantime, our status having been settled by the Confederates, we were, on the fourth day, taken out of Libby and marched again to United States Ford, a distance, I suppose, of about fifty miles. This was close to where we had been made prisoners, and we had been able to see something of the country between there and the Confederate capital.

This time, to our very great joy, we were passed through the lines at the Ford without delay. We were not paroled prisoners and our next destination was Camp Parole, at Annapolis, where we were to remain until formally exchanged. This was another surprise to us. This was about the middle of June. Three of our party, all from Pittsburg, decided to take "French leave" and go home, and we were not long in starting.

The three of us remained at home for six weeks. The writer, weary of the monotony of this kind of military life, went on duty with the provost guard, being prevented from service with his company at the front until duly exchanged. Comrade Landsburger, the writer's fellow-nurse on this detail, on being exchanged some time afterward, returned to the Regiment, and remained on duty with his company until badly wounded in the first day's battle in the Wilderness.

Chapter II

THE ROAD TO GETTYSBURG

Hooker's defeat at Chancellorsville opened the way for Lee to launch his second great invasion above the waters of the Potomac. Charged to meet this dire threat to the north was George Gordon Meade who was given command of the Army of the Potomac after Hooker's removal. On 1 July, detachments from both Union and Confederate forces met to the northwest of Gettysburg in a battle that continued to grow in intensity until two Federal and two Confederate corps were engaged in heavy fighting. By nightfall, the rest of the grand armies were gravitating towards that small Pennsylvania town to play out one of the greatest moments in American military history.

Despite being sworn enemies on the field of battle, a Confederate and a Union picket meet on the "neutral ground" of the Rappahannock River to confer about recent events.

★★★

W. W. BLACKFORD

Riding with J. E. B. Stuart

*One of the most controversial perfor-
mances of the Gettysburg Campaign was
J.E.B. Stuart's handling or rather
mishandling of the cavalry of the Army of
Northern Virginia. After being roughed
up by mounted Yankee troopers at Brandy
Station, Stuart attempted to redeem himself by embarking on one of his famous
rides entirely around the Federal army.*

*While it was a spectacular performance,
Stuart's move failed to keep Lee informed
about the movements of the enemy thus
allowing the Confederates to blunder into
a major engagement at Gettysburg. One
of Stuart's commanders, W.W. Blackford
gives this account of Brandy Station and
Stuart's controversial ride in his* War Years
with J.E.B. Stuart.

A grand review was ordered for the 5th of June and all at headquarters were exerting themselves to the utmost to make it a success. Invitations were issued far and near, and as the time approached every train came loaded with visitors. I wrote to the University, and Mary Minor and a troop of Charlottesville girls attended. I was very sorry that my wife could not attend, but she was over three hundred miles away in Abingdon, and dreaded the journey.

When the day of review arrived the Secretary of War, General Randolph, came from Richmond to see it, and many infantry Generals and prominent men. The staff was resplendent in new uniforms, and horses were in splendid condition as we rode to the field on the level plains near Brandy Station. The ground was admirably adapted to the purpose, a hill in the centre affording a reviewing stand from which the twelve thousand men present could be seen to great advantage. It must be borne in mind that cavalry show much larger than infantry, and that these twelve thousand mounted men produced the effect of at least three times their number of infantry. General Stuart, accompanied by his brilliant staff, passed down the front and back by the rear at a gallop in the usual way, the general officers and their staff joining us as we passed, so that by the time we got back to the stand there were nearly a hundred horsemen, all officers, dashing through the field. Then the lines broke into column of squadrons and marched by at a walk, mak-ing the entire circuit; then they came by at a trot, taking the gallop a hundred yards before reaching the reviewing stand; and then the "charge" at full speed past the reviewing stand, yelling just as they do in a real charge, and brandishing their sabres over their heads. The effect was thrilling, even to us, while the ladies clasped their hands and sank into the arms, sometimes, of their escorts in a swoon, if the escorts

were handy, but if not they did not. While the charg-ing was going on, Beckham with the horse artillery was firing rapidly and this heightened the effect. It would make your hair stand on end to see them. How little did we then think that on this very ground a few days later just such charges would be made in reality in the greatest cavalry action of modern times.

That night we gave a ball at headquarters on the turf by moonlight, assisted by huge wood fires, fire-light to dance by and moonlight for the strolls.

General Lee arrived rather unexpectedly and on the 7th we moved to "Fleetwood," an old plantation

*The most flamboyant, if not one of the best, cavalry
commanders of the war, James Ewell Brown Stuart.*

residence near Brandy Station. The next day we had another cavalry review for General Lee's benefit. This was a business affair, the spectators being all soldiers. Many men from Hood's division were present who enjoyed it immensely. During the charges past the reviewing stand the hats and caps of the charging column would sometimes blow off, and then, just as the charging squadron passed and before the owners could come back, Hood's men would have a race for them and bear them off in triumph. This was the last of our frolics for a long time, for on the morrow we were to begin the fighting which was kept up almost daily until two weeks after the battle of Gettysburg, and we were to begin it in a severe action.

Up to this time the cavalry of the enemy had not been able to stand before us, but during the past winter great attention had been bestowed upon that branch of their service and it had become much more formidable. We were to meet the next day in nearly equal numbers upon the plain around Fleetwood in the great cavalry action, Fleetwood Fight, June 9, '63.

General Stuart's headquarters, as I have before stated, were at Fleetwood, an old homestead, situated on a hill half a mile from Brandy Station and four miles from the Rappahannock, and our cavalry was encamped for the most part along the river in front. Pleasanton then commanded the cavalry of the enemy and had been encamped twelve miles north of the river, but under pressing orders from Hooker to find out something of Lee's movements, he had the night before moved down to the river with the intention of crossing at daylight the next morning to attack Stuart at the Court House. Thus each commander was nearer the river than the other thought. Pleasanton moved in two columns, one under Buford to cross at Beverly's ford nearly in our front, and the other under Gregg at Kelly's ford six miles below. Both of these columns bivouacked about two miles north of the river.

At daylight our camp was aroused by a rattling fire proceeding from the bank of fog which hung over the valley. Stuart awaited impatiently the news, and presently a courier from General Jones, who was opposite Beverly's ford, reported that the enemy had charged through the ford, had driven in the picket there and had attacked the camp with great fury. Jones had met them with dismounted men and held them in check until his command could saddle up, had then struck his camp, packed his wagons and sent everything to the rear and was awaiting further developments. A sharp action followed without further advance on the part of the enemy. They were disconcerted at meeting such a force at that place, and awaited the movements of Gregg with the other wing six miles away.

Everything remaining quiet, Stuart accompanied by his staff rode down to the scene of action about the middle of the day, having previously sent Gen. Beverly Robertson with his brigade off to our right towards Kelly's ford to guard against an advance from that direction. This move was made on general principles of military strategy, he not having at that time knowledge of the movements of Gregg's column, and if

General Robertson had done his duty we would have had ample notice of any advance on that flank. Major McClellan, our Adjutant General, had been left by Stuart on Fleetwood hill with some couriers to receive any communications arriving and to forward them to him. Time rolled on, and Stuart with his shrewdness suspected that some scheme was brewing and sent one of his aides, Lieutenant Goldsborough, off to Colonel Butler near Stevensburg to find out if he knew anything of the enemy in his direction. Goldsborough was a fine, handsome and gallant young fellow but he had only joined the staff a few days before and was, as it turned out, inexperienced, and lacking in that habitual caution necessary for a staff officer in riding up to a body of troops on a battlefield; he must be sure who they are before he joins them, particularly in dusty weather when blue and gray are covered alike with dust so as not to be distinguishable. The roads were deep in dust and Goldsborough, poor fellow, had not gone far down the Kelly's ford road before he dashed full tilt into the head of a column of the enemy and was captured.

Federal cavalry troopers under Major General Alfred Pleasonton mix it up with J.E.B. Stuart's riders in perhaps the most epic cavalry confrontation of the war: Brandy Station.

I must now explain how this force came to be there close upon our flank and we not to know of their approach. Gregg had crossed at Kelly's ford without opposition and had then divided his force, bringing two brigades under Sir Percy Wyndham, an Englishman, and Colonel Kilpatrick up to form a junction with Buford and sending Colonel Duffie with the other part on towards Culpeper C. H. General Robertson, most unaccountably, did not attack either of these forces but allowed Gregg to go on towards our main army and Sir Percy Wyndham to pass him and go on towards Stuart's exposed flank and rear, and it was this latter column Goldsborough met. The first intimation any one had of this attack in flank and rear was their appearance in sight of Fleetwood. McClellan at once sent courier after courier to notify General Stuart, and as good luck would have it he was enabled to make some show of resistance by finding a piece of artillery accidentally passing the road across the hill. With this he immediately opened fire, the boom of the guns reaching us just as the courier brought the news to General Stuart, and satisfied him that McClellan was not mistaken, which at first he thought must be the case.

There now followed a passage of arms filled with romantic interest and splendor to a degree unequaled by anything our war produced. The waste of war had removed the obstacles to cavalry maneuvers usually met with in our country—fences and forests; and the ground was open, level and firm; conditions which led to the settlement of the affair with the sabre alone. Fleetwood hill was the key to the position. Artillery upon the commanding ground would render the surrounding plain untenable, and for its possession the battle was fought over its surface and on the levels beyond. There was here presented in a modern battle the striking phenomenon of gunpowder being ignored almost entirely. Not a man fought dismounted, and there was heard but an occasional pistol shot and but little artillery, for soon after the opening of the fight the contest was so close and the dust so thick that it was impossible to use either without risk to friends.

General Stuart turned to me and ordered me to gallop along the line and order every commanding officer of a regiment to move on Fleetwood at a gallop. It was a thrilling sight to see these dashing horsemen draw their sabres nd start for the hill a mile and a half in rear at a gallop. The enemy had gotten a battery almost to the top of the hill when they arrived. This was taken and retaken three times, we retaining it finally. The lines met on the hill. It was like what we read of in the days of chivalry, acres and acres of horsemen sparkling with sabres, and dotted with brilliant bits of color where their flags danced above them, hurled against each other at full speed and meeting with a shock that made the earth tremble. Sir Percy Wyndham after a gallant fight was repulsed before Buford, who was pushing Rooney Lee vigorously, could come to his assistance.

Col. M. C. Butler heard of Duffie's advance, and with great good judgment, without awaiting orders to that effect, threw his regiment in his front and ar-

rested his advance, falling desperately wounded himself. The same cannonball which took off his leg killed Captain Farley of our staff who was riding by his side.

As soon as this repulse was completed, General Stuart told me to watch closely to see if the enemy showed any infantry support, for if they did I must at once inform General Lee or General Longstreet. It was

not long before I found them with my powerful field glasses deployed as skirmishers and though they kept low in the grass I could see the color of their trimmings and their bayonet scabbards. Informing Stuart, he sent me to report the fact and after a hot ride of six miles I reached General Longstreet's quarters and reported the fact to him. General Lee then came down himself with some infantry but they were not brought into action. Gen. W. H. F. Lee charged and drove back Buford who was still advancing and then a final advance on our part pressed them back across the Rappahannock.

Cavalrymen duel and slash with sabres and cutlasses at Brandy Station. Though the Federals could hardly claim victory in the great battle, they finally managed to prove themselves the equal of their Southern adversaries.

By all the tests recognized in war the victory was fairly ours. We captured three cannon and five hundred prisoners, and held the field.

Colonel Hampton of the 2nd South Carolina, and Col. Sol. Williams of the 2nd North Carolina were killed, while Gen. W. H. F. Lee, Col. M. C. Butler and many others were wounded. Our loss on the staff was Captain Farley killed, Captain White wounded, and Lieutenant Goldsborough taken prisoner. Goldsborough's fate was a sad one. Taken prisoner in this his first battle, he remained in prison two years; he

was then exchanged, and in the first battle after his return, during the retreat from Richmond, only a few days before the surrender at Appomattox, he was killed. During his short stay on the staff he made warm friends of all of us by his gallant bearing and unassuming, attractive manners. He was a son of Commodore Goldsborough of the navy, and one of the handsomest young fellows in the army.

During the action, in galloping from one part of the field to the other carrying orders, friend and foe were so mixed together and all so closely engaged that I had

some capital pistol practice, and emptied every barrel of my revolver twice at close range. I could not tell with certainty what effect my shots had, for galloping by one cannot take a second glance, but at a target I seldom failed to hit a hat at that distance and in that manner. Pistol practice from the saddle at a gallop was our favorite amusement on the staff and it is surprising how accurately one can shoot in this way.

After the engagement Stuart ordered headquarters camp to be pitched on the same hill from which it had been moved in the morning, but when we reached the place it was covered so thickly with the dead horses and men, and the bluebottle flies were swarming so think over the blood stains on the ground that there was not room enough to pitch the tents among them. So the General reluctantly consented to camping at another place. He regretted this, for as a matter of pride he was inclined to hold the field as he held it in the morning even in this particular. The next morning we rode over the field and most of the dead bore wounds from the sabre, either by cut or thrust. I mean the field around Fleetwood; in other places this was not the case to so great an extent.

General Lee now began his march towards Pennsylvania. His proposed route was to cross the Blue Ridge and follow the valley of Virginia with his main army, while Stuart was to move on the east side of the mountains to cover his flank at least as far as Middleburg. Winchester was occupied by a strong force of the enemy and Ewell was sent on ahead to clear the valley. This he did gloriously, capturing four or five thousand prisoners and some thirty pieces of artillery.

Stuart pushed on up into Fauquier where Mosby met us. Mosby by this time had become famous. I had not seen him for more than a year and the change in his appearance was striking. When he was a member of my company and afterwards when he became Adjutant of our regiment, the 1st Virginia Cavalry, he was careless about his dress and mount and presented anything but a soldierly appearance. As we were riding along the road at the head of the column one evening we saw a horseman, handsomely dressed, gallop across the field towards us and lift his horse lightly over the fence a short distance ahead, and approach us. I could scarcely believe my eyes when I recognized in this dashing looking officer my old friend and the now celebrated guerrilla chief, Mosby. He had been scouting, and was fully posted as to the movements of the enemy, whose cavalry was following us in a parallel line some miles to the east of Bull Run Mountain. During all this period Mosby and his men kept us thoroughly informed of all movements of the enemy in that country.

On facing page, Pleasanton's cavalry drive the enemy back and give Stuart a good cause for much concern. Fortunately for the Confederates, reinforcements arrived to save the day.

Confederate and Yankee troopers engage in a massive effusion of blood at Brandy Station.

On the 18th of June we reached Middleburg and on the 19th their cavalry attacked us with great fury. The day before there had been several combats in which we had been in the main successful, capturing many prisoners. The fight at Upperville was a very hot one and at one time we were forced back. General Stuart with his staff around him was slowly leaving the field before the advance of a heavy line of dismounted skirmishers who were pouring their fire into us, the only group of horsemen they could see at that time. We were going up the side of a gently sloping hill and the bullets pattered around us on the hard, hoof-trodden ground like drops of rain. Just then I heard a thump very much like some one had struck a barrel a violent blow with a stick. I knew well enough what it meant, and I can never forget the agony of suspense with which I looked around to see which one of our group would fall. My first glance was towards General Stuart, but there he sat as firm as a rock in his saddle. I than saw von Borcke who was riding close by my side drop his bridle hand and become limp, his horse bounding forward as the rein was relaxed. I saw at once that his spur was going to hang in the blanket strapped behind his saddle, for he slowly slid sideways from his seat with both hands clutching the horse's

mane. I spurred Magic up alongside instantly, and, leaning over, took his foot in both hands and threw it over, clear of the saddle. His feet fell to the ground and this jerked loose his hold on the mane, letting him down easily on his back. Frank Robertson and myself sprang to the ground while someone caught the horse and brought him back. Seeing that our poor comrade was shot in the back of the neck I had little hope for him but determined to get his body off the field if possible. Von Borcke had often expressed his horror of filling a nameless grave and he once asked me, if the occasion should ever arise, to mark the place so that his friends could find it. The horse, as I have said, was brought to us but he was in a state of great excitement from the constant hissing of the bullets, for the approaching skirmish line, seeing the party halted, were bestowing special attention on us. I was at my wits' end to know how we were to throw our friend's body, weighing two hundred and fifty pounds, across the rearing, plunging charger, and how we were to keep it there if we succeeded in doing so. I then recollected a thing von Borcke had once told me was taught in the Prussian Cavalry schools for this very emergency, and I made a courier twist the horse's ear severely and keep it twisted while he led the horse off the field with von Borcke on him, the horse becoming perfectly quiet immediately. How strange that von Borcke's mentioning this little trick on a long night march in a general conversation to while away the time should have saved the narrator from capture, and quite likely from death from neglect in prison.

When we first lifted him von Borcke was as limp as a rag, but to our great surprise and pleasure he then showed signs of returning consciousness and stiffened himself on his legs enough for us to lift one foot to the stirrup, and then with a mighty effort to hoist him to the saddle, where with assistance on both sides he kept his balance until we could get him to an ambulance.

Von Borcke's strong constitution enabled him to survive this wound, though it was a very severe one. The bullet passed through the collar of his jacket an inch or two from the spine and entered his throat, and for months he coughed up pieces of his clothing which had been carried in. He was never able, however, to enter active service again with us. A few months before the surrender he returned to his own country and in the war with Austria held a position on Prince Frederick Charles' staff, though obliged to ride mostly in a carriage. In 1884 he visited this country and I dined with him at the Maryland Club in Baltimore, an elegant entertainment given in his honor at which there were present some twenty-odd old comrades of his, including Generals Wade Hampton and M. C. Butler of South Carolina, Gen. W. H. F. Lee of Virginia and Col. R. Snowden Andrews and Gen. Bradley T. Johnson of Baltimore. When I met him on this occasion he threw his arms around me and his eyes filled with tears. I spent a couple of days with him in Baltimore and we called to see the "New York rebel" who happened to be on a visit to the city at the time. She was still unmarried. This was the beautiful girl we met at Urbana, Maryland, during the Antietam Campaign in 1862, the one with whom I was dancing at our memorable ball when the wounded arrived. We had many pleasant memories to recall, but it was hard to realize that the middle-aged, matronly looking lady and the huge gentleman weighing between four and five hundred pounds were those who danced so gracefully then. Von Borcke told me he had not been able to reach his feet to tie his shoes for years on account of his corpulency. He was immense—his neck quite as large as his head, and all his manly beauty gone.

When he visited this country von Borcke had just lost his wife. He showed me her picture, and the picture of his two boys. She was a beautiful woman, judging by the photograph.

At the time of Lee's invasion of Pennsylvania, citizens of the Chambersburg were miffed by the decision of the commander of the Army of the Northern Virginia to live off the land at the expense of the Yankees.

When Col. Chas. Venable visited Prussia, von Borcke invited him to his castle and ran up the Prussian flag on one tower and the Confederate flag on the other.

The improvement in the cavalry of the enemy became painfully apparent in the fights around Upperville. It was mainly in their use of dismounted men, and in their horse artillery, however, for they could not stand before us yet in a charge on horseback. Around Upperville the fields were much enclosed by stone fences which greatly favored dismounted troops, and greatly impeded the mounted men. They were much better provided with long-range carbines than our cavalry, which gave them an advantage dismounted. Their cavalry too had been largely recruited from the infantry and had seen service and been drilled as such, which of course was greatly to their advantage serving on foot, while our cavalry had served from the beginning in their branch of the service, and had been drilled mainly mounted.

In the series of combats from Aldie to Middleburg from the 17th to the 21st it must be borne in mind that we were following a *defensive* policy, Stuart's only object being to cover the gaps of the Blue Ridge. This of course places cavalry at a disadvantage as it is mainly an *offensive* arm of the service and our object was successfully obtained, for the enemy never even entered a gap of the mountain. From a captured dispatch Stuart found that a strong force of infantry was supporting their attack and he then called upon General Longstreet for a detachment. These reached us, or rather reached a point within supporting distance in Ashby's Gap, but were not brought into action, nor even in sight of the enemy, as shown by General Pleasanton's report of the action.

We were not about to start on an expedition which for audacious boldness equaled if it did not exceed any of our dashing leader's exploits; but before entering upon the subject we must take a glance at the position of the contending forces: Lee occupied the valley from Winchester to the Potomac, and Meade awaited his movements in Loudoun and Fauquier, the two counties opposite, on the eastern side of the Blue Ridge. Stuart, as I have stated, guarded the passes of the mountain, and occupied the space between the Blue Ridge and the low range of hills parallel thereto called Bull Run Mountain, with headquarters at Rector's crossroads. General Lee being now ready to begin his march northwards, Early crossed the Potomac with his division as the advanced guard on June 22nd.

The question now arose as to how Stuart was to reach the head of Lee's advancing column, now entering Pennsylvania. It was impossible for him to move along the eastern slope of the Blue Ridge between the mountain and Meade's forces, and all the roads leading northward through the valley were densely filled with the trains of artillery, and quartermaster, commissary and ordnance wagons, to say nothing of the infantry columns. Two plans were presented by Stuart and submitted to General Lee's consideration: one, to take the route through the valley, and the other, which Stuart was ardently in favor of, to sweep around the rear of Meade's army and dash northward past him, and between him and Washington, cutting his communications, breaking up the railroads, doing all the damage possible, and then to join Early in Pennsylvania. General Lee left the decision of the question to Stuart, and Stuart immediately prepared to carry it into execution.

It was clearly necessary to leave a strong force of cavalry to guard the passes until Meade had left his position, else their cavalry could pour through and fall upon Lee's rear. Stuart had with him about five thousand men. This force he divided, leaving Wm. E. Jones' and Robertson's brigades, three thousand men, under command of Robertson to hold the passes until their front was clear and then to operate with the main army as Gen. R. E. Lee might direct; and he took three brigades, Hampton's, Fitz Lee's and W. H. F. Lee's, the latter under the command of Colonel Chambliss, numbering about two thousand men.

These three brigades were ordered to rendezvous at Salem on the night of the 24th, and a little after midnight on the morning of the 25th of June we started. No one could ride along the lines of this splendid body of men and not be struck with the spirit which animated them. They knew they were starting on some bold enterprise, but their confidence in their leader was so unbounded that they were as gay and lively as it was possible for them to be, for up to that time no reverse had crossed their path and they believed themselves and their leader invincible. Often have I heard, when some danger threatened and Stuart galloped by to the front, the remark, "Ah boys! I feel all right now, there is General Stuart."

Mosby had reported the enemy still in their encampments the day before and Stuart expected to move eastward through Haymarket and thence direct to Fairfax C. H., but at Haymarket, early in the first day's march, he found Hancock's corps on the march occupying the road he wished to cross for many miles each way. After shelling them awhile and capturing some prisoners, he had to wait most of the morning for them to pass, and then by a detour he passed around their rear and by a more circuitous route pushed on, crossing the Occoquan at Wolf Run shoals, capturing a small force at Fairfax C. H., passing through Dranesville, and reaching Rowser's Ford of the Potomac on the night of the 27th. The ford was wide and deep and might well have daunted a less determined man than our indomitable General, for the water swept over the pommels of our saddles. To pass the artillery without wetting the ammunition in the chests was impossible, provided it was left in them, but Stuart had the cartridges distributed among the horsemen and it was thus taken over in safety. The guns and caissons went clean out of sight beneath the surface of the rapid torrent, but all came out without the loss of a piece or a man, though the night was dark, and by three o'clock on the morning of the 28th of June we all stood wet and dripping on the Maryland shore.

Oh, what a change! From the hoof-trodden, war-wasted lands of old Virginia to a country fresh and plentiful. The march for three days had been through a country naturally poor at its best, but stripped by war of all the little it once had. Not a mouthful of grain had even I been able to beg, borrow, or steal for my horses; and where I could not find it there was apt to be none to find. Poor Magic looked as thin as a snake but cocked her ear as gayly as ever. Manassas had been wounded during our attack on Hancock's corps at Haymarket, but could still do duty, though much in want of food. The necessity for stopping to graze the horses on this march had delayed us a good deal, both in the time it took and the weakening of the animals from such light diet. I rode Manassas on the march and had Magic led, saving her for the big battle that we knew was brewing. It was absolutely necessary, though time was so precious, to allow the artillery horses some rest and a chance to eat the fine grass around us after their hard night's work; so it was nearly the middle of the day before we reached Rockville, a pretty village on the main road leading from Washington and nine or ten miles from that city. We had just arrived when a long wagon train of a hundred and fifty wagons appeared on the road slowly approaching from the direction of Washington, and a detail from Hampton's brigade was at once sent to capture it, which I accompanied. Galloping full tilt into the head of the train, we captured a small guard and a lot of gayly dressed quartermasters, and over half the wagons, before they could turn round; but then those beyond took the alarm, turned and fled as fast as their splendid mule teams could go. After them we flew, popping away with our pistols at such drivers as did not pull up, but the more we popped the faster those in front plied the whip; finally, coming to a sharp turn in the road, one upset and a dozen or two other piled up on top of it, until you could see nothing but the long ears and kicking legs of the mules sticking above bags of oats emptied from the wagons upon them. All behind this blockade were effectually stopped, but half a dozen wagons had made the turn

before this happened and after them two or three of us dashed. It was as exciting as a fox chase for several miles, until when the last was taken I found myself on a hill in full view of Washington. One hundred and twenty-five uninjured wagons were taken and safely brought into our lines, together with the animals of the others. Here was a godsend to our poor horses, for every wagon was loaded with oats intended for Meade's army and it did one's heart good to see the way the poor brutes got on the outside of those oats. After giving my horses all they could eat I slung half a bag, saddle-bag fashion, across my saddle for future use, and my horse seemed to know what this additional load was, for he occasionally turned an affectionate glance back towards it.

There was a large female academy in Rockville, and flocks of the pretty maidens congregated on the front to greet us, showing strong sympathy for our cause, and cutting off all the buttons they could get hold of from our uniforms as souvenirs. In passing along the street I saw a very duplicate of my little daughter Lizzie. Never have I seen so remarkable a likeness between two people. Frank Robertson was as much struck with it as I was. Twenty years after he met her there, a grown woman.

With the exception of a squadron of the enemy, encountered at Winchester, we met no opposition until Hanover was reached about noon on the 30th. It seems remarkable that the enemy should not have used more enterprise than this, for we were destroying his communications as we advanced. At Hanover, however, we met Kilpatrick's division of cavalry and had a hot affair with them. We were just opposite Gettysburg and if we could have made our way direct, the fifteen miles of distance to that place would have passed that day, and we would have effected a junction with General Lee the day before the battle began. It was here the wagon train began to interfere with our movements, and if General Stuart could only have known what we do now it would have been burned;

Stuart's troopers wreak havoc in the Federal rear. During the Gettysburg Campaign, J.E.B. Stuart managed to make a customary nuisance of himself to the Army of the Potomac at the expense of leaving Lee completely blind to his enemy's movements.

but he knew nothing of the concentration which accidental circumstances were to bring about at Gettysburg in the next two days, and as he expected to meet Early at York very soon, he held on to them.

The 2nd North Carolina Regiment made the first charge through the town, driving the enemy out, but receiving strong reinforcements they rallied and drove the North Carolinians back in their turn in great confusion. As General Stuart saw them rushing out of the place, he started down the road to meet them, calling me to follow him. We tried to rally them, but the long charge *in* and the repulse *out* and the hot skirmish fire opened upon them from the windows on the street by citizens had thrown them into utter confusion, and in spite of all we could do they got by us, and before we were aware of it we found ourselves at the head of the enemy's charging column.

The road was lined on each side by an ill-kept hedge grown up high, but at some places, fortunately for us, there were gaps of lower growth. Stuart pulled up and waving his sabre with a merry laugh, shouted to me, "Rally them, Blackford!" and then lifted his

mare, Virginia, over the hedge into the field. I knew that he only said what he did to let me know that he was off, so I followed him. I had only that morning, fortunately, mounted Magic, having had her led previously, and Stuart had done the same with Virginia, so they were fresh. As we alighted in the field, we found ourselves within ten paces of the front of a flanking party of twenty-five or thirty men which was accompanying the charging regiment, and they called to us to halt; but as we let our two thoroughbreds out, they followed in hot pursuit, firing as fast as they could cock their pistols. The field was in tall timothy grass and we did not see, nor did our horses until close to it, a huge gully fifteen feet wide and as many deep stretched across our path. There were only a couple of strides of distance for our horses to regulate their step, and Magic had to rise at least six feet from the brink. Stuart and myself were riding side by side and as soon as Magic rose I turned my head to see how Virginia had done it, and I shall never forget the glimpse I then saw of this beautiful animal away up in mid-air over the chasm and Stuart's fine figure sitting erect and

A Confederate cavalryman receives a blade thrust through his jugular during a gripping struggle for his guidon.

firm in the saddle. Magic, seeing the size of the place and having received a very unusual sharp application of my spurs, had put out her strength to its full in this leap and she landed six or seven feet beyond the further bank, making a stride of certainly twenty-seven feet. The moment our horses rose, our pursuers saw that there was something there, and it was with difficulty they could pull up in time to avoid plunging headlong into it, and their firing was of course arrested. This time Magic's activity had saved me from capture, but ten minutes later her quickness saved my life.

General Stuart galloped on up towards the top of a hill to direct the fire of a battery on the pursuing regiment, while I, wishing to get Magic cooled down away from the excitement of other horses, took a path which would round the foot of the hill. I had just quieted her, so that she had put her head down and was walking with the reins on her neck, when I heard the clatter of a horse's hoofs behind me at full speed. Thinking it was someone who wished to join company, I did not turn to look until I found the horse was not going slower as it approached. I then looked back, and there, within a couple of horses' lengths, came dashing a Yankee sergeant bending low on his horse's neck with his sabre "encarte" ready to run me through. It was the work of a second to seize the slackened reins, pulls them over to the right and plunge my left spur into her flank. As quick as lightning Magic bounded to the right, so quickly that my left arm was lifted a little from my side, and at the same instant there gleamed the bright blade of a sabre between my arm and body as my pursuer made his thrust; but by the time I could gather the reins and turn, the man was fifty yards away. Then I heard some cheering, and looking up the left, on a hill nearby saw a general officer and his staff, towards whom my man was making his way. It was evident that, seeing me alone, this man had made the pass as a little sword practice for the amusement of his comrades and his own glorification. I would have given anything if I could only have had half a minute's notice of his coming, for I don't think there would have been then anything for them to cheer. From where they stood it looked exactly as if he had succeeded in running me through, and he no doubt did not disabuse their minds as to the facts. I could only show my feelings upon the subject by shaking my fist at them as I moved slowly on to the battery on our hill.

It was night before we withdrew from Hanover, and Kilpatrick had been so roughly handled that he did not follow us on the first. On approaching York, Stuart found that Early had left there, moving westward, and he sent Maj. Andrew R. Venable of his staff on his trail to get orders from General Lee. Later in the day Capt. Henry Lee of Fitz Lee's staff was sent on a similar errand. During our night march the wagon train and nearly four hundred prisoners, who had been taken since the first batch of four hundred were paroled four days before, were a source of unmitigated annoyance. The mules in the captured wagon trains could neither be fed nor watered, and had not been for

Federal cavalry on patrol in the attempt to discover the movements of Lee's army as the Rebel force invades Union soil.

several days, while the prisoners fared nearly as badly. The consequence was great difficulty in moving them. Expecting to get rations in Carlisle, Stuart sent his commissary on ahead to make a requisition on the town, but since the withdrawal of Early the place had been occupied by the enemy. Stuart reached the place on the evening of July 1, and found it occupied by two brigades of militia under command of Gen. W. F. Smith. Of this officer he demanded a surrender, which was refused; whereupon Stuart opened his batteries and shelled the town and burned the barracks.

About midnight Venable and Lee returned with the first information we had received from our army and with orders from Gen. R. E. Lee for Stuart to march to Gettysburg at once. They also brought us intelligence of the successful combat of that day at Gettysburg.

We started from Carlisle about one o'clock A.M. on July 2, and effected a junction with our army at Gettysburg early in the day, Hampton becoming engaged in a sharp conflict with Kilpatrick's division before reaching there.

The brigades of Jones and Robertson, left at Upperville when Stuart started on his expedition, remained there long after the enemy left their front, and did not rejoin us until after the Battle of Gettysburg was fought and we were withdrawing towards the Potomac. Whose fault this was I cannot say, but certainly not Stuarts. If Robertson had not been a West Pointer he would have been deprived of his command for his inactivity in letting General Wyndham's command pass him as he did at Fleetwood Fight on the 9th of June, and the same qualities in the man which made him play such a part there may have been the cause of the delay on this occasion. General Robertson was an excellent man in camp to train troops, but in the field, in the presence of the enemy, he lost all self-possession, and was perfectly unreliable. But had he not sat upon the benches at West Point? Certainly he had, and he must consequently be made a general without ever having done one single thing in action to deserve that promotion. Our cause died of West Point as much as of any one thing. General Lee and General Stuart must have been convinced of his incapacity by this affair, for he was relieved of his command soon after and sent elsewhere.

It is easy enough to say that some other course would have been better than the one Stuart followed, looking back now with the knowledge of *what has since happened;* but is it fair to blame him for acting for the best with the *knowledge he then had?* If the Battle of Gettysburg had been won by us, as it very nearly was, this expedition would have been called a magnificent achievement. As it was the injury inflicted on the enemy by the diversion of troops was alone enough to justify it. Maj. H. B. McClellan gives a very able defence of Stuart on this point in his book, *The Campaigns of Stuart's Cavalry,* and shows clearly that the effect of Stuart's movement accomplished as much, if not more, diversion and neutralization of the forces of the enemy as any plan he could have pursued.

★★★

SIR ARTHUR FREEMANTLE

On to Gettysburg

One of the more lively accounts of the battle of Gettysburg belongs to Sir Arthur Freemantle, a colonel of the Coldstream Guards serving as a British observer with the Army of Northern Virginia at the time. His diary during his term of service in this position was published in 1863 and entitled Three Months in the Southern States. *In it the colonel presumptuously predicts a Southern victory in the Civil War. Here he describes Lee's path to Gettysburg.*

This morning, before marching from Chambersburg, General Longstreet introduced me to the Commander-in-Chief. General Lee is, almost without exception, the handsomest man of his age I ever saw. He

*Robert E. Lee in 1863. With his tremendous victory at —
Chancellorsville in May, "Bobby" Lee attained the
apex of his military career only to see his gains shattered a few months later with the defeat at
Gettysburg.*

is fifty-six years old, tall, broad-shouldered, very well
made, well set up—-a thorough soldier in appearance;
and his manners are most courteous and full of dig-
nity. He is a perfect gentleman in every respect. I
imagine no man has so few enemies, or is so univer-
sally esteemed. Throughout the South, all agree in
pronouncing him to be as near perfection as a man
can be. He has none of the small vices, such as smoking, drinking, chewing, or swearing, and his bitterest
enemy never accused him of any of the greater ones.
He generally wears a well-worn long grey jacket, a
high black felt hat, and blue trousers bucked into his
Wellington boots. I never saw him carry arms; and the

only mark of his military rank are the three stars on
his collar. He rides a handsome horse, which is ex-
tremely well groomed. He himself is very neat in his
dress and person, and in the most arduous marches he
always looks smart and clean.

In the old army he was always considered one of its
best officers; and at the outbreak of these troubles, he
was Lieutenant-Colonel of the 2d cavalry. He was a
rich man, but his fine estate was one of the first to fall
into the enemy's hands. I believe he has never slept in
a house since he has commanded the Virginian army,
and he invariably declines all offers of hospitality, for
fear the person offering it may afterwards get into
trouble for having sheltered the Rebel General. The
relations between him and Longstreet are quite touching—they are almost always together. Longstreet's
corps complain of this sometimes, as they say that
they seldom get a chance of detached service, which
falls to the lot of Ewell. It is impossible to please
Longstreet more than by praising Lee. I believe these
two Generals to be as little ambitious and as thoroughly unselfish as any men in the world. Both long
for a successful termination of the war, in order that
they may retire into obscurity.

Soon after starting we got into a pass in the South
mountain, a continuation, I believe, of the Blue Ridge
range, which is broken by the Potomac at Harper's
Ferry. The scenery through the pass is very fine. The
first troops, alongside of whom we rode, belonged to
Johnson's division of Ewell's corps. Among them I
saw, for the first time, the celebrated "Stonewall" Brigade, formerly commanded by Jackson. In appearance
the men differ little from other Confederate soldiers,
except, perhaps, that the brigade contains more el-
derly men and fewer boys. All (except, I think, one
regiment) are Virginians. As they have nearly always
been on detached duty, few of them knew General
Longstreet, except by reputation. Numbers of them
asked me whether the General in front was Longstreet; and when I answered in the affirmative, many
would run on a hundred yards in order to take a good
look at him. This I take to be an immense compliment from any soldier on a long march.

At 2 P.M. firing became distinctly audible in our
front, but although it increased as we progressed, it
did not seem to be very heavy. A spy who was with us
insisted upon there being "a pretty tidy bunch of *blue-
bellies* in or near Gettysburg," and he declared that he
was in their society three days ago.

After passing Johnson's division, we came up to a
Florida Brigade, which is now in Hill's corps; but as it
had formerly served under Longstreet, the men knew
him well. Some of them (after the General had passed)
called out to their comrades, "Look out for work now,
boys, for here's the old bull-dog again."

*On facing page, foreign observers of the American
Civil War in pose and at play. During the great conflict, many nations including Great Britain, France,
and Austria sent representatives from their armies to
observe the world's first truly modern war.*

At 3 P.M. we began to meet wounded men coming to the rear, and the number of these soon increased most rapidly, some hobbling alone, others on stretchers carried by the ambulance corps, and others in the ambulance wagons; many of the latter were stripped nearly naked, and displayed very bad wounds. This spectacle, so revolting to a person unaccustomed to such sights, produced no impression whatever upon the advancing troops, who certainly go under fire with the most perfect nonchalance: they show no enthusiasm or excitement, but the most complete indifference. This is the effect of two years' almost uninterrupted fighting.

We now began to meet Yankee prisoners coming to the rear in considerable numbers: many of them were wounded, but they seemed already to be on excellent terms with their captors, with whom they had commenced swapping canteens, tobacco, &c. Among them was a Pennsylvanian colonel, a miserable object from a wound in his face. In answer to a question, I heard one of them remark, with a laugh, "We're pretty nigh whipped already." We next came to a Confederate soldier carrying a Yankee colour, belonging, I think, to a Pennsylvanian regiment, which he told us he had just captured.

At 4:30 P.M. we came in sight of Gettysburg and joined General Lee and General Hill, who were on the top of one of the ridges which form the peculiar feature of the country round Gettysburg. We could see the enemy retreating up one of the opposite ridges, pursued by the Confederates with loud yells. The position into which the enemy had been driven was evidently a strong one. His right appeared to rest on a cemetery, on the top of a high ridge to the right of Gettysburg, as we looked at it.

General Hill now came up and told me he had been very unwell all day, and in fact he looks very delicate. He said he had had two of his divisions engaged, and had driven the enemy four miles into his present position, capturing a great many prisoners, some cannon, and some colours; he said, however, that the Yankees had fought with a determination unusual to them. He pointed out a railway cutting, in which they had made a good stand; also, a field in the centre of which he had seen a man plant the regimental colour, round which the regiment had fought for some time with much obstinacy, and when at last it was obliged to retreat, the colour-bearer retired last of all, turning round every now and then to shake his fist at the advancing rebels. General Hill said he felt quite sorry when he saw this gallant Yankee meet his doom.

General Ewell had come up at 3:30, on the enemy's right (with part of his corps), and completed his discomfiture. General Reynolds, one of the best Yankee generals, was reported killed. Whilst we were talking, a message arrived from General Ewell, requesting Hill to press the enemy in the front, whilst he performed the same operation on his right. The pressure was accordingly applied in a mild degree, but the enemy were too strongly posted, and it was too late in the evening for a regular attack. The town of Gettysburg

Always on the move, Johnny Rebs prepare to cross a ford while on the march in Pennsylvania.

was now occupied by Ewell, and was full of Yankee dead and wounded. I climbed up a tree in the most commanding place I could find, and could form a pretty good general idea of the enemy's position, although, the tops of the ridges being covered with pinewoods, it was very difficult to see anything of the troops concealed in them. The firing ceased about dark, at which time I rode back with General Longstreet and his Staff to his headquarters at Cashtown, a little village eight miles from Gettysburg. At that time troops were pouring along the road, and were being marched towards the position they are to occupy to-morrow. In the fight to-day nearly 6000 prisoners had been taken, and 10 guns. About 20,000 men must have been on the field on the Confederate side. The enemy had two *corps d'armée* engaged. All the prisoners belong, I think, to the 1st and 11th corps. This day's work is called a "brisk little scurry," and all anticipate a "big battle" to-morrow.

I observed that the artillerymen in charge of the horses dig themselves little holes like graves, throwing up the earth at the upper end. They ensconce themselves in these holes when under fire.

At supper this evening, General Longstreet spoke of the enemy's position as being "very formidable." He also said that they would doubtless intrench themselves strongly during the night. The Staff officers spoke of the battle as a certainty, and the universal feeling in the army was one of profound contempt for an enemy whom they have beaten so constantly, and under so many disadvantages.

On 24 June 1863, Lee brought his army north of the Potomac in his second invasion of the Yankee heartland. His first attempt had met failure on the Maryland farmland near Antietam less than a year before.

Gettysburg, sleepy town where the two great armies of the Civil War met in their most epic confrontation.

★★★

RUFUS R. DAWES

The Iron Brigade's Great Battle

Perhaps the most famous unit in the Army of the Potomac was a brigade of hard fighting Westerners from Wisconsin, Michigan and Indiana, called the Iron Brigade for their fierce tenacity in combat. In a term of glorious service which began at the battle of Groveton just preceding Second Bull Run, the Iron Brigade's greatest fight was on McPherson Ridge on the first day of the Battle of Gettysburg on 1 July. This selection was taken from The Sixth Wisconsin Volunteers *by Colonel Rufus R. Dawes, skipper of the 6th Wisconsin.*

When General James S. Wadsworth's division of the first army corps marched toward Gettysburg on the morning of July first, 1863, the sixth Wisconsin was the last regiment in the order of march for the day. The brigade guard, two officers and one hundred men, marched immediately behind us, which accounts for their assignment to the regiment for duty when we became involved in battle. The column moved on the Emmitsburg Road. Three hundred and forty officers and enlisted men marched in the ranks of the regiment. All were in the highest spirits. To make a show in the streets of Gettysburg, I brought our drum corps to the front and had the colors unfurled. The drum major, R. N. Smith, had begun to play "The Campbells are Coming," and the regiment had closed its ranks and swung into the step, when we first heard the cannon of the enemy, firing on the cavalry of General Buford. The troops ahead turned across the fields to the left of Gettysburg, toward the Seminary Ridge. We stopped our music, which had at least done something to arouse the martial spirit of old John Burns, and turned to engage in the sterner duties involved in war. When the head of the regimental column reached the crest of Seminary Ridge, an aide of General Meredity, Lieutenant Gilbert M. Woodward, came on a gallop with the order, "Colonel, form

After resting up from their defeat at Chancellorsville, weary Yankee soldiers prepare to take up the pursuit of the enemy.

Two Rebel spies discover a major liability in their profession after being captured by the enemy: death by hanging.

McPherson's Woods where Major General John F. Reynolds fell after receiving a deadly bullet in the back of the head shot from a Confederate marksman. Arriving on the field of battle on 1 July, Reynolds, the commander of the I Corps, decided to make a stand against a strong force of the Confederates under A.P. Hill.

your line, and prepare for action." I turned my horse and gave the necessary orders. The evolution of the line was performed on the double quick, the men loading their muskets as they ran. Hastening forward on a run to get to our position on the left flank of the "Iron Brigade," which, regiment after regiment, *en echelon*, was dashing into the McPherson woods, another aide, Lieutenant Marten, came galloping up and said, "Colonel, *General Doubleday is now in command of the first corps, and he directs that you halt your regiment." General John F. Reynolds had been killed, but the fact was not disclosed to us by Lieutenant Marten. I halted the men and directed them to lie down on the ground. The brigade guard now reported to me for duty in the impending battle, and I divided them into two companies of fifty men each, and placed them upon the right and left flanks of the regiment.

The brigade guard comprised twenty men from each of the five regiments of the "Iron Brigade." The two officers, Lieutenant Lloyd G. Harris, sixth Wisconsin, were capable men and excellent leaders. Eighty-one men of the other regiments of the brigade were thus, by the emergency of sudden and unexpected battle, brought into the ranks of our regiment.

The situation on the field of battle of all the troops now engaged, will be made clear by a diagram. Two

brigades of each army confronted each other. Archer's brigade opposed the "Iron Brigade," and Joseph R. Davis's brigade opposed Cutler's brigade of Wadsworth's division. Hall's battery was with Cutler's brigade.

Excepting the sixth Wisconsin, the whole of Wadsworth's division was hotly engaged in battle with the enemy. Lieutenant Meredith Jones came with orders from General Doubleday. He said, "General Doubleday directs that you move your regiment at once to the right." I immediately gave the order to move in that direction at a double quick. Captain J. D. Wood came and rode beside me, repeating the order from General Meredith and saying the rebels were "driving Cutler's men." The guns of Hall's battery could be seen driving to the rear, and Cutler's men were manifestly in full retreat.

Across our track we passed some officers carrying the body of our corps commander, General John F. Reynolds. We did not then know that he had been shot.

Suddenly my horse reared and plunged. It did not occur to me that she had been shot. I drew a tight rein and spurred her when she fell heavily on her haunches. I scrambled from the ground, where I had been thrown sprawling, in front of the regiment, and the men gave a hearty cheer. The gallant old mare also struggled to her feet and hobbled toward the rear on three legs. She had been struck in the breast by a minnie ball, which penetrated seventeen inches. For years she carried the bullet, which could be felt under the skin behind the left shoulder blade—but woe to the man who felt it, as her temper had been spoiled. For the rest of the battle I was on foot. The regiment halted at the fence along the Cashtown Turnpike, a long line of yelling Confederates could be seen running forward and firing, and our troops of Cutler's brigade were running back in disorder. The fire of our carefully aimed muskets, resting on the fence rails, striking their flank, soon checked the rebels in their headlong pursuit. The rebel line swayed and bent, and suddenly stopped firing and the men ran into the

Confederates of Colonel J. M. Brockenbrough's Brigade driving the Federals before the McPherson Barn on 1 July 1863.

railroad cut, parallel to the Cashtown Turnpike. I ordered my men to climb over the turnpike fences and advance. I was not aware of the existence of the railroad cut, and at first mistook the manuever of the enemy for retreat, but was undeceived by the heavy fire which they began at once to pour upon us from their cover in the cut. Captain John Ticknor, always a dashing leader, fell dead while climbing the second fence, and many were struck on the fences, but the line pushed on. When over the fences and in the field, and subjected to an infernal fire, I first saw the ninety-fifth New York regiment coming gallantly into line upon our left. I did not then know or care where they came from, but was rejoiced to see them. Farther to the left was the fourteenth Brooklyn regiment, but I was then ignorant of the fact. Major Edward Pye appeared to be in command of the ninety-fifth New York. Running to the major, I said, "We must charge." The gallant major replied, "Charge it is." "Forward, charge!" was the order I gave, and Major Pye gave the same command. We were receiving a fearfully destructive fire from the hidden enemy. Men who had been shot were leaving the ranks in crowds. With the colors at the advance point, the regiment firmly and hurriedly moved forward, while the whole field behind streamed with men who had been shot, and who were struggling to the rear or sinking in death upon the ground. The only commands I gave, as we advanced, were, "Align on the colors! Close up on the colors! Close up on the colors!" The regiment was being so broken up that this order alone could hold the body together. Meanwhile the colors fell upon the ground several times but were raised again by the heroes of the color guard. Four hundred and twenty men started in the regiment from the turnpike fence, of whom about two hundred and forty reached the railroad cut. Years afterward I found the distance passed over to be one hundred and seventy-five paces. Every officer proved brave, true, and heroic in encouraging the men to breast the deadly storm, but the real impetus was the eager and determined valor of our men who carried muskets in the ranks. I noticed the

Members of Brigadier General John Buford's cavalry brigade take a desperate stand against the powerful Confederate division under Major General Henry Heth.

motions of our "Tall Sycamore," Captain J. H. Marston, who commanded company "E." His long arms were stretched out as if to gather his men together and push them forward. At a crisis he rose to his full height, and he was the tallest man in the regiment, excepting Levi Steadman of company "I," who was killed on this charge. How the rebels happened to miss Captain Marston I cannot comprehend. Second Lieutenant O. B. Chapman, commanding company "C," fell dead while on the charge. The commission of Lieutenant Thomas Kerr as captain of company "D," bears the proud date of July first, 1863—in recognition of his conduct. The rebel color was seen waving defiantly above the edge of the railroad cut. A heroic ambition to capture it took possession of several of our men. Corporal Eggleston, of company "H," sprang forward to seize it, and was shot and mortally wounded. Private Anderson. of his company, furious at the killing of his brave young comrade, recked little for the rebel color, but he swung aloft his musket and with a terrific blow split the skull of the rebel who had shot young Eggleston. This soldier was well known in the regiment as "Rocky Mountain Anderson." Lieutenant William N. Remington was shot and severely wounded in the shoulder, while rushing for the color. Into this deadly melee came Corporal Francis A. Waller, who seized and held the rebel battle flag. His name will forever remain upon the historic record, as he received from Congress a medal for this deed.

My notice that we were upon the enemy, was a general cry from our men of: "Throw down your muskets! Down with your muskets!" Running forward through our line of men, I found myself face to face with hundreds of rebels, whom I looked down upon in the railroad cut, which was, where I stood, four feet deep. Adjutant Brooks, equal to the emergency, quickly placed about twenty men across the cut in position to fire through it. I have always congratulated myself upon getting the first word. I shouted: "Where is the colonel of this regiment?" An officer in gray, with stars on his collar, who stood among the men in the cut, said: "Who are you?" I said: "I command this regiment. Surrender, or I will fire." The officer replied not a word, but promptly handed me his sword, and his men, who still held them, threw down their muskets. The coolness, self-possession, and discipline which held back our men from pouring in a general volley saved a hundred lives of the enemy, and as my mind goes back to the fearful excitement of the moment, I marvel at it. The fighting around the rebel colors had not ceased when this surrender took place. I took the sword. It would have been the handsome thing to say, "Keep your sword, sir," but I was new to such occasions, and when six other officers came up and handed me their swords, I took them also. I held this awkward bundle in my arms until relieved by Adjutant Brooks. I directed the officer in command, Major John A. Blair, of the second Mississippi regiment, to have his men fall in without arms. He gave

Members of Reynolds' I Corps skirmish with the Confederate III Corps under Lieutenant General A.P. Hill. Though holding under intense pressure, the Federals were eventually forced to fall back through Gettysburg even after receiving reinforcements.

Gettysburg as seen from Oak Hill. Confederate batteries stationed here played havoc on the Federal lines of battle.

the command, and his men, (seven officers and two hundred and twenty-five enlisted men) obeyed: To Major John F. Hauser I assigned the duty of marching this body to the provost-guard. Lieutenant William Goltermann of Company "F," volunteered to command a line of volunteer skirmishers, which I called for as soon as Major Hauser moved his prisoners away. This line of men took possession of the ridge toward the enemy and guarded against a surprise by a return of the enemy to attack. One gun of Hall's second Maine battery stood upon the field before the railroad cut and between the hostile lines. After the surrender, Captain Rollin P. Converse took men enough for the purpose and pulled this gun to the turnpike, where Captain Hall took it again in charge.

Corporal Frank Asbury Waller brought me the captured battle flag. It was the flag of the second Mississippi Volunteers, one of the oldest and most distinguished regiments in the Confederate army. It belonged to the brigade commanded by Joseph R. Davis, the nephew of Jefferson Davis. It is a rule in battle not to allow sound men to leave the ranks. Sergeant William Evans of company "H," a brave and true man, had been severely wounded in the thighs. He was obliged to use two muskets as crutches. To him I intrusted the battle-flag, and I took it from the staff and wrapped it around his body.

Adjutant E. P. Brooks buckled on one of the captured swords, and he still retains it, but the other six were given to a wounded man and delivered to our chief surgeon, A. W. Preston. The enemy, when they took the town, captured the hospital and the swords. No discredit to the doctor is implied, as his hands were full of work with wounded men.

After this capture of prisoners in the railroad cut there was a lull in the battle. Our comrades of the "Iron Brigade," who had charged so brilliantly into the McPherson woods, had been completely victorious. They had routed Archer's brigade, capturing its commander and many of its men, and then they had changed front to move to the relief of Cutler's brigade, but our charge upon the railroad cut, and its success, obviated that necessity. By this charge Joseph R. Davis' brigade was scattered or captured. We had fairly defeated, upon an open field, a superior force of the veterans of the army of General Lee. It was a short, sharp, and desperate fight, but the honors were easily with the boys in blue.

While the regiment is being reorganized, let us follow Sergeant William Evans. Weak and faint from loss of blood, he painfully hobbled to Gettysburg, and became exhausted in the street. Brave and faithful friends came to his relief. Two young women assisted this wounded soldier into their home, and placed him upon a bed. The Union troops soon began to retreat in confusion through the town, and the cheers of the victorious enemy could be plainly heard. Evans begged of his friends to hide the rebel flag. They cut a hole in the bed-tick beneath him thrust in the flag, and sewed up the rent. The flag was thus safely concealed until the enemy retreated from Gettysburg, and on the morning of July 4th Evans brought his precious trophy to Culp's Hill and gave it to me there.

In his official report General Doubleday says that when Cutler's regiments were overpowered and driven back, "the moment was a critical one, involving the defeat, perhaps the utter rout of our forces." Later in the day we marched through the railroad cut, and about one thousand muskets lay in the bottom of it. Only one regiment suffered as an organization, and that was the second Mississippi Volunteers. The ninety-fifth New York took prisoners, as did also the fourteenth Brooklyn. All the troops in the railroad cut threw down their muskets, and the men either surrendered themselves, or ran away out of the other end of the cut.

We next advanced, by order of General Wadsworth, to the ridge west of the Seminary Ridge. Here we encountered a heavy line of rebel skirmishers, upon whom we opened fire, and drove them into Willoughby Run. But the enemy turned upon us the fire of six pieces of artillery in position just south of the Cashtown Turnpike beyond Willoughby Run, and beyond the houses in the picture. The shell flew over

Under heavy fire, Lieutenant Bayard Wilkeson 4th U.S. Artillery blasts away at Heth's men.

us and burst around us so thickly that I was obliged to order the men to lie upon the ground under the brow of the ridge. The "Iron Brigade" was in the McPherson Woods, half a mile to our left. The space between us and that brigade was occupied by Colonel Roy Stone's Pennsylvania Bucktails. General Lysander Cutler's brigade was now upon our right. This was our position when the general attack was made by the rebel army

McPherson's Woods, where the Iron Brigade destroyed most of Brigadier General James J. Archer's brigade of Alabamians and Tennesseans while capturing the unit's commander.

The Lutheran Seminary at Gettysburg atop the ridge that bears its name. After the Confederates seized Seminary Ridge, Lee used the building to observe Union movements across the way on Cemetery Ridge.

corps of Hill and Ewell combined, at half past one o'clock in the afternoon. The first brunt of it struck the gallant brigade of Bucktails. They were fighting on Pennsylvania soil. Their conduct was more than heroic, it was glorious. I can not describe the charges and counter-charges which took place, but we all saw the banner of the one hundred and forty-ninth Pennsylvania planted in the ground and waving between the hostile lines of battle, while the desperate fight went on. This color was taken by the enemy.

Under presure of the battle, the whole line of Union troops fell back to the Seminary Ridge. I could plainly see the entire movement. I saw Captain Hollon Richardson who acted as an aide to Colonel W. W. Robinson, now in command of the "Iron Brigade," carrying on his horse and waving aloft, the colors of the seventh Wisconsin, as the proud brigade slowly drew back from the McPherson Woods to the Seminary Ridge. We received no orders. Being a detached regiment it is likely that we were overlooked. The enemy (Ewell's corps) advanced so that the low ground between us and the Seminary Ridge in our rear was swept by their fire. It would cost many lives to march in line of battle through this fire. I adopted the tactics of the rebels earlier in the day, and ordered my men to run into the railroad cut. Then instructing the men to follow in single file, I led the way, as fast as I could run, from this cut to the cut in the Seminary Ridge. About a cart load of dirt was ploughed over us by the rebel shell, but otherwise not a man was struck. The ranks were promptly reformed, and we marched into the woods on the Seminary Ridge to the same position from which we had advanced. The whole first army corps was now in line of battle on the Seminary Ridge, and here that grand body of veteran soldiers made a heroic effort to stay the overwhelming tide that swept against them.

Battery "B," fourth U. S. artillery, under command of Lieutenant James Stewart, came up, and General Wadsworth directed me to support it with my regiment. James Stewart was as brave and efficient a man as ever fought upon a battle field. His battery was manned by men detailed from the volunteers, many of them from our brigade. And now came the grand advance of the enemy. During this time the attack was progressing, I stood among the guns of battery "B." Along the Seminary Ridge, flat upon their bellies, lay mixed up together in one line of battle, the "Iron Brigade" and Roy Stone's "Bucktails." For a mile up and down the open fields in front, the splendid lines of the veterans of the army of Northern Virginia swept down upon us. Their bearing was magnificent. They maintained their alignments with great precision. In many cases the colors of regiments were advanced several paces in front of the line. Stewart fired shell until they appeared on the ridge east of Willoughby Run; when on this ridge they came forward with a rush. The musketry burst from the Seminary Ridge, every shot fired with care, and Stewart's men, with the regularity of a machine, worked their guns upon the enemy. The rebels came half way down the opposite slope, wavered, began to fire, then to scatter

Brigade commander, Brigadier General James T. Archer.

Probably one of the persons most responsible for bringing about the cataclysmic battle at Gettysburg was Major General Henry Heth. His quest for shoes led his division into a skirmish with John Buford's cavalry which eventually mushroomed into the greatest battle of the war.

and then to run, and how our men did yell, "Come on, Johnny! come on!" Falling back over the ridge they came on again more cautiously, and pouring upon us from the start a steady fire of deadly musketry. This killed Stewart's men and horses in great numbers, but did not seem to check his fire.

Lieutenant Clayton E. Rogers, aide on General Wadsworth's staff, came riding rapidly to me. Leaning over from his horse, he said very quietly: "The orders, colonel, are to retreat beyond the town. Hold your men together." I was astonished. The cheers of defiance along the line of the first corps, on Seminary Ridge, had scarcely died away. But a glance over the field to our right and rear was sufficient. There the troops of the eleventh corps appeared in full retreat, and long lines of Confederates, with fluttering banners and shining steel, were sweeping forward in pursuit of them without let or hindrance. It was a close race which could reach Gettysburg first, ourselves, or the rebel troops of Ewell's corps, who pursued our eleventh corps. Facing the regiment to the rear, I marched in line of battle over the open fields toward the town. We were north of the railroad, and our direction separated us from other regiments of our corps. If we had desired to attack Ewell's twenty thousand men with our two hundred, we could not have moved more directly toward them. We knew nothing about a Cemetery Hill. We could see only that the on-coming lines of the enemy were encircling us in a horseshoe. But with the flag of the Union and of Wisconsin held aloft, the little regiment marched firmly and steadily. As we approached the town, the buildings of the Pennsylvania College screened us from the view of the enemy. We could now see that our troops were retreating in a direction at right angles to our line of march. We reached a street extending through Gettysburg from the college to Cemetery Hill, and crossed it. We were now faced by the enemy, and I turned the course toward the Cemetery Hill, although then unconscious of the fact. The first cross street was swept by the musketry fire of the enemy. There was a close board fence, inclosing a barn-yard, on the opposite side of the street. A board or two off from the fence made what the men called a "hog-hole." Instructing the regiment to follow in single file on the run, I took a color, ran across the street, and jumped through this opening in the fence. Officers and men followed rapidly. Taking position at the fence, when any man obstructed the passage-way through it, I jerked him away without ceremony or apology, the object being to keep the track clear for those yet to come. Two men were shot in this street crossing. The regiment was reformed in the barn-yard, and I marched back again to the street leading from the Pennsylvania College to the Cemetery Hill. To understand why the street was crossed in the manner described, it should be remembered that men running at full speed, scattered in single file, were safer from the fire of the enemy than if marching in a compact body. By going into the inclosure, the regiment came together, to be at once formed into compact order. It

was in compliance with the order, to keep my men together. The weather was sultry. The sweat steamed from the faces of the men. There was not a drop of water in the canteens, and there had been none for hours. The streets were jammed with crowds of retreating soldiers, and with ambulances, artillery, and wagons. The cellars were crowded with men, sound in body, but craven in spirit, who had gone there to surrender. I saw no men wearing badges of the first army corps in this disgraceful company. In one case, these miscreants, mistaking us for the rebels, cried out from the cellar, "Don't fire, Johnny, we'll surrender." These surroundings were depressing to my hot and thirsty men. Finding the street blocked, I formed my men in two lines across it. The rebels began to fire

Westerners fighting out east. Two soldiers of the 4th Michigan. At Gettysburg, they engaged Longstreet's men at close quarters near the Peach Orchard.

on us from houses and cross-lots. Here came to us a friend in need. It was an old citizen with two buckets of fresh water. The inestimable value of this cup of cold water to those true, unyielding soldiers, I would that our old friend could know.

After this drink, in response to my call, the men gave three cheers for the good and glorious cause for which we stood in battle. The enemy fired on us sharply, and the men returned their fire, shooting wherever the enemy appeared. This firing had a good effect. It cleared the street of stragglers in short order. The way being open I marched again toward the Cemetery Hill. The enemy did not pursue; they had found it dangerous business. We hurried along, not knowing certainly that we might not be marching into the clutches of the enemy. But the colors of the Union, floating over a well ordered line of men in blue, who were arrayed along the slope of Cemetery Hill, became visible. This was the seventy-third Ohio, of Steinwehr's division of the eleventh army corps. With swifter steps we now pressed on up the hill, and, passing in through the ranks open to receive us, officers and men threw themselves in a state of almost perfect exhaustion on the green grass and the graves of

the cemetery. The condition of affairs on Cemetery Hill at this time has been a subject of discussion. If fresh troops had attacked us then, we unquestionably would have fared badly. The troops were scattered over the hill in much disorder, while a stream of stragglers and wounded men pushed along the Baltimore Turnpike toward the rear. But this perilous condition of affairs was of short duration. There was no appearance of panic on the Cemetery Hill. After a short breathing spell my men again promptly responded to the order to "fall in." Lieutenant Rogers brought us orders from General Wadsworth, to join our own brigade, which had been sent to occupy Culp's Hill. As we marched toward the hill our regimental wagon joined us. In the wagon were a dozen spades and shovels. Taking our place on the right of the line of the brigade, I ordered the regiment to intrench. The men worked with great energy. A man would dig with all his strength till out of breath, when another would seize the spade and push on the work. There were no orders to construct these breastworks, but the situation plainly dictated their necessity. The men now lay down to rest after the arduous labors of this great and terrible day. Sad and solemn reflections

A row of dead Westerners from the 24th Michigan of the Iron Brigade lie on the field on the first day of the battle. Of the 496 men of the Wolverine Regiment, 399 were lost on 1 July alone.

The dead of the first day's battle were members of the I and XI Corps lost their lives desperately fighting the Confederates on McPherson's Ridge and Seminary Ridge.

The bloated bodies of several members of the Iron Brigade lie exposed to the cruel heat of the summer sun. The corpses have been stripped of shoes, ammunition and other articles that these unfortunate fellows will no longer have a use for.

possessed, at least, the writer of these papers. Our dead lay unburied and beyond our sight or reach. Our wounded were in the hands of the enemy. Our bravest and best were numbered with them. Of eighteen hundred men who marched with the splendid brigade in the morning, but seven hundred were here. More than one thousand men had been shot. There was to us a terrible reality in the figures which represent our loss. We had been driven, also, by the enemy, and the shadow of defeat seemed to be hanging over us. But that afternoon, under the burning sun and through the stifling clouds of dust, the Army of the Potomac had marched to the sound of our cannon. We had lost the ground on which we had fought, we had lost our commander and our comrades, but our fight had held the Cemetery Hill and forced the decision for history that the crowning battle of the war should be at Gettysburg.

It is a troubled and dreamy sleep at best that comes to the soldier on a battle field. About one o'clock at night we had a great alarm. A man in the seventh Indiana regiment, next on right, cried so loudly in his sleep that he aroused all the troops in the vicinity. Springing up, half bewildered, I ordered my regiment to "fall in," and a heavy fire of musketry broke out from along the whole line of men. At three o'clock in the morning, according to orders, the men were aroused. The morning of the second day found us lying quietly in our breastworks near the summit of Culp's Hill. We were in the shade of some fine oak trees, and enjoyed an excellent view of nearly the whole battle field. Our situation would have been delightful, and our rest in the cool shade would have been refreshing, if it had not been for the crack, crack, of the deadly sharpshooters on the rebel skirmish line. Owing, probably, to the crooked line of our army, the shots came from all directions, and the peculiarly mournful wail of the spent bullet was constantly heard.

★════════════════════ **Chapter III** ════════════════════★

THE SECOND DAY OF SLAUGHTER

On 1 July, Confederates had managed to drive the Federals into a fishhook like formation on and around Cemetery Ridge. Though outnumbered and facing an enemy holding a strong position, Lee elected to launch a brutal attack on Meade's left the next day. His forces badly mangled the enemy, but the Confederate general found to his irritation that the Army of the Potomac refused to budge and almost patiently awaited his next move.

Soldiers in butternut count the bullet holes in their battle torn colors.

★★★

JAMES LONGSTREET

Gettysburg—The Second Day

Another controversial aspect of the Battle of Gettysburg was General James Longstreet's handling of his forces during the massive conflict. Because he was against the idea of engaging the Army of the Potomac at Gettysburg, Longstreet disagreed with his commander over the viability of making an assault against the overpowering numbers of entrenched Fed-erals. Lee's lieutenant, who was charged to assail the unsteady Federal left, has often been harshly criticized for his delays in getting his troops into position and for launching a tardy attack on the enemy. Longstreet's view of the second day of the battle is taken from his epic memoirs of the war, From Manassas to Appomattox.

The stars were shining brightly on the morning of the 2d when I reported at General Lee's head-quarters and asked for orders. After a time Generals McLaws and Hood, with their staffs, rode up, and at sunrise their commands filed off the road to the right and rested. The Washington Artillery was with them, and about nine o'clock, after an all-night march, Alexander's batteries were up as far as Willoughby's Run, where he parked and fed, and rode to head-quarters to report.

As indicated by these movements, General Lee was not ready with his plans. He had not heard from his cavalry, nor of the movements of the enemy further than the information from a despatch captured during the night, that the Fifth Corps was in camp about five miles from Gettysburg, and the Twelfth Corps was reported near Culp's Hill. As soon as it was light enough to see, however, the enemy was found in position on his formidable heights awaiting us.

The result of efforts during the night and early morning to secure Culp's Hill had not been reported, and General Lee sent Colonel Venable of his staff to confer with the commander of the Second Corps as to opportunity to make the battle by his left. He was still in doubt whether it would be better to move to his far-off right. About nine o'clock he rode to his left to be assured of the position there, and of the general temper of affairs in that quarter. After viewing the field, he held conference with the corps and division commanders. They preferred to accept his judgment and orders, except General Early, who claimed to have learned of the topographical features of the country during his march towards York, and recommended the right of the line as the point at which strong battle should be made. About ten o'clock General Lee returned to his head-quarters, but his engineer who had been sent to reconnoitre on his right had not come

back. To be at hand for orders, I remained with the troops at his head-quarters. The infantry had arms stacked; the artillery was at rest.

The enemy occupied the commanding heights of the city cemetery, from which point, in irregular grade, the ridge slopes southward two miles and a half to a bold outcropping height of three hundred feet called Little Round Top, and farther south half a mile ends in the greater elevation called Round Top. The former is covered from base to top by formidable boulders. From the cemetery to Little Round Top was the long main front of General Meade's position. At the cemetery his line turned to the northeast and east and southeast in an elliptical curve, with his right on Culp's Hill.

At an early hour of the 2d the Union army was posted: the Twelfth Corps at Culp's Hill, extending its left to Wadsworth's division of the First; on Wadsworth's left the Eleventh Corps; on the left of the Eleventh the other troops of the First; on their left the Second, and left of that to Little Round Top the Third Corps; the Fifth Corps stood in reserve across the bend from the right of the Twelfth to the left of the Second Corps. Thus there was formed a field of tremendous power upon a convex curve, which gave the benefit of rapid concentration at any point or points. The natural defences had been improved during the night and early morning. The Sixth Corps was marching from Manchester, twenty-two miles from Gettysburg. Its first order, received near Manchester before night of the 1st, was to march for Taneytown, but after passing the Baltimore pike the orders were changed, directing a prompt march to Gettysburg. The march has been variously estimated from thirty to thirty-five miles, but the distance from Manchester *via* Taneytown to Gettysburg is only twenty-nine miles, and as the ground for which the corps marched was three miles east of Gettysburg, the march would have been only twenty-six miles *via* Taneytown; as the corps marched back and took the Baltimore pike, some distance must have been saved. It was on the field at three o'clock of the afternoon,—the Union cavalry under General Pleasonton in reach.

The Confederate left was covering the north and east curve of the enemy's line, Johnson's division near Culp's Hill, Early's and Rodes's extending the line to the right through Gettysburg; Pender's division on the right of Rodes's; the other divisions of the Third Corps resting on Seminary Ridge, with McLaws's division and Hood's three brigades near general headquarters; Pickett's brigades and Law's of Hood's division at Chambersburg and New Guilford, twenty-two and twenty-four miles away. Law had received orders to join his division, and was on the march. The cavalry was not yet heard from. The line so extended and twisted about the rough ground that concentration at any point was not posible.

It was some little time after General Lee's return from his ride to the left before he received the reports of the reconnoissance ordered from his centre to his right. His mind, previously settled to the purpose to fight where the enemy stood, now accepted the explicit plan of making the opening on his right, and to have the engagement general. He ordered the commander of the Third Corps to extend the centre by Anderson's division, McLaws's and Hood's divisions to extend the deployment to his right. Heth's division of the Third was drawn nearer the front, and notice of

James "Old Pete" Longstreet, the general charged with breaking the Federal left at Gettysburg on the second day of the battle. Longstreet strongly disagreed over the viability of launching just such an attack and recommended Lee take a more defensive posture.

The man who thwarted Lee at Gettysburg, (sitting at center with legs crossed) George Gordon Meade. After fighting under such military failures as McClellan, Burnside and Hooker, the Army of the Potomac found a solid fighting commander in Meade.

his plans was sent the commander of the Second Corps.

At the intimation that the battle would be opened on the right by part of the First Corps, Colonel Alexander was asked to act as director of artillery, and sent to view the field in time to assign the batteries as they were up. It was eleven o'clock when General Lee's order was issued, but he had ordered Law's brigade to its division, and a wait of thirty minutes was necessary for it to get up. Law had received his orders at three in the morning, and had marched twenty-three miles. The battle-ground was still five miles off by the route of march, but Law completed his march of twenty-eight miles in eleven hours,—the best marching done in either army to reach the field of Gettysburg.

The battle was to be opened on the right by two divisions of the First Corps, supported on their left by four of the brigades of Anderson's division; the opening to be promptly followed on Lee's left by the Second Corps, and continued to real attack if the opportunity occurred; the Third (centre) Corps to move to severe threatening and take advantage of opportunity to attack; the movements of the Second and Third Corps to be prompt, and in close, severe cooperation, so as to prevent concentration against the battle of the right. The little cavalry that was with the army was kept on the extreme left. Not so much as one trooper was sent us.

General Lee ordered his reconnoitring officer to lead the troops of the First Corps and conduct them by a route concealed from view of the enemy. As I was relieved for the time from the march, I rode near the middle of the line. General Lee rode with me a mile or more. General Anderson marched by a route nearer the enemy's line, and was discovered by General Sickles, who commanded the Third Corps, the left of the Union line. A little uncomfortable at his retired position, and seeing that the battle was forming against him, General Sickles thought to put the Third Maine Regiment and the Berdan Sharpshooters on outpost in a bold woodland cover, to develop somewhat of the approaching battle, and presently threw his corps forward as far as the Peach Orchard, half a mile forward of the position assigned to it in the general line. The Tenth Alabama Regiment was sent against the outpost guard, and, reinforced by the Eleventh Regiment, drove it back, and Anderson's division found its place in proper line.

General Birney's account of the affair at the outpost puts it at twelve o'clock, and the signal accounts, the only papers dated on the field, reported, "The enemy's skirmishers advancing from the west one mile from here—11.45." And presently, "The rebels are in force; our skirmishers give way—12.55." There is no room for doubt of the accuracy of these reports, which go to show that it was one o'clock in the afternoon when the Third Corps, upon which the First Corps was to form, was in position.

Under the conduct of the reconnoitring officer, our march seemed slow,—there were some halts and

William Barksdale

countermarches. To save time, I ordered the rear division to double on the front, and we were near the affair of Anderson's regiments with the outpost guard of Sickles. Anderson's division deployed,—Wilcox's, Perry's, Wright's, Posey's, and Mahone's brigades from right to left.

General Hood was ordered to send his select scouts in advance, to go through the woodlands and act as vedettes, in the absence of cavalry, and give information of the enemy, if there. The double line marched up the slope and deployed,—McLaws on the right of Anderson, Hood's division on his right, McLaws near the crest of the plateau in front of the Peach Orchard, Hood spreading and enveloping Sickles's left. The former was readily adjusted to ground from which to advance or defend. Hood's front was very rugged, with no field for artillery, and very rough for advance of infantry. As soon as he passed the Emmitsburg road, he sent to report of the great advantage of moving on by his right around to the enemy's rear. His scouting parties had reported that there was nothing between them and the enemy's trains. He was told that the move to the right had been proposed the day before and rejected; that General Lee's orders were to guide my left by the Emmitsburg road.

In our immediate front were the divisions of the Third Corps under Generals Humphreys and Birney, from right to left, with orders for supports of the flanks by divisions of the Second and Fifth Corps. The ground on the left of Birney's division was so broken and obstructed by boulders that his left was dropped off to the rear, forming a broken line. In rear of the enemy, and between his lines and Little Round Top, was a very rough elevation of eighty feet formed by upheavals that left open passage deep down Devil's Den. Smith's battery was on Birney's left, Winslow's between the right and next brigade. Other batteries in position were Clark's, Ames's, Randolph's, Seeley's, and Turnbull's.

As McLaws's division came up on line, Barksdale's brigade was in front of a battery about six hundred yards off. He appealed for permission to charge and capture it, but was told to wait. On his right was Kershaw's brigade, the brigades of Semmes and Wofford on the second line. Hood's division was in two lines,—Law's and Robertson's brigades in front, G. T. Anderson's and Benning's in the second line. The batteries were with the divisions,—four to the division. One of G. T. Anderson's regiments was put on picket down the Emmitsburg road.

General Hood appealed again and again for the move to the right, but, to give more confidence to his attack, he was reminded that the move to the right had been carefully considered by our chief and rejected in favor of his present orders.

The opportunity for our right was in the air. General Halleck saw it from Washington. General Meade saw and was apprehensive of it. Even General Pendleton refers to it in favorable mention in his official report. Failing to adopt it, General Lee should have gone with us to his right. He had seen and carefully examined the left of his line, and only gave us a guide to show the way to the right, leaving the battle to be adjusted to formidable and difficult grounds without his assistance. If he had been with us, General Hood's messengers could have been referred to general headquarters, but to delay and send messengers five miles in favor of a move that he had rejected would have been contumacious. The opportunity was with the Confederates from the assembling on Cemetery Hill. It was inviting of their preconceived plans. It was the object of and excuse for the invasion as a substitute for more direct efforts for the relief of Vicksburg. Confederate writers and talkers claim that General Meade could have escaped without making aggressive battle, but that is equivalent to confession of the inertia that failed to grasp the opportunity.

Beaten in the battle of the 1st, dislodged of position, and outgeneralled, the Union army would have felt the want of spirit and confidence important to aggressive battle; but the call was in the hands of the Confederates, and these circumstances would have made their work more facile, while the Union commander would have felt the call to save his capital most imperative. Even as events passed it was thought helpful to the Union side to give out the report that General McClellan was at hand and would command the army.

Four of the brigades of Anderson's division were ordered to advance in echelon in support of my left.

At three o'clock the artillery was ordered to open practice. General Meade was then with General Sickles discussing the feasibility of withdrawing his corps to the position to which it was originally assigned, but the opening admonished him that it was too late. He had just sent a cipher telegram to inform General Halleck, commander-in-chief, that in the event of his having no opportunity to attack, and should he find the Confederates moving to interpose between him and Washington, he would fall back on his supplies at Westminster. But my right division was then nearer to Westminster, and our scouting parties of infantry were within rifle range of the road leading to that point and to Washington. So it would have been convenient, after holding our threatening attitude till night, to march across his line at dark, in time to draw

The summit of Little Round Top. Originally the site of a signal station during the second day, the prominence soon became a vital position as both sides recognized it as the anchor of the Federal left.

Cluttered with boulders and rocks, Little Round Top played havoc on the attacking formations of Confederate soldiers.

The controversial Major General Daniel Sickles (left) sits with a previous commander of the III Corps, Major General S. P. Heintzelman.

other troops to close connection before the next morning.

Prompt to the order the combat opened, followed by artillery of the other corps, and our artillerists measured up to the better metal of the enemy by vigilant work. Hood's lines were not yet ready. After a little practice by the artillery, he was properly adjusted and ordered to bear down upon the enemy's left, but he was not prompt, and the order was repeated before he woudl strike down.

In his usual gallant style he led his troops through the rocky fastnesses against the strong lines of his earnest adversary, and encountered battle that called for all of his power and skill. The enemy was tenacious of his strong ground; his skilfully-handled batteries swept through the passes between the rocks; the more deadly fire of infantry concentrated as our men bore upon the angle of the enemy's line and stemmed the fiercest onset, until it became necessary to shorten their work by a desperate charge. This pressing struggle and the cross-fire of our batteries broke in the salient angle, but the thickening fire, as the angle was pressed back, hurt Hood's left and held him in steady fight. His right brigade was drawn towards Round Top by the heavy fire pouring from that quarter, Benning's brigade was pressed to the thickening line at the angle, and G. T. Anderson's was put in support of the battle growing against Hood's right.

I rode to McLaws, found him ready for his opportunity, and Barksdale chafing in his wait for the order to seize the battery in his front. Kershaw's brigade of his right first advanced and struck near the angle of the enemy's line where his forces were gathering strength. After additional caution to hold his ranks closed, McLaws ordered Barksdale in. With glorious bearing he sprang to his work, overriding obstacles and dangers. Without a pause to deliver a shot, he had the battery. Kershaw, joined by Semmes's brigade, responded, and Hood's men, feeling the impulsion of relief, resumed their bold fight, and presently the en-

emy's line was broken through its length. But his well-seasoned troops knew how to utilize the advantage of their grounds and put back their dreadful fires from rocks, depressions, and stone fences, as they went for shelter about Little Round Top.

That point had not been occupied by the enemy, nor marked as an important feature of the field. The broken ranks sought shelter under its rocks and defiles as birds fly to cover. General Hood fell seriously hurt, and General Law succeeded to command of the division, but the well-seasoned troops were not in need of a close guiding hand. The battle was on, and they knew how to press its hottest contention.

General Warren, chief engineer of the Federal army, was sent at the critical moment to Little Round Top, and found that it was the citadel of the field. He called for troops to occupy it. The Fifth Corps (Sykes's) was hurried to him, and General Hancock sent him Caldwell's division of the Second Corps. At the Brick House, away from his right, General Sickles had a detachment that had been reinforced by General Hancock. This fire drew Anderson's brigade of direction (Wilcox) a little off from support of Barksdale's left. General Humphreys, seeing the opportunity, rallied such of his troops as he could, and, reinforced by Hays's division (Willard's brigade) of Hancock's corps, came against Barksdale's flank, but the latter moved bravely on, the guiding spirit of the battle. Wright's Georgia and Perry's Florida brigades were drawn in behind Wilcox and thrown against Humphreys, pushing him off and breaking him up.

The fighting had by this time become tremendous, and brave men and officers were stricken by hundreds. Posey and Wilcox dislodged the forces about the Brick House.

General Sickles was desperately wounded!

General Willard was dead!

General Semmes, of McLaws's division, was mortally wounded!

Our left relieved, the brigades of Anderson's division moved on with Barksdale's, passed the swale, and moved up the slope. Caldwell's division, and presently those of Ayres and Barnes of the Fifth Corps, met and held our strongest battle. While thus engaged, General Sykes succeeded in putting Vincent's and Weed's brigades and Hazlett's battery on the summit of Little Round Top, but presently we overreached Caldwell's division, broke it off, and pushed it from the field. Of his brigade commanders, Zook was killed, and Brooke and Cross were wounded, the latter mortally. General Hancock reported sixty percent of his men lost. On our side, Barksdale was down dying, and G. T. Anderson wounded.

We had carried Devil's Den, were at the Round Tops and the Wheat-Field, but Ayres's division of regulars and Barnes's division were holding us in equal battle. The struggle throughout the field seemed at its tension. The brigades of R. H. Anderson's division could hold off other troops of Hancock's, but were not strong enough to step to the enemy's lines. When Caldwell's division was pushed away, Ayres's flank and the gorge at Little Round Top were only covered by a sharp line of picket men behind the boulders. If we could drive in the sharp-shooters and strike Ayres's flank to advantage, we could dislodge his and Barnes's divisions, occupy the gorge behind Sykes's brigades on Round Top, force them to retreat, and lift our desperate fighters to the summit. I had one brigade—Wofford's—that had not been engaged in the hottest battle. To urge the troops to their reserve power in the precious moments, I rode with Wofford. The rugged field, the rough plunge of artillery fire, and the piercing musket-shots delayed somewhat the march, but Alexander dashed up with his batteries and gave new spirit to the worn infantry ranks. By a fortunate strike upon Ayres's flank we broke his line and pushed him and Barnes so closely that they were obliged to use most strenuous efforts to get away without losing in prisoners as well as their killed and wounded. We gained the Wheat-Field, and were so close upon the gorge that our artillery could no longer venture their fire into it. We were on Little Round Top grappling for the crowning point. The brigade commanders there, Vincent and Weed, were killed, also

the battery commander, Hazlett, and others, but their troops were holding to their work as firmly as the mighty boulders that helped them. General Meade thought that the Confederate army was working on my part of the field. He led some regiments of the Twelfth Corps and posted them against us, called a division of Newton's corps (First) from beyond Hancock's, and sent Crawford's division, the last of the Fifth Corps, splitting through the gorge, forming solid lines, in places behind stone fences, and making steady battle, as veterans fresh in action know so well how to make. While Meade's lines were growing my men were dropping; we had no others to call to their aid, and the weight against us was too heavy to carry. The extreme left of our lines was only about a mile from us across the enemy's concentric position, which brought us within hearing of that battle, if engaged, and near enough to feel its swell, but nothing was heard or felt but the clear ring of the enemy's fresh metal as he came against us. No other part of our army had engaged! My seventeen thousand against the Army of the Potomac! The sun was down,

The bloody remains of a destroyed artillery battery lie before the Trostle Farmhouse which served as the head quarters for the commander of the III Corps, Major General Daniel Sickles.

and with it went down the severe battle. I ordered recall of the troops to the line of Plum Run and Devil's Den, leaving picket lines near the foot of the Round Tops. My loss was about six thousand, Meade's between twelve and fourteen thousand; but his loss in general and field officers was frightful. When General Humphreys, who succeeded to Barksdale's brigade, was called back to the new line, he thought there was some mistake in the orders, and only withdrew as far as a captured battery, and when the order was repeated, retired under protest.

General Stuart came down from Carlisle with his column of cavalry late in the afternoon of the 2d. As he approached he met a cavalry force of the enemy moving towards the Confederate left rear, and was successful in arresting it. He was posted with Jenkins' three thousand cavalry on the Confederate left.

Notwithstanding the supreme order of the day for general battle, and the reinforcement of the cavalry on our left, the Second and Third Corps remained idle during all of the severe battle of the Confederate right, except the artillery, and the part of that on the extreme left was only in practice long enough to feel the superior metal of the enemy, when it retired, leaving a battery of four guns in position. General Early failed to even form his division in battle order, leaving a brigade in position remote from the line, and sending, later, another to be near Stuart's cavalry. The latter returned, however, before night.

At eight o'clock in the evening the division on our extreme left, E. Johnson's, advanced. The brigades were J. M. Jones's, Nicholls's, Steuart's, and Walker's. Walker's was detached, as they moved, to look for a detachment of the enemy reported threatening the far away left. When the three brigades crossed Rock Creek it was night. The enemy's line to be assaulted was occupied by Greene's brigade of the Twelfth Corps. It was reinforced by three regiments of Wadsworth's division and three from the Eleventh Corps. After brave attack and defence, part of the line was carried, when the fight, after a severe fusillade between the infantry lines, quieted, and Walker's brigade returned to the division. Part of the enemy's trenches, east of the point attacked (across a swale), vacated when the corps moved over to the left, General Johnson failed to occupy.

Before this, General Rodes discovered that the enemy, in front of his division, was drawing off his artillery and infantry to my battle of the right, and suggested to General Early that the moment had come for the divisions to attack, and drew his forces from entanglements about the streets to be ready. After E. Johnson's fight on our extreme left, General Early ordered two brigades under General Harry T. Hays to attack. Hays had with his Louisiana brigade Hoke's North Carolina brigade under Colonel Avery. He made as gallant a fight as was ever made. Mounting to the top of the hill, he captured a battery, and

The Louisiana Tigers manage to gain a hole in the Union line while storming a battery of the Federal XI Corps. Unsupported, the Louisianians were forced to relinquish their gains in blood as their efforts went for naught.

pushed on in brave order, taking some prisoners and colors, until he discovered that his two brigades were advancing in a night affair against a grand army, when he found that he was fortunate in having night to cover his weakness, and withdrew. The gallant Colonel Avery, mortally wounded and dying, wrote on a slip of paper, *"Tell father that I died with my face to the enemy."* When Rodes was prepared, Hays had retired, and the former did not see that it was part of the order for general engagement to put his division in night attack that could not be supported.

Thus the general engagement of the day was dwarfed into the battle of the right at three o'clock, that on the left at eight by a single division, and that nearer the centre at nine o'clock by two brigades.

There was a man on the left of the line who did not care to make the battle win. He knew where it was, had viewed it from its earliest formation, had orders for his part in it, but so withheld part of his command from it as to make co-operative concert of action impracticable. He had a pruriency for the honors of the field of Mars, was eloquent, before the fires of the bivouac and his chief, of the glory of war's gory shield; but when its envied laurels were dipping to the grasp, when the heavy field called for bloody work, he found the placid horizon, far and away beyond the cavalry, more lovely and inviting. He wanted command of the Second Corps, and, succeeding to it, held the honored position until General Lee found, at last, that he must dismiss him from field service.

General Lee ordered Johnson's division of his left, occupying part of the enemy's trenches about Culp's Hill, to be reinforced during the night of the 2d by two brigades of Rodes's division and one of Early's division. Why the other brigades of those divisions were not sent does not appear, but it does appear that there was a place for them on Johnson's left, in the trenches that were vacated by the Federal Twelfth Corps when called over to reinforce the battle of Meade's left. Culp's Hill bore the same relations to the enemy's right as Little Round Top did to his left. General Fitzhugh Lee quotes evidence from General Meade that had Culp's Hill been occupied, in force, by Confederates, it would have compelled the withdrawal of the Federal troops.

General Meade, after the battle of his left, ordered the divisions of his Twelfth Corps back to their trenches, to recover the parts occupied by the Confederate left. It was night when the First Division approached. General Ruger, commanding, thought to feel his way through the dark by a line of skirmishers. He found the east end of his trenches, across the swale, unoccupied, and took possession. Pressing his adventure, he found the main line of his works occupied by the Confederates in force, and disposed his command to wait for daylight. The Second Division came during the night, when General Williams, commanding the corps, posted it on the left of the First,

The gate to the Gettysburg Cemetery for which Cemetery Ridge won its name.

and the division commanders ordered batteries in proper positions.

During the night, General Meade held a council, which decided to fight it out. So it began to look as if the vicissitudes of the day had so worked as to call General Meade from defensive to aggressive battle for Culp's Hill. But the Confederates failed to see the opportunity and force the issue as it was presented.

In General Meade's evidence before the Committee on the Conduct of the War, he puts his losses of the first and second days at twenty thousand and assigns two-thirds of these to the battle of the 2d. As the fighting against the three brigades of our left after night, and two brigades, later in the night, from our centre, could not have been very severe, I claim that his loss in the battle of his left was from twelve to fourteen thousand.

As events of the battle of the 2d passed, it seems fair to claim that with Pickett's brigades present at the moment of Wofford's advance for the gorge at Little Round Top, we could have had it before Crawford was there.

Under ordinary circumstances this account of the second day, made from the records, would be complete and conclusive; but the battle of Gettysburg, which may be called the epitome of the war, has been the subject of many contentions of words. Knights of the quill have consumed many of their peaceful hours in publishing, through books, periodicals, and newspapers, their plans for the battle, endeavoring to forestall the records and to find a scapegoat, and their representations may be given, though they do not deserve it, a word of reply.

General W. N. Pendleton led off when making a lecturing tour through the South for a memorial church for General Lee. He claims that he made a reconnoissance on the afternoon of the 1st of July, and that upon his reporting it, General Lee ordered General Longstreet to attack at sunrise the next day. He did not venture to charge that the Second and Third Corps, that were on the field and had had a good night's rest, were part of the command ordered for the early battle, for the commanders, both Virginians, and not under the political ban, could have brought confusing evidence against him; nor did he intend to put General Lee in the anomalous position, inferentially, of ordering part of the First Corps—that should march through the night and all night—to make the battle alone. The point of battle was east of the Emmitsburg road; to find it, it was necessary to cross that road, but General Sickles was moving part of his corps over the road during that afternoon, and rested there the latter part of the day and during the night. So, to make the reconnoissance, General Pendleton passed the Union troops in Confederate uniform—he was military in his dress—and found the point of battle. Giving him credit, for the moment, for this delicate work and the mythical order, let us find the end to which it would lead.

The only troops that could come under the order were McLaws's division, part of Hood's, and the artil-

lery,—about ten thousand men. These, after a hurried all-night's march, reached General Lee's head-quarters about sunrise of the 2d, and by continued forced march could have reached the point of battle, about five miles away, by seven o'clock, where they would have encountered a division of the Third Corps (Birney's); presently the Second and Fifth Corps under Hancock and Sykes; then the First, Eleventh, and Twelfth under Newton, Howard, and Slocum; then the balance of the Third coming in on our rear along the Emmitsburg road,—making sixty thousand men and more. There was reason to be proud of the prowess of the troops of the First Corps, but to credit a part of it with success under the circumstances was not reasonable.

That the Confederate Second Corps did not have orders for the alleged sunrise battle is evidenced by the report of its commander, who, accounting for his work about Culp's Hill during the night of the 1st and morning of the 2d, reported of the morning, "It was now daylight, and too late," meaning that it was too late for him to attack and carry that hill, as General Lee had authorized and expected him to do during the night before. If he had been ordered to take part in the sunrise battle, he would have been in the nick of time. That the Third Corps was not to be in it is evidenced by the position of the greater part of it on Seminary Ridge until near noon of the 2d. So General Lee must have orderd a position carried, at sunrise, by ten thousand men, after it had gathered strength all night—a position that he would not assault on the afternoon of the 1st with forty thousand men, lest they should encounter "overwhelming numbers."

As the other corps, after receiving their orders for the afternoon battle of the 2d, failed to engage until after nightfall, it is not probable that they would have found the sunrise battle without orders.

General Pendleton's official report is in conflict with his memorial lecture. In the former he makes no reference to the sunrise-battle order, but mentions a route by which the left of the enemy could be turned.

Letters from the active members of General Lee's staff and from his military secretary, General A. L. Long, show that the sunrise battle was not ordered, and a letter from Colonel Fairfax shows that the claim that it was so ordered was set up after General Lee's death.

Colonel Taylor claims that the attack by the Confederate right should have been sooner, and should have met the enemy back on his first or original line, and before Little Round Top was occupied. But Little Round Top was not occupied in force until after my battle opened, and General Sickles's advance to his forward lines was made in consequence of the Confederate threatening, and would have been sooner or later according as that threatening was made. He calls the message of General Lee to General Ewell on the afternoon of the 1st an order. General Lee says,

> The strong position which the enemy had
> assumed could not be attacked without danger of

Result of Rebel cannon fire on Culp's Hill. Though Ewell's Rebels managed to threaten the Federal right on the evening of 2 July, they were forced to retreat the next morning in the face of a strong Federal counter-attack.

Victims of a well placed artillery shell: a wrecked caisson and murdered horse.

exposing the four divisions present, exhausted by a long and bloody struggle, to overwhelming numbers of fresh troops. General Ewell was thereupon instructed to carry the hill occupied by the enemy if he found it practicable."

It is the custom of military service to accept instructions of a commander as orders, but when they are coupled with conditions that transfer the responsibility of battle and defeat to the subordinate, they are not orders, and General Ewell was justifiable in not making attack that his commander would not order, and the censure of his failure is unjust and *very ungenerous.*

The Virginia writers have been so eager in their search for a flaw in the conduct of the battle of the First Corps that they overlook the only point into vhich they could have thrust their pens.

At the opening of the fight, General Meade was with General Sickles discussing the feasibility of moving the Third Corps back to the line originally assigned for it, but the discussion was cut short by the opening of the Confederate battle. If that opening had been delayed thirty or forty minutes the corps would have been drawn back to the general line, and my first deployment would have enveloped Little Round Top and carried it before it could have been strongly manned, and General Meade would have drawn off to his line selected behind Pipe Creek. The point should

have been that the battle was opened too soon.

Another point from which they seek comfort is that Sedgwick's corps (Sixth) was not up until a late hour of the 2d, and would not have been on the field for an earlier battle. But Sedgwick was not engaged in the late battle, and could have been back at Manchester, so far as the afternoon battle was concerned. And they harp a little on the delay of thirty minutes for Law's brigade to join its division. But General Lee called for the two divisions, and had called for Law's brigade to join his division. It was therefore his order for the division that delayed the march. To have gone without it would have justified censure. As we were not strong enough for the work with that brigade, it is not probable that we could have accomplished more without it.

Colonel Taylor says that General Lee urged that the march of my troops should be hastened, and was chafed at their non-appearance. Not one word did he utter to me of their march until he gave his orders at eleven o'clock for the move to his right. Orders for the troops to hasten their march of the 1st were sent without even a suggestion from him, but upon his announcement that he intended to fight the next day, if the enemy was there. That he was excited and off his balance was evident on the afternoon of the 1st, and he labored under that oppression until enough blood was shed to appease him.

★★★

THEODORE GARRISH

The Stand of the 20th Maine

win College, Colonel Joshua Chamberlain. Despite being hard pressed, outnumbered, and low on ammunition, the soldiers from the Pine Tree State held their position and fiercely drove back the enemy. The story of this episode is related in this selection penned by a private of the 20th Maine, Theodore Garrish, in his work, Army Life: A Private's Reminiscences of the Civil War.

On the 28th of June, General Hooker, at his own request, was relieved of his command, and it was given to General Meade. The latter had been in command of our corps. We knew him to be a brave and gallant officer, but feared a mistake had been made in

The anchor for the Federal line at Gettysburg was a steep prominence studded with rocky outcroppings, a hill known as Little Round Top. Had the Confederates ever managed to take it, Meade's position would have become untenable and he would be forced to retreat in ignominious defeat. Instrumental in the defense of this position was the gallant stand of the 20th Maine led by a former professor at Bado-

changing commanders just as a battle was to be fought. Many rumors came back to us from the front, and from these we learned that Lee's troops numbered at least one hundred thousand, that he was concentrating his forces near Gettysburgh, and that a

A battery of Federal light artillery anxiously awaits the order to go into action during the epic conflict at Gettysburg.

desperate battle would probably be fought near that place. We knew that the army of the Potomac did not number over eighty thousand men, that the authorities of the states of Pennsylvania and New York were moving so slowly in raising troops that but little aid would be received from them, and that unaided we must cope with our old foe.

On the first day of July we crossed the state line of Pennsylvania, and noted the event by loud cheering and much enthusiasm. And here, on the border of the state, we learned that our cavalry under General Buford, and our old First corps, under General Reynolds, had on that day encountered the rebels at Gettysburgh, and that on the morrow the great battle would be fought. Night came on, but we halted not. We knew that our comrades on the distant battle-field needed our aid, and we hastened on. It was a beautiful evening. The moon shone from a cloudless sky, and flooded our way with its glorious light. The people rushed from their homes and stood by the roadside to welcome us, men, women, and children all gazing on the strange spectacle. Bands played, the soldiers and the people cheered, banners waved, and white handkerchiefs fluttered from doors and windows, as the

blue, dusty column surged on. That moonlight march will always be remembered by its survivors. A staff officer sat on his horse by the roadside. In a low voice he spoke to our colonel as he passed. "What did he say?" anxiously inquired the men. "McClellan is to command us on the morrow,"—McClellan, our first commander, who had been removed, criticised, and we thought he was forgotten; but our old love for him broke out afresh. He had never seemed one-half so dear to us before. Men waved their hats and cheered until they were hoarse and wild with excitement. It is strange what a hold little Mac had on the hearts of his soldiers. At midnight we halted, having marched more than thirty miles on that eventful day. The men threw themselves upon the ground to get a little rest and sleep. Sleep on, brave fellows, for the morrow's struggle will call for both strength and courage! While they are sleeping, we will step across the country for a few miles and view Gettysburgh in the moonlight, that we may better understand the battle-ground of to-morrow. It has been a bloody day around this little country village. Early in the morning the cavalry under General Buford had met the enemy advancing in great force, and bravely contested the ground with him. General Reynolds, hearing the heavy firing, had pushed the First corps forward to Buford's support, and formed his line of battle upon an eminence west of Seminary Ridge. The conflict soon became general. The gallant Reynolds was killed at the first volley, as he was riding to the front to ascertain the position of the enemy. General Doubleday assumed command of the corps. It was a fearful struggle. Hill's corps of the rebel army on the one side, and the First corps, much the inferior in numbers, upon the other.

General Howard arrives with the Eleventh corps. The rebels also receive reinforcements. Back and forth the contending lines press each other until late in the afternoon, when the Union troops are overpowered, and are hurled, bleeding and mangled, through the streets of Gettysburgh, and up the slopes of Cemetery Ridge. General Hancock arrives at this moment from the headquarters of General Meade, and assumes the command, and in concert with General Howard, selected the line of battle. The village is filled with the highly elated rebels, who loudly boast that they can easily whip the Yankees on the morrow.

Things look a little desperate on Cemetery Hill. Reynolds and thousands of his gallant men have fallen, but their courage saved the position for the Union army, and on that hill our line of battle is being formed under the supervision of our brave generals,—Howard, the one-armed hero, Hancock the brilliant leader, Dan Sickles the irresistible commander of the Third corps, and brave Slocum of the Twelfth. Sykes and Sedgwick with their respective corps will put in an appearance on the morrow. At midnight General Meade arrives and assumes command of the entire line. It is evident at a glance that the old army of the Potomac is "on deck," and that if General Lee expects to win Gettysburgh by fighting a few brigades of raw militia, he is very much mistaken. The ridge on which our line of battle is being formed somewhat resembles a horseshoe in shape. Cemetery Hill, facing the northwest, is the point nearest Gettysburgh and Lee's headquarters, and that point we will call the toe calk of the horseshoe. To the left and rear is Round Top, which represents one heel calk, while Wolf's Hill to the right and rear represents the other. Howard, with the Eleventh corps, is stationed at Cemetery Hill. The First and Twelfth corps, under Generals Slocum and Wadsworth, formed our right, reaching from Howard to our extreme right at Wolf's Hill. At the left of Howard is Hancock and the Second corps, and at his left Sickles with the Third, in a somewhat advanced position, reaching unto our extreme left, near Little Round Top. It has been decided that General Sykes and Sedgwick shall be held in reserve to reinforce any part of our line upon which Lee may mass his troops. And thus through the hours of that night our preparations for the battle were being made.

If General Lee had pushed on his forces, and followed up his advantage gained in the afternoon, he would have been master of the situation, but this delay was fatal to him. The Union line is formed, the artillery is in position. The rebels outnumber us both in men and guns, but we have the ridge, and are on the

The hero of the 20th Maine, Colonel Joshua L. Chamberlain.

defensive. The tired men sink upon the ground to catch a few moments' sleep before the battle opens. All is still in Gettysburgh save the groans of the wounded and dying. It is an anxious night throughout the great loyal North. Telegrams have been flashing all over the country, bearing the sad tidings of the death of Reynolds and the repulse of his troops. Every one knows that this battle is to decide, to a large extent, the fortunes of war. There is no sleep for the people. Strong men are pale with excitement and anxiety, as through the hours of night they talk of the coming conflict; Christians gather in their sanctuaries to pray that success may be ours on the morrow; mothers, wives and sisters, with pale, upturned faces, pray to God to protect their loved ones in the dangers of the battle. It is the most anxious night through which America ever passed. God grant that we shall never pass through another like it!

At daylight, on the morning of July 2d, we resumed our march, and in a few hours halted within supporting distance of the left flank of our army, about a mile to the right of Little Round Top. The long forenoon passed away, and to our surprise the enemy made no attack. This was very fortunate for our army, as it enabled our men to strengthen our lines of fortifications, and also to obtain a little rest, of which they were in great need. The rebels were also engaged in throwing up rude lines of defenses, hurrying up reinforcements, and in discussing the line of action they should pursue, for, to use General Lee's own words in his report of the battle, they "unexpectedly found themselves confronted by the Federal army."

The hour of noon passed, and the sun had measured nearly one-half the distance across the western sky, before the assault was made. Then, as suddenly as a bolt of fire flies from the storm cloud, a hundred pieces of rebel artillery open upon our left flank, and under the thick canopy of screaming, hissing, bursting shells, Longstreet's corps was hurled upon the troops of General Sickles. Instantly our commanders discerned the intention of General Lee. It was to turn and crush our left flank, as he had crushed our right at Chancellorsville. It was a terrible onslaught. The brave sons of the South never displayed more gallant courage than on that fatal afternoon of July 2d. But brave Dan Sickles and the old Third corps were equal to the emergency, and stood as immovable against the surging tides as blocks of granite. But a new and appalling danger suddenly threatened the Union army. Little Round Top was the key to the entire position. Rebel batteries planted on that rocky bluff could shell any portion of our line at their pleasure. For some reason Sickles had not placed any infantry upon this

A Confederate sharpshooter lies dead at Devil's Den, the victim of a well placed shot from the enemy.

Yankees on the rocky face of Little Round Top attempt to blunt the vicious offensive of John Bell Hood's division. It was here that Colonel Joshua Chamberlain and his 20th Maine Regiment made their famous stand facing heavy odds while desperately low on ammunition.

important position. A few batteries were scattered along its ragged side, but they had no infantry support. Lee saw at a glance that Little Round Top was the prize for which the two armies were contending, and with skillful audacity he determined to wrest it from his opponent. While the terrible charge was being made upon the line of General Sickles, Longstreet threw out a whole division, by extending his line to his right, for the purpose of seizing the coveted prize. The danger was at once seen by our officers, and our brigade was ordered forward, to hold the hill against the assault of the enemy. In a moment all was excitement. Every soldier seemed to understand the situation, and to be inspired by its danger. "Fall in! Fall in! By the right flank! Double-quick! March!" and away we went, under the terrible artillery fire. It was a moment of thrilling interest. Shells were exploding on every side. Sickles' corps was enveloped in sheets of flame, and looked like a vast windrow of fire. But so intense was the excitement that we hardly noticed these surroundings. Up the steep hillside we ran, and reached the crest. "On the right by file into line," was the command, and our regiment had assumed the position to which it had been assigned. We were on the left of our brigade, and consequently on the ex-

treme left of all our line of battle. The ground sloped to our front and left, and was sparsely covered with a growth of oak trees, which were too small to afford us any protection. Shells were crashing through the air above our heads, making so much noise that we could hardly hear the commands of our officers; the air was filled with fragments of exploding shells and splinters torn from mangled trees; but our men appeared to be as cool and deliberate in their movements as if they had been forming a line upon the parade ground in camp. Our regiment mustered about three hundred and fifty men. Company B, from Piscataquis county, commanded by the gallant Captain Morrill, was ordered to deploy in our front as skirmishers. They boldly advanced down the slope and disappeared from our view. Ten minutes have passed since we formed the line; the skirmishers must have advanced some thirty or forty rods through the rocks and trees, but we have seen no indications of the enemy; "But look!" "Look!" "Look!" exclaimed half a hundred men in our regiment at the same moment; and no wonder, for right in our front, between us and our skirmishers, whom they have probably captured, we see the lines of the enemy. They have paid no attention to the rest of the brigade stationed on our right, but they are rushing on, determined to turn and crush the left of our line. Colonel Chamberlain with rare sagacity understood the movement they were making, and bent back the left flank of our regiment until the line formed almost a right angle with the colors at the point, all these movements requiring a much less space of time than it requires for me to write of them.

How can I describe the scenes that followed? Imagine, if you can, nine small companies of infantry, numbering perhaps three hundred men, in the form of a right angle, on the extreme flank of an army of eighty thousand men, put there to hold the key of the entire position against a force at least ten times their number, and who are desperately determined to succeed in the mission upon which they came. Stand firm, ye boys from Maine, for not once in a century are men permitted to bear such responsibilities for freedom and justice, for God and humanity, as are now placed upon you.

The conflict opens. I know not who gave the first fire, or which line received the first lead. I only know that the carnage began. Our regiment was mantled in fire and smoke. I wish that I could picture with my pen the awful details of that hour,—how rapidly the cartridges were torn from the boxes and stuffed in the smoking muzzles of the guns; how the steel rammers clashed and clanged in the heated barrels; how the man's hands and faces grew grim and black with burning powder; how our little line, baptized with fire, reeled to and fro as it advanced or was pressed back; how our officers bravely encouraged the men to hold on and recklessly exposed themselves to the enemy's fire,—a terrible medley of cries, shouts, cheers, groans, prayers, curses, bursting shells, whizzing rifle bullets and clanging steel. And if that was all, my heart would not be so sad and heavy as I write. But the enemy was pouring a terrible fire upon us, his superior forces giving him a great advantage. Ten to one are fearful odds where men are contending for so great a prize. The air seemed to be alive with lead. The lines at times were so near each other that the hostile gun barrels almost touched. As the contest continued, the rebels grew desperate that so insignificant a force should so long hold them in check. At one time there was a brief lull in the carnage, and our shattered line was closed up, but soon the contest raged again with renewed fierceness. The rebels had been reinforced, and were now determined to sweep our regiment from the crest of Little Round Top.

Many of our companies have suffered fearfully. Look at Company H for a moment. Charley, my old tent-mate, with a fatal wound in his breast, staggered up to brave Captain Land. "My God, Sergeant Steele!" ejaculated the agonized captain as he saw the fate of his beloved sergeant. "I am going, Captain," cried the noble fellow, and fell dead, weltering in his blood. Sergeant Lathrop, with his brave heart and gigantic frame, fell dying with a frightful wound. Sergeant Buck, reduced to the ranks at Stoneman's Switch, lay down to die, and was promoted as his life blood ebbed away. Adams, Ireland, and Lamson, all heroes, are lying dead at the feet of their comrades. Libby, French,

View from Little Round Top.

Clifford, Hilt, Ham, Chesly, Morrison, West, and Walker are all severely wounded, and nearly all disabled. But there is no relief, and the carnage goes on. Our line is pressed back so far that our dead are within the lines of the enemy. The pressure made by the superior weight of the enemy's line is severely felt. Our ammunition is nearly all gone, and we are using the cartridges from the boxes of our wounded comrades. A critical moment has arrived, and we can remain as we are no longer; we must advance or retreat. It must not be the latter, but how can it be the former? Colonel Chamberlain understands how it can be done. The order is given "Fix bayonets!" and the steel shanks of the bayonets rattle upon the rifle barrels. "Charge bayonets, charge!" Every man understood in a moment that the movement was our only salvation, but there is a limit to human endurance, and I do not dishonor those brave men when I write that for a brief moment the order was not obeyed, and the little line seemed to quail under the fearful fire that was being poured upon it. O for some man reckless of life, and all else save his country's honor and safety, who would rush far out to the front, lead the way, and inspire the hearts of his exhausted comrades! In that moment of supreme need the want was supplied. Lieut. H. S. Melcher, an officer who had worked his way up from the ranks, and was then in command of Co. F, at that time the color company, saw the situation, and did not hesitate, and for his gallant act deserves as much as any other man the honor of the victory on Round Top. With a cheer, and a flash of his sword, that sent an inspiration along the line, full ten paces to the front he sprang—ten paces—more than half the distance between the hostile lines. "Come on! Come on! Come on, boys!" he shouts. The color sergeant and the brave color guard follow, and with one wild yell of anguish wrung from its tortured heart, the regiment charged.

The rebels were confounded at the movement. We struck them with a fearful shock. They recoil, stagger, break and run, and like avenging demons our men pursue. The rebels rush toward a stone wall, but, to our mutual surprise, two scores of rifle barrels gleam over the rocks, and a murderous volley was poured in upon them at close quarters. A band of men leap over the wall and capture at least a hundred prisoners. Piscataquis has been heard from, and as usual it was a good report. This unlooked-for reinforcement was Company B, whom we supposed were all captured.

Our Colonel's commands were simply to hold the hill, and we did not follow the retreating rebels but a short distance. After dark an order came to advance and capture a hill in our front. Through the trees, among the rocks, up the steep hillside, we made our way, captured the position, and also a number of prisoners.

★★★

JAMES O. BRADFIELD

"Until God stopped them . . ."

The Division belonging to Kentuckian John Bell Hood was charged with assaulting Little Round Top. Among Bell's ranks was Hood's old brigade composed of an ornery group of Texans and Arkansasians, infamously known as the Texas Brigade. James O. Bradfield, a private in Company E of the First Texas Regiment, describes the attack of his unit on the Yankee line in a selection from comrade J.B. Polley's Hood's Texas Brigade.

Hood's division held the right flank of our army. . . . We began forming our line of battle on a wide plateau leading back to the rear, while in front about 200 yards distant was a skirt of timber on the brow of a hill which led down to the valley below. In this timber, our batteries were posted, and as the Texas Brigade was forming immediately in the rear, we were in direct range of the enemy's guns on the mountain beyond. As our artillery began feeling for their batteries, the answering shells struck our lines with cruel effect. The Fourth Texas suffered most severely. As they were passing this zone of fire, one shell killed and wounded fifteen men. It certainly tries a man's nerve to have to stand still and receive such a fire without being able to return it.

Just here occurred one of the little incidents that, happening at times like this, are never forgotten. In our company was a tall, robust young fellow named Dick Childers, who was noted for the energy and talent he displayed in procuring rations. On this occasion Dick's haversack was well stocked with nice biscuits which a kind Dutch lady had given him. As we were marching by the right flank, our left sides were turned towards the enemy. A shell from the mountain in front struck the ground near our batteries, and came bouncing along across the field, and as Dick happened to be just in the line of fire, it struck him, or rather, his haversack, fairly, and scattered biscuits all over that end of Pennsylvania. But the strange part of it is, that it did not knock the man down, but so paralyzed him that he fell, after it had passed, and lay there unable to move a muscle. The litter bearers picked him up and laid him on a stretcher, as if he had been a log. The boys all contended, however, that it was the destruction of Dick's rations, and not any shock the shell gave, that paralyzed him.

We marched onward by the right flank, about a quarter of a mile, moving parallel with the enemy's lines, and halting, left-faced and formed for work. We were on the brow of a hill which here sloped quite abruptly down into the narrow valley. We could see the enemy's lines of battle—the first on the level space below us, behind a heavy rock fence; the second, at the top of a ridge a hundred or two yards further on, while still further, and entirely out of our reach, at the summit of the higher range, their batteries were posted so as to sweep the whole space over which we were to advance. Their battle flags floated proudly in the breeze, above the almost perfect natu-

Federal batteries unloading canister into the ranks of oncoming Confederates.

Big Round Top as seen from Little Round Top. Though dominating most of the surrounding countryside, the rugged terrain of Big Round Top denied its use to either army.

Commander of a brigade of Georgians, Brigadier General Henry L. Benning was a major participant in Hood's crushing attack on Meade's left. All told after the battle, Benning's brigade lost the elite of its ranks, almost 500 men.

ral breastworks formed by the fence and the large rocks that crowned the low ridge upon which they stood. There were but two small cannon on the lower ridge, and these were captured and pulled off the hill by the First Texas regiment.

About 2 o'clock in the afternoon, the order was given to advance all along the line. We moved quietly dorward down the steep decline, gaining impetus as we reached the more level ground below. The enemy had already opened fire on us, but we did not stop to return it. 'Forward—double quick,' rang out, and then Texas turned loose. Across the valley and over the little stream that ran through it, they swept, every man for himself. The first man down was my right file man, William Langley, a noble, brave boy, with a minie-ball straight through the brain. I caught him as he fell against me, and laid him down, dead. As I straightened up to move on, that same familiar 'spat' which always means something, sounded near, and looking around, I saw Bose Perry double over and catch on his gun. He did not fall, however, but came on, dragging his wounded leg, and firing as he advanced. But it was getting too hot, now, to pay attention to details.

The enemy stood their ground bravely, until we were close on them, but did not await the bayonet. They broke away from the rock fence as we closed in with a rush and a wild rebel yell, and fell back to the top of the ridge, where they halted and formed on their second line. Having passed the rock fence, and as we were moving on up the hill, an order came to halt. No one seemed to know whence it came, nor from

Below, victims of the bloody fighting near Little Round Top

whom. It cost us dearly, for as we lay in close range of their now double lines, the enemy poured a hail of bullets on us, and in a few minutes a number of our men were killed or wounded. We saw that this would never do, and so, without awaiting orders, every man became his own commander and sprang forward toward the top of the hill at full speed.

By this time, Benning's brigade, which had been held in reserve, joined us and together we swept on to where the Blue Coats stood behind the sheltering rocks to receive us. Just here, and to our right, in a little cove called the 'Devil's Den,' which was covered by the Fourth and Fifth Texas, Law's Alabama and Anderson's Georgia brigades, occurred one of the wildest, fiercest struggles of the war—a struggle such as it is given to few men to pass through and live.

The opposing lines stood with only the sheltering rocks between them—breast to breast, and so close that the clothing of many of the enemy was set on fire by the blaze from the Confederate rifles. This continued for some time, but finally, our fire grew so hot that brave as they were, the Federals could no longer endure it, but gave way and fled down the slope, leaving us in possession of the field. The Lone Star flag crowned the hill, and Texas was there to stay. Not alone, however, for just to our right stood Benning—

'Old Rock'—that peerless old hero than whom no braver man ever lived. Striding back and forth in front of his line, he was calling to his gallant Georgians: 'Give them h—ll, boys—give them h—ll,' and the 'boys' were giving it to them according to instructions.

On the right of Benning stood Anderson and Law, and the Fourth and Fifth Texas, as firm as the rocks which sheltered them. I cannot hope to describe the deeds of daring and heroism that were enacted. Beyond the valley in our front, on the summit of the practically impregnable ridge that stretched north toward Gettysburg, stood the enemy's batteries, 200 guns. Of these, about forty were playing in close range upon the position we occupied. Their fire and that of our own batteries, and the constant roar and rattle of thousands of muskets, made the earth tremble beneath our feet, while the fierce, angry shriek of shells, the strident swirl of grape and canister as they tore hurtling through the air and broke like a wave from the ocean of death upon that devoted spot, the hissing bullets, and their 'spat' as they struck rock, tree or human flesh—all this, with the shouts and imprecations, the leaping to and fro and from boulder to boulder of powder-begrimed men, seemingly gone wild with rage and excitement, created a scene of

Federal batteries at the center of the Union line shell advancing legions of Confederates at the second day of Gettysburg.

such indescribable, awe-inspiring confusion that an on-looker might well believe that a storm from the Infernal regions was spending its fury in and around a spot so fitly named, 'The Devil's Den.' Had it not been for the protection afforded us by the large rocks and boulders which lay scattered over the hill-top, no living thing could have remained on its summit.

The fearful artillery fire of the enemy was intended to cover the massing of their infantry, who were now to make one more grand effort to regain the ground they had lost. Our boys prepared for this by gathering up all abandoned muskets within reach, and loading them. Some of us had as many as five or six lying by us, as we awaited the attack.

We had not long to wait, for soon the long blue line came in view, moving in gallant style up the valley. The Federals were led by splendid officers, and made a noble charge: but when they met the murderous fire from behind the rocks where we crouched, they faltered. Only for a moment, though, and on they came right up to the rocks. Again they faltered, for now, most of their officers were down. Again it was but for a second, and cheered on by some of the bravest men I have ever seen, they rallied in the very face of death, and charged right up to the muzzles of our guns.

There was one officer, a major, who won our admiration by his courage and gallantry. He was a very handsome man, and rode a beautiful, high-spirited gray horse. The animal seemed to partake of the spirit of the rider, and as he came on with a free, graceful stride into that hell of death and carnage, head erect and ears pointed, horse and man offered a picture such as is seldom seen. The two seemed the very impersonation of heroic courage. As the withering, scathing volleys from behind the rocks cut into the ranks of the regiment the major led, and his gallant men went down like grain before a scythe, he followed close at their heels, and when, time and again, they stopped and would have fled the merciless fire, each time he rallied them as if his puissant arm alone could stay the storm. But his efforts were, in the end, unavailing; the pluck of himself and his men only made the carnage the more dreadful, for the Lone Star banner and the flag of Georgia continued floating from the hill, showing who stood, defiant and unyielding, beneath their folds.

In the last and most determined charge they made on us, the gallant officer made his supreme effort. Riding into our very midst, seeming to bear a charmed life, he sat proudly on the noble gray, and

Remnants of the fateful charge of the 1st Minnesota which lost 262 men out of 309 the regiment had taken into action.

A Confederate sharpshooter killed at Devil's Den. The marksmen within the cover of the immense boulders of Devil's Den played havoc with the Federals at Little Round Top as they continuously picked off officers, gunners, and regular soldiers with their deadly aim.

still cheered on his men. 'Don't shoot at him—don't kill him,' our boys shouted to each other; 'he is too brave a man to die—shoot his horse and capture the man.' But it could not be. In a second or two, horse and rider went down together, pierced by a dozen balls. Thus died a hero—one of the most gallent men that ever gave up his life on the red field of carnage. Though it was that of an enemy, we honored the dead body as if it had been that of one of our own men. Such courage belongs not to any one army or country, but to mankind.

It was about this time that a spectacular display of reckless courage was made by a young Texan, Will Barbee, of the First Texas. Under twenty years old, he was ordinarily a jolly, whole-souled lad, not at all given to extraordinary performances. But when a fight was going on, he went wild, seemed to have no sense of fear whatever, and was a reckless dare-devil. Although a courier for General Hood, he never failed to join his regiment, if possible, and go into battle with it. On the present occasion, when General Hood was wounded, Barbee hunted us up. In the hottest of the

Remnants of Hood's struggle to take Little Round Top. After driving the Federals from Devil's Den and the Wheat Field, the Kentuckian's advance was only arrested by the quick thinking and action of Gouverneur K. Warren who rushed reinforcements to the scene to avert possible disaster.

fight, I heard some one say, 'Here comes Barbee,' and looking down from the rock on which I was lying I saw him coming as fast as his little sorrel horse could run, and waving his hat as he came. Just before reaching us, the sorrel fell, but Barbee did not stop to see what had happened to the brute. He hit the ground running, and snatching up a gun as he came, was soon in line.

About five paces to my left was a large, high rock behind which several of our wounded were sheltering themselves. To the top of that, where the very air was alive with missiles of death, Barbee sprang, and standing there, erect and fearless, began firing—the wounded men below him pasing up loaded guns as fast as he emptied them. But no living being could stay unhurt long in such a fire. In a few minutes, Barbee was knocked off the rock by a ball that struck him in the right leg. Climbing instantly back, he again commenced shooting. In less than two minutes, he was tumbled off the rock by a ball in the other leg. Still unsatisfied, he crawled back a second time, but was not there more than a minute before, being wounded in the body, he again fell, this time dropping on his back between the rock that had been his perch, and that which was my shelter. Too seriously wounded this time to extricate himself from the narrow passageway, he called for help, and the last time I saw him that day, he was lying there, crying and cursing because the boys would not come to his relief and help him back on to the rock.

There were many in the regiment as brave as Barbee, but none so reckless. The best blood of Texas was there, and in the Fourth and Fifth Texas, and General Lee could safely place the confidence he did in Hood's Texas Brigade. But God must have ordained our defeat. As was said by one of the speakers at a reunion of 'the Mountain Remnant Brigade': 'At the first roll of the war drum, Texas sent forth her noblest and best. She gave the Army of Northern Virginia Hood's matchless brigade—a band of heroes who bore their country's flag to victory on every field, until God stopped them at Little Round Top.'

★★★

VAL C. GILES

"Both sides were whipped . . ."

Another member of the Texas Brigade to view the combat was private Val C. Giles who, in a selection also taken from

Polley's Hood's Texas Brigade, *presents a lighter side to the destructive slaughter at Little Round Top.*

It was near 5 o'clock when we began the assault against an enemy strongly fortified behind logs and stones on the crest of a mountain, in many places perpendicular. It was more than half a mile from our starting point to the edge of the timber at the base of the ridge, comparatively open ground all the way. We started off at quick time, the officers keeping the column in pretty good line until we passed through the peach orchard and reached the level ground beyond. We were now about four hundred yards from the timber and the fire from the enemy, both artillery and musketry, was fearful.

In making that long charge our brigade got 'jammed.' Regiments overlapped each other and when we reached the woods and climbed the mountains as far as we could go, we were a badly mixed crowd.

Confusion reigned supreme everywhere. Nearly all our field officers were gone. Hood, our major general, had been shot from his horse. Robertson, our brigadier, had been carried from the field. Colonel Powell of the Fifth Texas was riddled with bullets. Colonel Van Manning of the Third Arkansas was disabled and Colonel Carter of my regiment lay dying at the foot of the mountain.

An overly romantic view of the charge of the 1st Minnesota Regiment against an advancing column of Confederates. Though achieving initial success in forcing the enemy back, the Rebels managed to catch the Yankee regiment with fire on both flanks and incurred a casualty loss of 82 percent.

Casualties on Little Round Top. In order to meet the threat to Little Round Top, Colonel Strong Vincent's Brigade, including the 20th Maine, took the rocky crest of the hill and was later joined by Brigadier General Stephen H. Weed's Brigade, including the 155th Pennsylvania. The Confederates were repulsed but only at a heavy cost.

Hoke's Brigade under Colonel Isaac E. Avery storm enemy batteries in Early's attack on the Federal right.

The sides of the mountain were heavily timbered and covered with great boulders, that had tumbled from the cliffs above years before, which afforded great protection to the men.

Every tree, rock and stump that gave any protection from the rain of minie-balls, that was poured down upon us, from the crest above us, were soon appropriated. John Griffith and myself pre-empted behind a moss-covered old boulder about the size of a 500-pound cotton bale.

By this time order and discipline were gone. Every fellow was his own general. Private soldiers gave commands as loud as the officers—nobody paying any attention to either. To add to this confusion, our artillery on the hill in our rear was cutting its fuse too short. The shells were bursting behind us, in the tree-tops, over our heads, and all around us.

Nothing demoralizes troops quicker than to be fired into by their friends. I saw it occur twice during the war. The first time we ran, but at Gettysburg we couldn't.

This mistake was soon corrected and the shells burst high on a mountain or went over it.

Major Rogers, then in command of the Fifth Texas regiment, mounted an old log near my boulder and began a Fourth of July speech. He was a little ahead of time, for that was about 6:30 o'clock on the evening of the 2d. Of course, nobody was paying any attention to the oration as he appealed to the men to 'stand fast.' He and Captain Cussons of the Fourth Alabama were the only two men I saw standing. The balance of us had settled down behind rocks, logs and trees. While the speech was going on, John Haggerty, one of Hood's couriers, then acting for General Law, dashed up the side of the mountains, saluted the major and said: 'General Law presents his compliments and says hold the place at all hazards.' The major checked up, glared down at Haggerty from his perch and shouted: 'Compliments, hell! Who wants compliments in such a damned place as this? Go back and ask General Law if he expects me to hold the world in check with the Fifth Texas regiment.'

The major evidently thought he had his regiment with him, while, in fact, these men were from every regiment in the Texas Brigade all around him.

But I must back to my boulder at Gettysburg. It was a ragged line of battle, strung out along the side of Cemetery Ridge and in front of Little Round Top. Night began settling around us, but the carnage went on. It is of that night that I started out to speak.

There seemed to be a viciousness in the very air we breathed. Things had gone wrong all the day and now pandemonium came with the darkness.

Alexander Dumas says the devil gets in a man seven times a day, and if the average is not over seven times he is almost a saint.

At Gettysburg that night it was about seven devils to each man. Officers were cross to the men, and the men were equally cross to the officers. It was the same way with the enemy. We could hear the Yankee officer on the crest of the ridge in front of us cursing the men by platoons, and the men telling them to go to a country not very far from them just at that time. If that old satanic dragon has ever been on earth since he offered our Saviour the world if He would serve him, he was at Gettysburg that night.

Every characteristic of the human race was presented there, the cruelty of the Turk, the courage of the Greek (old style), the endurance of the Arab, the dash of the Cossack, the fearlessness of the Bashibazouk, the ignorance of the Zulu, the cunning of the Comanche, the recklessness of the American volunteers and the wickedness of the devil thrown in to make the thing complete.

The advance lines of the two armies in many places were not more than fifty yards apart. Everything was on the shoot; no favors asked, and none offered.

My gun was so dirty that the ramrod hung in the barrel, and I could neither get it down nor out. I slammed the rod against a rock a few times and drove home ramrod, cartridge and all, laid the gun on a boulder, elevated the muzzle, ducked my head, halloed 'Look out!' and pulled the trigger. She roared like a young cannon and flew over my shoulder, the barrel striking John Griffith a smart whack on the left ear. John roared, too, and abused me like a pickpocket for my carelessness. It was no trouble to get another gun there. The mountain side was covered with them.

Just to our left was a little fellow from the Third Arkansas regiment. He was comfortably located behind a big stump, loading and firing as fast as he could, and between biting cartridges and taking aim, he was singing at the top of his voice:

> 'Now, let the wide world wag as it will,
> I'll be gay and happy still.'

The world was wagging all right—no mistake about that, but I failed to see where the 'gay and happy' part came in.

That was a fearful night. There was no sweet music to soothe the savage beast. The 'tooters' had left the shooters to fight it out, and taken 'Home, Sweet Home' and 'The Girl I Left Behind Me' off with them.

Our spiritual advisers, chaplains of regiments, were in the rear, caring for the wounded and dying soldiers. With seven devils to each man, it was no place for a preacher, anyhow.

A little red paint and a few eagle feathers were all that was necessary to make that crowd on both sides the most veritable savages on earth. 'White-winged Peace' didn't roost at Little Round Top that night. There was not a man there who cared a snap for the Golden Rule or that could have remembered one line of the Lord's Prayer. Both sides were whipped and all were mad about it.

★★★

D. AUGUST DICKERT

On the Attack against Sickles

Kershaw's brigade was charged with attacking elements of Sickles' corps that held the Peach Orchard. After pummeling through Union lines, they were hit in the flank. Brigadier Paul J. Semmes called for more reinforcements as his brigade joined the fray with assistance from Barkesdale's and Wofford's brigades. While they almost drove a gap in the Union line, the Federals were able to throw some forces to push back the enemy threat. Once again, D. Augustus Dickert relates the action in History of Kershaw's Brigade.

When the troops were aroused from their slumbers on that beautiful clear morning of the 2d of July, the sun had long since shot its rays over the quaint old, now historic, town of Gettysburg, sleeping down among the hills and spurs of the Blue Ridge. After an all-night's march, and a hard day's work before them, the troops were allowed all the rest and repose possible. I will here state that Longstreet had with him only two divisions of his corps, with four regiments to a division. Pickett was left near Chambersburg to protect the numerous supply trains. Jenkins' South Carolina brigade of his division had been left in Virginia to guard the mountain passes against a possible cavalry raid, and thus had not the opportunity of sharing with the other South Carolinians in the glories that will forever cluster around Gettysburg. They would, too, had they been present, have enjoyed and deserved the halo that will for all time surround the "charge of Pickett," a charge that will go down in history with Balaclava and Hohenlinden.

A. P. Hill, aided by part of Ewell's corps, had fought a winning fight the day before, and had driven the enemy from the field through the streets of the sleepy old town of Gettysburg to the high ground on the east. But this was only the advance guard of General Meade, thrown forward to gain time in order to bring up his main army. He was now concentrating it with all haste, and forming in rear of the rugged ridge running south of Gettysburg and culminating in the promontories at the Round Top. Behind this ridge was soon to assemble an army, if not the largest, yet the grandest, best disciplined, best equipped of all time, with an incentive to do successful battle as seldom falls to the lot of an army, and on its success or defeat depended the fate of two nations.

There was a kind of intuition, an apparent settled

fact, among the soldiers of Longstreet's corps, that after all the other troops had made their long marches, tugged at the flanks of the enemy, threatened his rear, and all the display of strategy and generalship had been exhausted in the dislodgement of the foe, and all these failed, then when the hard, stubborn, decisive blow was to be struck, the troops of the first corps were called upon to strike it. Longstreet had informed Lee at the outset, "My crops is as solid as a rock—a great rock. I will strike the blow, and win, if the other troops gather the fruits of victory."

How confident the old "War Horse," as General Lee called him, was in the solidity and courage of his troops. Little did he know when he made the assertion that so soon his seventeen thousand men were to be pitted against the whole army of the Potomac. Still, no battle was ever considered decisive until Longstreet, with his cool, steady head, his heart of steel and troops who acknowledged no superior, or scarcely equal, in ancient or modern times, in endurance and courage, had measured strength with the enemy. This I give, not as a personal view, but as the feelings, the confidence and pardonable pride of the troops of the 1st corps.

As A. P. Hill and Ewell had had their bout the day before, it was a foregone conclusion that Longstreet's time to measure strength was near at hand, and the men braced themselves accordingly for the ordeal.

A ridge running parallel with that behind which the enemy stood, but not near so precipitous or rugged, and about a mile distant, with a gentle decline towards the base of the opposite ridge, was to be the base of the battle ground of the day. This plain or gentle slope between the two armies, a mile in extent, was mostly open fields covered with grain or other crops, with here and there a farm house, orchard and garden. It seems from reports since made that Lee had not matured his plan of battle until late in the forenoon. He called a council of war of his principal Lieutenant to discuss plans and feasibilities. It was a long time undecided whether Ewell should lead the battle on the right, or allow Longstreet to throw his whole corps on the Round Top and break away these strongholds, the very citadel to Meade's whole line. The latter was agreed upon, much against the judgment of General Longstreet but Lee's orders were imperative, and obeyed with alacrity. At ten o'clock the movement began for the formation of the columns of assault. Along and in rear of the ridge we marched at a slow and halting gait. The Washington artillery had preceded us, and soon afterwards Alexander's battery passed to select positions. We marched and countermarched, first to the right, then to the left. As we thus marched we had little opportunity as yet to view the strongholds of the enemy on the opposite ridge, nor the incline between, which was soon to be strewn with the dead and dying. Occasionally a General would ride to the crest and take a survey of the surroundings. No cannon had yet been fired on either side, and everything was quiet and still save the tread of the thousands in motion, as if preparing for a great review.

Gunners of Battery D, Second U.S. Artillery, load and prime their pieces in preparation to fire upon the enemy. This unit served with Sedgwick's VI Corps at both Chancellorsville and Gettysburg.

Longstreet passed us once or twice, but he had his eyes cast to the ground, as if in a deep study, his mind disturbed, and had more the look of gloom than I had ever noticed before. Well might the great chieftain look cast down with the weight of this great responsibility resting upon him. There seemed to be an air of heaviness hanging around all. The soldiers trod with a firm but seeming heavy tread. Not that there was any want of confidence or doubt of ultimate success, but each felt within himself that this was to be the decisive battle of the war, and as a consequence it would be stubborn and bloody. Soldiers looked in the faces of their fellow-soldiers with a silent sympathy that spoke more eloquently than words an exhibition of brotherly love never before witnessed in the 1st corps. They felt a sympathy for those whom they knew, before the setting of the sun, would feel touch of the elbow for the last time, and who must fall upon this distant field and in an enemy's country.

About now we were moved over the crest and halted behind a stone wall that ran parallel to a county road, our center being near a gateway in the wall. As soon as the halt was made the soldiers fell down, and soon the most of them were fast asleep. While here, it was necessary for some troops of Hill's to pass over up and through the gate. The head of the column was lead by a doughty General clad in a brilliant new uniform, a crimson sash encircling his waist, its deep, heavy hanging down to his sword scabbard, while great golden curls hung in maiden ringlets to his very shoulders. His movement was

The rocky terrain of Devil's Den which provided a strong position for the expert Confederate marksmen to strike against the Yankees of the Federal left.

Confederate gunners take time out to enjoy a meager dinner.

superb and he sat his horse in true Knightly manner. On the whole, such a turn-out was a sight seldom witnessed by the staid soldiers of the First Corps. As he was passing a man in Company D, 3d South Carolina, roused up from his broken sleep, saw for the first time the soldier wonder with the long curls. He called out to him, not knowing he was an officer of such rank, "Say, Mister, come right down out of that hair," a foolish and unnecessary expression that was common throughout the army when anything unusual hove in sight.

This hail roused all the ire in the flashy General, he became as "mad as a March hare," and wheeling his horse, dashed up to where the challenge appeared to have come from and demanded in an angry tone, "Who was that spoke? Who commands this company?" And as no reply was given he turned away, saying, "D—d if I only knew who it was that insulted me, I would put a ball in him." But as he rode off the soldier gave him a Parthian shot by calling after him, "Say, Mister, don't get so mad about it, I thought you were some d—n wagon master."

Slowly again our column began moving to the right. The center of the division was halted in front of little Round Top. Kershaw was then on the right, Barksdale with his Mississippians on his left, Wofford and Sumner with their Georgians in rear as support. Everything was quiet in our front, as if the enemy had put his horse in order and awaited our coming. Kershaw took position behind a tumbled down wall to await Hood's movements on our right, and who was to open the battle by the assault on Round Top. The country on our right, through which Hood had to manœuvre, was very much broken and thickly studded with trees and mountain undergrowth, which delayed that General in getting in battle line. Anderson's Georgians, with Hood's old Texas Brigade under Robertson, was on McLaws' immediate right, next to Kershaw. Law's Alabama Brigade was on the extreme right, and made the first advance. On McLaws' left was Wilcox, of General "Tige" Anderson's Division of the 3d Corps, with Posey and other troops to his left, these to act more as a brace to Longstreet as he advanced to the assault; however, most of them were

Members of the 71st New York, one of the five regiments raised by Daniel Sickles that formed his Excelsior Brigade. The unit was fearfully cut up at Gettysburg where it lost 778 men.

drawn into the vortex of battle before the close of the day. In Kershaw's Brigade, the 2d under Colonel John D. Kennedy and Lieutenant Colonel Frank Gilliard, the 15th under Colonel W. D. Dessausure and Major Wm. Gist, the 3d under Colonel James D. Nance and Major R. C. Maffett, the 7th under Colonel D. Wyatt Aiken and Lieutenant Colonel Elbert Bland, the 3d Battallion under Lieutenant Colonel W. G. Rice, the 8th under Colonel John W. Henegan, Lieutenant Colonel Hood and Major McLeod, went into battle in the order named, as far as I remember Major Wm. Wallace of the 2d commanded the brigade skirmish line or sharpshooters, now some distance in our front. A battery of ten guns was immediately in our rear, in a grove of oaks, and drew on us a heavy fire when the artillery duel began. All troops in line, the batteries in position, nothing was wanting but the signal gun to put these mighty forces in motion. Ewell had been engaged during the morning in a desultory battle far to our left and beyond the town, but had now quieted down. A blue puff of smoke, a deafening report from one of the guns of the Washington Artil-

lery of New Orleans, followed in quick succession by others, gave the signal to both armies—the battle was now on.

It was the plan of action for Hood to move forward first and engage the enemy, and when once the combat was well under way on the right, McLaws to press his columns to the front. Law, with his Alabamians, was closing around the southern base of greater Round Top, while Robertson, with his three Texas regiments and one Arkansas, and Anderson with his Georgians, were pushing their way through thickets and over boulders to the front base of the Round Tops and the gorges between the two. We could easily determine their progress by the "rebel yell" as it rang out in triumph along the mountain sides.

The battery in our rear was drawing a fearful fire upon us, as we lay behind the stone fence, and all were but too anxious to be ordered forward. Barksdale, on our left, moved out first, just in front of the famous Peach Orchard. A heavy battery was posted there, supported by McCandless' and Willard's Divisions, and began raking Barksdale from the start. The brave

A group of Federals in Virginia.

old Mississippian, who was so soon to lose his life, asked permission to charge and take the battery, but was refused. Kershaw next gave the command, "forward," and the men sprang to their work with a will and determination and spread their steps to the right and left as they advanced. Kershaw was on foot, prepared to follow the line of battle immediately in rear, looking cool, composed and grand, his steel-gray eyes flashing the fire he felt in his soul.

The shelling from the enemy on the ridge in front had, up to this time, been mostly confined to replying to our batteries, but as soon as this long array of bristling bayonets moved over the crest and burst out suddenly in the open, in full view of the cannon-crowned battlements, all guns were turned upon us. The shelling from Round Top was terrific enough to make the stontest hearts quake, while the battery down at the base of the ridge, in the orchard, was raking Barksdale and Kershaw right and left with grape and shrapnell. Semms' Georgians soon moved up on our right and between Kershaw and Hood's left, but its brave commander fell mortally wounded at the very commencement of the attack. Kershaw advanced directly against little Round Top, the strongest point in the enemy's line, and defended by Ayer's Regulars, the best disciplined and most stubborn fighters in the Federal army. The battery in the orchard began grape-

ing Kershaw's left as soon as it came in range, the right being protected by a depression in the ground over which they marched. Not a gun was allowed to be fired either at sharpshooters that were firing on our front from behind boulders and trees in a grove we were nearing, or at the commoners who were raking our flank on the left. Men fell here and there from the deadly minnie-balls, while great gaps or swaths were swept away in our ranks by shells from the batteries on the hills, or by the destructive grape and canister from the orchard. On marched the determined men across this open expanse, closing together as their comrades fell out. Barksdale had fallen, but his troops were still moving to the front and over the battery that was making such havoc in their ranks. Semms, too, had fallen, but his Georgians never wavered nor faltered, but moved like a huge machine in the face of these myriads of death-dealing missiles. Just as we entered the woods the infantry opened upon us a withering fire, especially from up the gorge that ran in the direction of Round Top. Firing now became general along the whole line on both sides. The Fifteenth Regiment met a heavy obstruction, a mock-orange hedge, and it was just after passing this obstacle that Colonel Dessausure fell. The center of the Third Regiment and some parts of the other regiments, were practically protected by boulders and large trees, but

The once peaceful Pennsylvania countryside is shattered as the Army of Northern Virginia launches a series of bloody attacks against the entrenched Federals at Gettysburg on 2 July 1863. Though at times managing to drive the Yankees, victory proved elusive for Lee.

the greater part fought in the open field or in sparsely timbered groves of small trees. The fight now waged fast and furious.

Captain Malloy writes thus of the 8th: "We occupied the extreme left of the brigade, just fronting the celebrated 'Peach Orchard.' The order was given. We began the fatal charge, and soon had driven the enemy from their guns in the orchard, when a command was given to 'move to the right,' which fatal order was obeyed under a terrible fire, this leaving the 'Peach Orchard' partly uncovered. The enemy soon rallied to their guns and turned them on the flank of our brigade. Amid a storm of shot and shell from flank and front, our gallant old brigade pushed towards the Round Top, driving all before them, till night put an end to the awful slaughter. The regiment went in action with 215 in ranks, and lost more than half its number. We lost many gallant officers, among whom were Major McLeod, Captain Thomas E. Powe, Captain John McIver, and others." The move to the right was to let Wofford in between Barksdale and Kershaw.

Barksdale was pressing up the gorge that lay between little Round Top and the ridge, was making successful battle and in all likelihood would have succeeded had it not been for General Warren. General Meade's Chief Engineer being on the ground and seeing the danger, grasped the situation at once, called up all the available force and lined the stone walls that led along the gorge with infantry. Brigade after brigade of Federal infantry was now rushed to this citadel, while the crown of little Round Top was literally covered with artillery. Ayer's Regulars were found to be a stubborn set by Kershaw's troops. The Federal volunteers on our right and left gave way to Southern valor, but the regulars stood firm, protected as they were by the great boulders along their lines. Barksdale had passed beyond us as the enemy's line bent backward at this point, and was receiving the whole shock of battle in his front, while a terrific fire was coming from down the gorge and from behind hedges on the hill-side. But the Mississippians held on like grim death till Wofford, with his Georgians, who was moving in majestic style across the open field in the rear, came to his support.

General Wofford was a splendid officer, and equally as hard a fighter. He advanced his brigade through the deadly hail of bullets and took position on Barksdale's right and Kershaw's left, and soon the roar of his guns were mingling with those of their comrades. The whole division was now in action. The enemy began to give way and scamper up the hill-side. But Meade, by this time, had the bulk of his army around and in rear of the Round Top, and fresh troops were continually being rushed in to take the places of or reinforce those already in action. Hood's whole force was now also engaged, as well as a part of A. P. Hill's on our left. The smoke became so dense, the noise of small arms and the tumult raised by the "Rebel Yell," so great that the voices of officers attempting to give commands were hushed in the pandemonium. Along to the right of the 3d, especially up the little ravine, the fire was concentrated on those who held this position and was terrific beyond description, forcing a part of the line back to the stone house. This fearful shock of battle was kept up along the whole line without intermission till night threw her sable curtains over the scene of carnage and bloodshed and put an end to the strife. Wofford and Barksdale had none to reinforce them at the gorge, and had to fight it out single-handed and alone, while the Regulars, with their backs to the base of little Round Top, protected by natural formations, were too strong to be dislodged by Kershaw. As soon as the firing ceased the troops were withdrawn to near our position of the forenoon.

The work of gathering up the wounded lasted till late at night. Our loss in regimental and line officers was very great. Scarcely a regiment but what had lost one of its staff, nor a company some of its officers. Dr. Salmond, the Brigade Surgeon, came early upon the field and directed in person the movements of his assistants in their work of gathering up the wounded. "The dead were left to take care of the dead" until next day.

When the brigade was near the woodland in its advance, a most deadly fire was directed towards the center of the 3d both by the battery to our left, and sharpshooting in the front. It was thought by some that it was our flag that was drawing the fire, four color guards having gone down, some one called out "Lower the colors, down with the flag." Sergant Lamb, color bearer, waved the flag aloft, and moving to the front where all could see, called out in loud tones, "This flag never goes down until I am down."

Then the word went up and down the line "Shoot that officer, down him, shoot him," but still he continued to give those commands, "Ready, aim, fire," and the grape shot would come plunging into our very faces. The sharpshooters, who had joined our ranks, as we advanced, now commenced to blaze away, and the connoneers scattered to cover in the rear. This officer finding himself deserted by his men, waved his sword defiantly over his head and walked away as deliberately as on dress parade, while the sharpshooters were plowing up the dirt all around him, but all failed to bring him down. We bivouaced during the night just in rear of the battle ground.

★★★

HENRY F. WEAVER

Under Fire

To maintain his control of Little Round Top and bolster his increasingly beleaguered left, Meade was forced to rely on reinforcements tapped from his right which had remained unengaged for most of the day. The 155th Pennsylvania went into action at Little Round Top and fought elements of the Texas Brigade. Corporal Henry F. Weaver of Company B of the 155th Pennsylvania suffered a wound that day and lost his foot. He went on to serve as a notary public, auditor, and secretary of financial institutions in Pittsburgh. This short work originally entitled, At Gettysburg—Under Front and Rear Fire *was taken from* Under the Maltese Cross.

Weed's Brigade, Sykes' Division, Fifth Corps, and the One Hundred and Fifty-fifth Regiment Pennsylvania Volunteers, arrived on the field at Gettysburg early on the morning of July 2nd, somewhere near Culp's Hill, on the right of the Union line. Except to shift from one position to another, we did nothing for several hours. The order announcing that General George G. Meade had taken charge of the Army of the Potomac was read to the troops while in line of battle in the woods, with skirmishers thrown out. While I do not think that any more impressive or patriotic order could be read to any troops on the eve of battle and the assumption of command by a new General, I confess that I was disappointed when the order was signed George G. Meade and not George B. McClellan, but Providence directed otherwise.

We remained in this position for some time, the men making coffee—many of them bathing in the creek. So the hours passed pleasantly away. The command had rested and taken short naps at halts. It was ominously quiet along our front, the quietness being broken only by some desultory infantry and artillery firing, doubtless both armies being occupied in getting ready to renew the contest.

About 4 P.M., the report of a solitary cannon was heard away over to the left. It was from Sickles, and the battle of the 2nd of July had commenced. This single cannon firing was followed by more and then *one, two,* somewhat broken. Then came the final crash and roar of musketry and booming of artillery together.

Sykes' Fifth Corps was then ordered to Little Round Top, following no roadway. Tearing down fences, the men double-quicked out past Little Round Top, near where two brigades of Regulars of Ayres' Division were already engaged. Weed's Brigade halted behind a battery actively engaged. The One Hundred and Fifty-fifth men loaded muskets and then by orders countermarched, left in front, and took position on Little Round Top. The One Hundred and Fifty-fifth, of Weed's Brigade, was on the right of the line and Company B on the right of the Regiment. A good view of that portion of the field, when not obscured by the smoke of battle, was afforded. The two small brigades of United States Regulars of Ayres' Division had advanced beyond the position of the One Hundred and Fifty-fifth on Little Round Top, toward the Wheatfield, this movement being made by the United States Regulars to support General Sickles. The Regulars fought with determined skill and bravery for nearly an hour, and then reluctantly fell back as if on drill, but sharply and bravely contesting every foot of the ground. These things I saw, and I am glad, as a volunteer, to bear tribute to the United States Regulars.

The remaining portion of the Third Corps and Regulars were overwhelmed, and fell back to Little Round Top. There were two batteries of artillery, one of steel and the other of brass pieces, one in front and one over to the right of the Regiment, which kept up their fire until the very last, two of the steel guns being captured, and one of them recaptured later from the enemy. In the meantime the Regulars reformed in line of battle a little below the position of the One Hundred and Fifty-fifth on the crest of Little Round Top, and the fire in our immediate front slackened temporarily. The enemy appeared and advanced from the Devil's Den and to the left of it, and owing to the formation of the ground, struck the left of the line of Weed's Brigade at its extended concave portion, and the fight became terrific.

Just then Robertson's Brigade of Texans swung across the foot of the hill and advanced to attack the positions occupied by the One Hundred and Fortieth

Strong Vincent   *Brigadier General*
                         Stephen H. Weed

and One Hundred and Forty-sixth New York, and the Ninety-first and One Hundred and Fifty-fifth Pennsylvania Volunteers. I wondered why our battery immediately above us did not open fire. Five minutes pass away. What is the matter? Then the battery opened, and over our head went a screaming, whistling shell followed by another and another and so on. Still the enemy kept on advancing on the positions of the four regiments mentioned which formed Weed's Brigade. Impatiently waiting as we were, it was hard to repress our fire. At last the order came to us, "Steady—Ready—Aim—Fire!" We arose and delivered our fire at close buck-and-ball range of our muskets, and reloaded and fired again, but still the Confederates kept advancing, halting to fire volleys as they advanced.

The Confederates were brave, resolute, and determined men. At this time I was wounded in the ball of the right ankle joint. I felt a stinging sensation extending to the thigh, but no pain. The enemy's bullets kept coming as numerous apparently as the drops of rain in a heavy storm. As I lay there wounded I expected to get a bullet in my head at any moment, but fortunately did not. Looking in front of my position, I say Corporal David M. Smith, of our company, lying mortally wounded behind a shelving rock about five yards from my position. Being hit in the left groin, the ball must have severed the femoral artery. He turned to me and said, "Oh! I am shot." The stretcher-bearers carried him back a short time after, but he died just as they reached the foot of the hill. While I was trying all in my power to encourage Corporal Smith, a bullet struck Comrade William Douglass, of my company, fairly in the center of the forehead, and with a terrible shriek, he fell back dead. I shall never forget the sight.

In the light of "After discovered evidence" a charge, which Major A. L. Pearson sought permission to make at that time and was refused, would have been wrong, Weed's Brigade having been assigned and ordered to hold that portion of Little Round Top only. General Meade wisely provided other troops for that purpose, and ordered them to do the charging.

Lieutenant Luke J. Dooling, of Company I, seeing

that I was wounded and unable to stand, the pain having become excruciating, ran up to me exclaiming, "Poor boy! are you hurt—are you wounded?" I threw my arms around his and Comrade Pat Lyon's necks, and was thus taken back some distance, until we met some stretcher-bearers from the Sixth Corps, who carried me a short distance to the rear, at the foot of Little Round Top, passing what was evidently a brigade of the Sixth Corps being formed in line of battle one behind the other in perfect formation, which did me good to see, as the musketry fire at the front occupied by Weed's Brigade was still severe, and the battle by no means decided. General Meade's provision for the reserve line of battle was perfect. Shells and balls from the enemy were coming through the trees and knocking off the branches here and there, during the passage of the wounded to the rear. We also passed two members of our company bearing the body of Corporal Smith, who had just died from his wounds.

I was next placed in an ambulance, which, after receiving other wounded soldiers, not of our Regiment, started back along the Taneytown road and we were deposited on the ground near Meade's headquarters, on the left center of the Union lines, where we lay all night.

Some time later the Union batteries on the ridge in front of where the wounded were placed opened on the enemy. I never could understand this, as our yellow hospital flags were flying and plainly visible from the small buildings. Why our artillerists at that time should draw the enemy's fire at a point where their answering missiles would fall among the already wounded men seemed incomprehensible. The enemy at once responded, and their fire became so warm as to compel the removal of the wounded, who were taken in ambulances to our right and laid under trees and woods. Escaping from the fire of the enemy in this position, the wounded were not so fortunate otherwise, as during the night one terrific thunderstorm after another broke out over our heads, followed by vivid flashes of lightning, continuing through the night. I pulled my gum blanket over my head and wrapped it around my body the best I could, and was thus afforded some protection from the rain. Early in the morning I was carried and laid on the ground a short distance from the field-hospital operating table. The rain still continuing, I made a pillow of my haversack, and again pulling my gum blanket over my face, lay there as patiently as I could, waiting my turn to be operated on. During a lull in the battle, Pat Lyon and Isaac Craig, of our Company, hunted me up, and Pat, taking his blanket from his shoulder, threw it over me, as I, being well-drenched, was shivering with cold.

At right, a group of Federal Telegraph operators lounge about after witnessing the Battle of Gettysburg. One of the vital improvements in military communications was the use of the telegraph to rapidly dispatch information from army headquarters to the field.

A period of several hours followed, during which we heard but little firing at the front. Suddenly the artillery fire from a hundred guns opened and the din was terrific, evidently being the initial attack on our side to repel Pickett's charge. During all this noise and confusion, I was removed and placed on the operating table, and had my foot amputated by Doctor Reed, Regimental Surgeon of the One Hundred and Fifty-fifth, assisted by the surgeon of the Ninety-first Pennsylvania Volunteers. As they were about to administer the chloroform to me, I heard Dr. Billings, a Regular army surgeon, say, "Let us be as quick as we can, as some of us may be killed during the operation." The shells and stray balls from the Confederates at that time were whistling through the location of the field hospital and the limbs of the trees were falling in every direction. There did not seem to be safety at any place in this trying period of the battle.

After the operation had been performed in this exposed field hospital in the immediate rear of Little Round Top, and the shelling and noise had subsided at the front, and I was lifted from the operating table still in a semiconscious state, I was again laid on the ground which had been covered with straw taken by "eminent domain" from neighboring barns. Soon after small tents were erected, and all the wounded were placed in them as fast as they were put up, so as to guard against drenching rains.

Color-Corporals Thomas J. Tomer, of Company E, and John H. Mackin, of Company F, who also had been wounded while with the colors, about the same time I was wounded, secured quarters in one of these tents. Privates Charles F. McKenna, of Company E, and Samuel W. Hill, of Company F, as soon as the firing in front ceased, were allowed to leave the ranks to visit Corporals Tomer, Mackin, myself and other companions in a field hospital in rear of Little Round Top and their visit cheered us very much.

From the tents the wounded could see most grewsome sights. Amputations of arms and legs by the army surgeons, to save the lives of the wounded, ran up into thousands; and for want of assistance these dissevered members, the first few days, were suffered to accumulate in piles several feet in height. The bodies of the poor comrades not surviving these operations, and the hundreds of dead from wounds or blood poisoning were placed in the dead-house close by, to await burial. These harrowing environments were not conducive towards cheering or comforting the suffering wounded.

Night, letting her sable mantle down, shut from view the terrible scenes of human wrath. Everything quieted down, and we slept fitfully until the next morning, the Fourth of July. Late in the day, the surgeon in charge came in and greeting the wounded, said, "Well, while you are all in pretty bad shape, you seem to be in good spirits, and I have good news for you. This battle is won, the rebels are retreating—Vicksburg has also fallen, and so this is a good and glorious Fourth of July after all. Don't you think so?"

It is needless to say we answered him with an affirmative shout.

At the scene of the struggle.

HIGHWATER MARK OF THE CONFEDERACY

Unhappy with his inability to crack Meade's line on 2 July, Lee planned a daring attack on the Federal center composed of 15,000 men of Pickett's and two of A.P. Hill's divisions. After a massive bombardment from 130 Confederate cannon, the mammoth force left the protective cover near Seminary Ridge and set off on a long and desperate march over a half a mile of clear ground to attack the enemy lines on Cemetery Ridge. In a battle lasting only one hour, the Confederates were forced to fall back after losing roughly 6,500 men. The high water mark of the Confederacy had been reached, Lee had met defeat, and there was nothing left for the Army of Northern Virginia to do but fall back across the Potomac and wait for the next major Federal offensive.

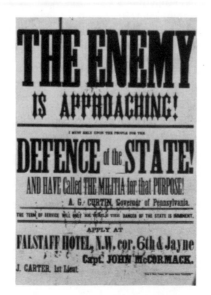

★★★

RAWLEY W. MARTIN
In Pickett's Ranks

On 3 July, after a tremendous bombardment around 1500, the doomed assault forever known as Pickett's Charge was launched on its impossible mission. As the picturesque lines of butternut and gray advanced against the enemy, their ranks were torn apart by the increasing swell of thundering cannon and eruptions of deadly musketry. Though some Southerners were able to break through the Yankee defenses, these gains were quickly lost and the survivors retreated to the safety of their own lines. Rawly Martin, member of the 53rd Virginia, wrote of his recollections of the doomed offensive in the Southern Society Historical Papers.

In the effort to comply with your request to describe Pickett's charge at Gettysburg, I may unavoidably repeat what has often been told before, as the position of troops, the cannonade, the advance, and the final disaster are familiar to all who have the interest or the curiosity to read. My story will be short, for I shall only attempt to describe what fell under my own observation.

You ask for a description of the "feelings of the brave Virginians who passed through that hell of fire in their heroic charge on Cemetery Ridge." The *esprit du corps* could not have been better; the men were in good physical condition, selfreliant and determined. They felt the gravity of the situation, for they knew well the metal of the foe in their front; they were serious and resolute, but not disheartened. None of the usual jokes, common on the eve of battle, were indulged in, for every man felt his individual responsibility, and realized that he had the most stupendous work of his life before him; officers and men knew at what cost and at what risk the advance was to be made, but they had deliberately made up their minds to attempt it. I believe the general sentiment of the division was that they would succeed in driving the Federal line from what was their objective point; they knew that many, very many, would go down under the storm of shot and shell which would greet them when their gray ranks were spread out to view, but it never occurred to them that disaster would come after they once placed their tattered banners upon the crest of Seminary Ridge.

I believe if those men had been told: "This day your lives will pay the penalty of your attack upon the Federal lines," they would have made the charge just as it was made. There was no straggling, no feigned sickness, no pretense of being overcome by the intense heat; every man felt that it was his duty to make that fight; that he was his own commander, and they

The man who led the fateful and fatal charge, Major General George E. Pickett.

would have made the charge without an officer of any description; they only needed to be told what they were expected to do. This is as near the feeling of the men of Pickett's Division on the morning of the battle as I can give, and with this feeling they went to their work. Many of them were veteran soldiers, who had followed the little cross of stars from Big Bethel to

Major General Winfield Scott Hancock who led the II Corps, the unit which received Pickett's Charge in such an unkind manner.

Gettysburg; they knew their own power, and they knew the temper of their adversary; they had often met before, and they knew the meeting before them would be desperate and deadly.

Pickett's three little Virginia brigades were drawn up in two lines, Kemper on the right (1st, 3d, 7th, 11th and 24), Garnett on the left (8th, 18th, 19th, 28th and 56th), and Armistead in the rear and center (9th, 14th, 38th, 53d and 57th) Virginia Regiments, covering the space between Kemper's left and Garnett's right flanks. This position was assigned Armistead, I suppose, that he might at the critical moment rush to the assistance of the two leading brigades, and if possible, put the capstone upon their work. We will see presently how he succeeded. The Confederate artillery was on the crest of Seminary Ridge, nearty in front of Pickett; only a part of the division had the friendly shelter of the woods; the rest endured the scorching rays of the July sun until the opening of the cannonade, when the dangers from the Federal batteries were added to their discomfort. About 1 o'clock two signal guns were fired by the Washington Artillery, and instantly a terrific cannonade was commenced, which lasted for more than an hour, when suddenly everything was silent. Every man knew what that silence portended. The grim blue battle line on Seminary Ridge began at once to prepare for the advance of its antagonists; both sides felt that the tug of war was about to come, and that Greek must meet Greek as they had never met before.

From this point, I shall confine my description to events connected with Armistead's brigade, with which I served. Soon after the cannonade ceased, a courier dashed up to General Armistead, who was pacing up and down in front of the 53d Virginia Regiment, his battalion of direction (which I commanded in the charge and at the head of which Armistead marched), and gave him the order from General Pickett to prepare for the advance. At once the command "Attention, battalion!" rang out clear and distinct. Instantly every man was on his feet and in his place; the alignment was made with as much coolness and precision as if preparing for dress parade. Then Armistead went up to the color sergeant of the 53d Virginia

Just after 1400 on 3 September, Pickett's troops charged across this ground towards the enemy positions over a mile away. As the Confederates emerged from their cover, their picturesque lines of battle were cut apart by Union cannon and later small arms fire.

Regiment and said: "Sergeant, are you going to put those colors on the enemy's works to-day?" The gallant fellow replied: "I will try, sir, and if mortal man can do it, it shall be done." It was done, but not until this brave man, and many others like him, had fallen with their faces to the foe; but never once did that banner trail in the dust, for some brave fellow invariably caught it as it was going down, and again bore it aloft, until Armistead saw its tattered folds unfurled on the very crest of Seminary Ridge.

After this exchange of confidence between the general and the color-bearer, Armistead commanded: "Right shoulder, shift arms. Forward, march." They stepped out at quick time, in perfect order and alignment—tramp, tramp, up to the Emmittsburg road; then the advancing Confederates saw the long line of blue, nearly a mile distant, ready and awaiting their coming. The scene was grand and terrible, and well calculated to demoralize the stoutest heart; but not a step faltered, not an elbow lost the touch of its neighbor, not a face blanched, for these men had determined to do their whole duty, and reckoned not the cost. On they go; at about 1,100 yards the Federal batteries opened fire; the advancing Confederates encounter and sweep before them the Federal skirmish line. Still forward they go; hissing, screaming shells break in their front, rear, on their flanks, all about them, but the devoted band, with the blue line in their front as their objective point, press forward, keeping step to the music of the battle. The distance between the opposing forces grows less and less, until suddenly the infantry behind the rock fence poured volley after volley into the advancing ranks. The men fell like stalks of grain before the reaper, but still they closed the gaps and pressed forward through that pitiless storm. The two advance brigades have thus far done the fighting. Armistead has endured the terrible ordeal without firing a gun; his brave followers have not changed their guns from the right shoulder. Great gaps have been torn in their ranks; their field and company officers have fallen; color-bearer after color-bearer has been shot down, but still they never faltered.

At the critical moment, in response to a request from Kemper, Armistead, bracing himself to the desperate blow, rushed forward to Kemper's and Garnett's line, delivered his fire, and with one supreme effort planted his colors on the famous rock fence. Armistead himself, with his hat on the point of his sword, that his men might see it through the smoke of battle, rushed forward, scaled the wall, and cried: "Boys, give them the cold steel!" By this time, the Federal hosts lapped around both flanks and made a counter advance in their front, and the remnant of those three little brigades melted away. Armistead himself had fallen, mortally wounded, under the guns he had captured, while the few who followed him over the fence were either dead or wounded. The charge was over, the sacrifice had been made, but, in the words of a Federal officer: "Banks of heroes they were; they fled not, but amidst that still continuous and terrible fire they slowly, sullenly recrossed the plain—all that was left of them—but few of the five thousand."

When the advance commenced General Pickett rode up and down in rear of Kemper and Garnett, and in this position he continued as long as there was opportunity of observing him. When the assault became so fierce that he had to superintend the whole line, I am sure he was in his proper place. A few years ago Pickett's staff held a meeting in the city of Richmond, Va., and after comparing recollections, they published a statement to the effect that he was with the division throughout the charge; that he made an effort to secure reinforcements when he saw his

The elite of the Confederacy wastes itself as Pickett's attack is blunted against a strong Union position that would not yield. With Pickett's Charge doomed, Lee lost Gettysburg and was forced to retreat to the safety of Virginia.

The ground over which the charge was made was an open terrene, with slight depressions and elevations, but insufficient to be serviceable to the advancing column. At the Emmertsburg road, where the parallel fences impeded the onward march, large numbers were shot down on account of the crowding at the openings where the fences had been thrown down, and on account of the halt in order to climb the fences. After passing these obstacles, the advancing column deliberately rearranged its lines and moved forward. Great gaps were made in their ranks as they moved on, but they were closed up as deliberately and promptly as if on the parade ground; the touch of elbows was always to the centre, the men keeping constantly in view the little emblem which was their beacon light to guide them to glory and to death.

I will mention a few instances of individual coolness and bravery exhibited in the charge. In the 53d Virginia Regiment, I saw every man of Company F (Captain Henry Edmunds, now a distinguished member of the Virginia bar) thrown flat to the earth by the explosion of a shell from Round Top, but every man who was not killed or desperately wounded sprang to his feet, collected himself and moved forward to close the gap made in the regimental front. A soldier from the same regiment was shot on the shin; he stopped in the midst of that terrific fire, rolled up his trousers leg, examined his wound, and went forward even to the rock fence. He escaped further injury, and was one of the few who returned to his friends, but so bad was his wound that it was nearly a year before he was fit for duty. When Kemper was riding off, after asking Armistead to move up to his support, Armistead called him, and, pointing to his brigade, said: "Did you ever see a more perfect line than that on dress parade?" It was, indeed, a lance

Brigadier General Lewis A. Armistead

flanks were being turned, and one of General Garnett's couriers testified that he carried orders from him almost to the rock fence. From my knowledge of General Pickett I am sure he was where his duty called him throughout the engagement. He was too fine a soldier, and had fought too many battles not to be where he was most needed on that supreme occasion of his military life.

This small humble abode served as Meade's headquarters during the epic battle of Gettysburg.

head of steel, whose metal had been tempered in the furnace of conflict. As they were about to enter upon their work, Armistead, as was invariably his custom on going into battle, said: "Men, remember your wives, your mothers, your sisters and you sweethearts." Such an appeal would have made those men assault the ramparts of the infernal regions.

You asked me to tell how the field looked after the charge, and how the men went back. This I am unable to do, as I was disabled at Armistead's side a moment after he had fallen, and left on the Federal side of the stone fence. I was picked up by the Union forces after their lines were reformed, and I take this occasion to express my grateful recollection of the attention I received on the field, particularly from Colonel Hess, of the 72d Pennsylvania (I think). If he still lives, I hope yet to have the pleasure of grasping his hand and expressing to him my gratitude for his kindness to me. Only the brave know how to treat a fallen foe.

I cannot close this letter without reference to the Confederate chief, General R. E. Lee. Somebody blundered at Gettysburg but not Lee. He was too great a master of the art of war to have hurled a handful of men against an army. It has been abundantly shown that the fault lay not with him, but with others, who failed to execute his orders.

★★★

SIR ARTHUR FREEMANTLE

"All this has been my fault . . ."

With the Confederate Commanders during the great attack, Sir Arthur Freemantle played witness to the reactions of Lee and Longstreet as the final drama of Pickett's Charge was played out. Despite suffering a disappointing and destructive defeat, the leaders and men of the Army of Northern Virginia remained calm even though the tide of battle as well as the entire war had turned against them.

At 6 A.M. I rode to the field with Colonel Manning, and went over that portion of the ground which, after a fierce contest, had been won from the enemy yesterday evening. The dead were being buried, but great numbers were still lying about; also many mortally wounded, for whom nothing could be done. Amongst the latter were a number of Yankees dressed in bad imitations of the Zouave costume. They opened their glazed eyes as I rode past in a painfully imploring manner.

We joined Generals Lee and Longstreet's Staff: they were reconnoitring and making preparations for renewing the attack. As we formed a pretty large party, we often drew upon ourselves the attention of the hostile sharpshooters, and were two or three times favoured with a shell. One of these shells set a brick building on fire which was situated between the lines. This building was filled with wounded, principally Yankees, who, I am afraid, must have perished miserably in the flames. Colonel Sorrel had been slightly wounded yesterday, but still did duty. Major Walton's horse was killed, but there were no other casualties amongst my particular friends.

The plan of yesterday's attack seems to have been very simple—first a heavy cannonade all along the line, followed by an advance of Longstreet's two divisions and part of Hill's corps. In consequence of the enemy's having been driven back some distance, Longstreet's corps (part of it) was in a much more forward situation than yesterday. But the range of heights to be gained was still most formidable, and evidently strongly intrenched.

The distance between the Confederate guns and the Yankee position—*i.e.*, between the woods crowning the opposite ridges—was at least a mile,—quite open, gently undulating, and exposed to artillery the whole distance. This was the ground which had to be crossed in to-day's attack. Pickett's division, which had just come up, was to bear the brunt in Longstreet's attack, together with Heth and Pettigrew in

Hill's corps. Pickett's division was a weak one (under 5000), owing to the absence of two brigades.

At noon all Longstreet's dispositions were made; his troops for attack were deployed into line, and lying down in the woods; his batteries were ready to open. The General then dismounted and went to sleep for a short time. The Austrian officer and I now rode off to get, if possible, into some commanding position from whence we could see the whole thing without being exposed to the tremendous fire which was about to commence. After riding about for half an hour without being able to discover so desirable a situation, we determined to make for the cupola, near Gettysburg, Ewell's headquarters. Just before we reached the entrance to the town, the cannonade opened with a fury which surpassed even that of yesterday.

Map of the third day of battle on 3 July 1863.

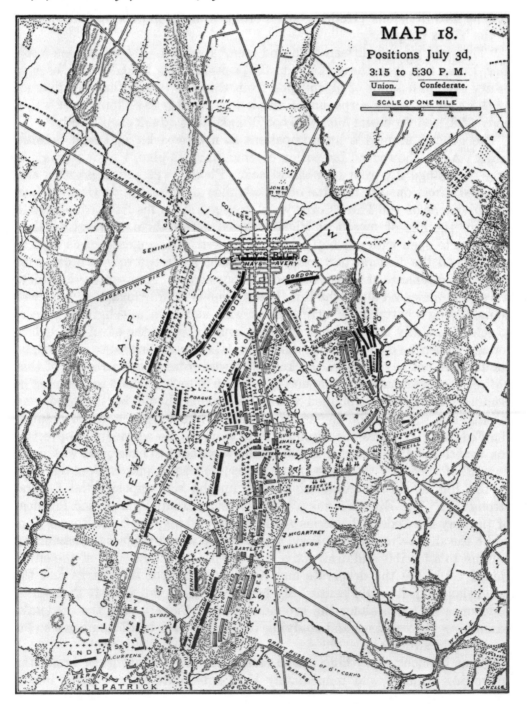

Soon after passing through the toll-gate at the entrance of Gettysburg, we found that we had got into a heavy cross-fire; shells both Federal and Confederate passing over our heads with great frequency. At length two shrapnel shells burst quite close to us, and a ball from one of them hit the officer who was conducting us. We then turned round and changed our views with regard to the cupola—the fire of one side being bad enough, but preferable to that of both sides. A small boy of twelve years was riding with us at the time: this urchin took a diabolical interest in the bursting of the shells, and screamed with delight when he saw them take effect. I never saw this boy again, or found out who he was. The road at Gettysburg was lined with Yankee dead, and as they had been killed on the 1st, the poor fellows had already begun to be very offensive. We then returned to the hill I was on yesterday. But finding that, to see the actual fighting, it was absolutely necessary to go into the thick of the thing, I determined to make my way to General Longstreet. It was then about 2.30. After passing General Lee and his Staff, I rode on through the woods in the direction in which I had left Longstreet. I soon began to meet many wounded men returning from the front; many of them asked in piteous tones the way to a doctor or an ambulance. The further I got, the greater became the number of the wounded. At last I came to a perfect stream of them flocking through the woods in numbers as great as the crowd in Oxford Street in the middle of the day. Some were walking alone on crutches composed of two rifles, others were supported by men less badly wounded than themselves, and others were carried on stretchers by the ambulance corps; but in no case did I see a sound man helping the wounded to the rear, unless he carried the red badge of the ambulance corps. They were still under a heavy fire; the shells were continually bringing down great limbs of trees, and carrying further destruction amongst this melancholy procession. I saw all this in much less time than it takes to write it, and although astonished to meet such vast numbers of wounded, I had not seen *enough* to give me any idea of the real extent of the mischief.

When I got close up to General Longstreet, I saw one of his regiments advancing through the woods in good order; so, thinking I was just in time to see the attack, I remarked to the General that *"I wouldn't have missed this for anything."* Longstreet was seated at the top of a snake fence at the edge of the wood, and looking perfectly calm and imperturbed. He replied, laughing, *"The devil you wouldn't! I would like to have missed it very much; we've attacked and been repulsed: look there!"*

For the first time I then had a view of the open space between the two positions, and saw it covered with Confederates slowly and sulkily returning towards us in small broken parties, under a heavy fire of artillery. But the fire where we were was not so bad as further to the rear; for although the air seemed alive with shell, yet the greater number burst behind us.

The General told me that Pickett's division had succeeded in carrying the enemy's position and cap-

turing his guns, but after remaining there twenty minutes, it had been forced to retire, on the retreat of Heth and Pettigrew on its left. No person could have been more calm or self-possessed than General Longstreet under these trying circumstances, aggravated as they now were by the movements of the enemy, who began to show a strong disposition to advance. I could now thoroughly appreciate the term bulldog, which I had heard applied to him by the soldiers. Difficulties seem to make no other impression upon him than to make him a little more savage.

Major Walton was the only officer with him when I came up—all the reset had been put into the charge. In a few minutes Major Latrobe arrived on foot, carrying his saddle, having just had his horse killed. Colonel Sorrel was also in the same predicament, and Captain Goree's horse was wounded in the mouth.

The General was making the best arrangements in his power to resist the threatened advance, by advancing some artillery, rallying the stragglers, &c. I remember seeing a General (Pettigrew, I think it was) come up to him, and report that "he was unable to bring his men up again." Longstreet turned upon him and replied with some sarcasm, *"Very well; never*

In a mighty charge tragically destined to fail, 15,000 Confederates under Major General George Pickett attempt to break through Meade's line at Cemetery Ridge. Only half of the attacking force returned to the safety of the Rebel position.

These members of Captain Andrew Cowan's 1st New York battery helped repulse Pickett's Charge. While the Confederates were just ten yards away, Cowan's battery opened up with a double load of canister massacring all those that stood within range of the blast.

mind, then, General; just let them remain where they are: the enemy's going to advance, and will spare you the trouble."

He asked for something to drink: I gave him some rum out of my silver flask, which I begged he would keep in remembrance of the occasion; he smiled, and, to my great satisfaction, accepted the memorial. He then went off to give some orders to M'Laws' division. Soon afterwards I joined General Lee, who had in the meanwhile come to that part of the field on becoming aware of the disaster. If Longstreet's conduct was admirable, that of General Lee was perfectly sublime. He was engaged in rallying and in encouraging the broken troops, and was riding about a little in front of the wood, quite alone—the whole of his Staff being engaged in a similar manner further to the rear. His face, which is always placid and cheerful, did not show signs of the slightest disappointment, care, or annoyance; and he was addressing to every soldier he met a few words of encouragement, such as, "All this will come right in the end: we'll talk it over afterwards; but, in the mean time, all good men must rally. We want all good and true men just now," &c. He spoke to all the wounded men that passed him, and the slightly wounded he exhorted "to bind up their hurts and take up a musket" in this emergency. Very few failed to answer his appeal, and I saw many badly wounded men take off their hats and cheer him. He said to me, "This has been a sad day for us, Colonel—a sad day; but we can't expect always to gain victories."

He was also kind enough to advise me to get into some more sheltered position, as the shells were bursting round us with considerable frequency.

Notwithstanding the misfortune which had so suddenly befallen him, General Lee seemed to observe everything, however trivial. When a mounted officer began licking his horse for shying at the bursting of a shell, he called out, "Don't whip him, Captain; don't whip him. I've got just such another foolish horse myself, and whipping does no good."

I happened to see a man lying flat on his face in a small ditch, and I remarked that I didn't think he seemed dead; this drew General Lee's attention to the man, who commenced groaning dismally. Finding appeals to his patriotism of no avail, General Lee had him ignominiously set on his legs by some neighbouring gunners.

I saw General Wilcox (an officer who wears a short round jacket and a battered straw hat) come up to him, and explain, almost crying, the state of his brigade. General Lee immediately shook hands with him and said, cheerfully, "Never mind, General, *all this has been* MY *fault*—it is *I* that have lost this fight, and you must help me out of it in the best way you can." In this manner I saw General Lee encourage and reanimate his somewhat dispirited troops, and magnanimously take upon his own shoulders the whole weight of the repulse. It was impossible to look at him or to listen to him without feeling the strongest admiration, and I never saw any man fail him except the man in the ditch.

Hancock's II Corps buckles under the tremendous assault by Major General George E. Pickett's division.

Veterans of Gettysburg. Seated is Major General Winfield Scott Hancock with (running clockwise) Brigadier Francis C. Barlow, commander in the XI Corps; Major General David Bell Birney, who led a division in Dan Sickles' III Corps; and Brigadier General John Gibbon of Hancock's II Corps. All four of these individuals fell wounded at the bloody field of Gettysburg.

It is difficult to exaggerate the critical state of affairs as they appeared about this time. If the enemy or their general had shown any enterprise, there is no saying what might have happened. General Lee and his officers were evidently fully impressed with a sense of the situation; yet there was much less noise, fuss, or confusion of orders than at an ordinary field-day: the men, as they were rallied in the wood, were brought up in detachments, and lay down quietly and coolly in the positions assigned to them.

We heard that Generals Garnett and Armistead were killed, and General Kemper mortally wounded; also, that Pickett's division had only one fieldofficer unhurt. Nearly all this slaughter took place in an open space about one mile square, and within one hour.

At 6 P.M. we heard a long and continuous Yankee cheer, which we at first imagined was an indication of an advance; but it turned out to be their reception of a general officer, whom we saw riding down the line, followed by about thirty horsemen. Soon afterwards I rode to the extreme front, where there were four pieces of rifled cannon almost without any infantry support. To the non-withdrawal of these guns is to be attributed the otherwise surprising inactivity of the enemy. I was immediately surrounded by a sergeant and about half-a-dozen gunners, who seemed in excellent spirits and full of confidence, in spite of their exposed situation. The sergeant expressed his ardent hope that the Yankees might have spirit enough to advance and receive the dose he had in readiness for them. They spoke in admiration of the advance of Pickett's division, and of the manner in which Pickett himself had led it. When they observed General Lee they said, "We've not lost confidence in the old man: this day's work won't do him no harm. 'Uncle Robert' will get us into Washington yet; you bet he will?" &c. Whilst we were talking, the enemy's skirmishers began to advance slowly, and several ominous sounds in quick succession told us that we were attracting their attention, and that it was necessary to break up the conclave. I therefore turned round and took leave of these cheery and plucky gunners.

At 7 P.M., General Lee received a report that Johnson's division of Ewell's corps had been successful on the left, and had gained important advantages there. Firing entirely ceased in our front about this time; but we now heard some brisk musketry on our right, which I afterwards learned proceeded from

Yankees of the 29th Pennsylvania prepare to go into battle on Culp's Hill on the third day of the battle.

Cemetery Ridge after Pickett's repulse

Brigadier General George H. Steurt's Brigade of Ewell's II Corps returns to the offensive on the morning of 3 July 1863.

Hood's Texans, who had managed to surround some enterprising Yankee cavalry, and were slaughtering them with great satisfaction. Only eighteen out of four hundred are said to have escaped.

At 7.30, all idea of a Yankee attack being over, I rode back to Moses's tent, and found that worthy commissary in very low spirits, all sorts of exaggerated rumours having reached him. On my way I met a great many wounded men, most anxious to inquire after Longstreet, who was reported killed; when I assured them he was quite well, they seemed to forget their own pain in the evident pleasure they felt in the safety of their chief. No words that I can use will adequately express the extraordinary patience and fortitude with which the wounded Confederates bore their sufferings.

I got something to eat with the doctors at 10 P.M., the first for fifteen hours.

I gave up my horse to-day to his owner, as from death and exhaustion the Staff are almost without horses.

═══════════ ★★★ ═══════════

JOHN D. IMBODEN
Retreat from Gettysburg

On the 87th anniversary of this nation's glorious birth, Robert E. Lee put his battered Army of Northern Virginia on the roads that led back to Virginia and safety. Guarding the wagon trains and ambulances during the retreat was Brigadier General John D. Imboden's cavalry command. A resourceful Virginian, Imboden rose from the ranks after winning a captains rank in the artillery. His reminiscences are take from Battles and Leaders of the Civil War.

During the Gettysburg campaign, my command—an independent brigade of cavalry—was engaged, by General Lee's confidential orders, in raids on the left flank of his advancing army, destroying railroad bridges and cutting the canal below Cumberland wherever I could—so that I did not reach the field till noon of the last day's battle. I reported direct to General Lee for orders, and was assigned a position to aid in repelling any cavalry demonstration on his rear. None of a serious character being made, my little force took no part in the battle, but were merely spectators of the scene, which transcended in grandeur any that I beheld in any other battle of the war.

When night closed the struggle, Lee's army was repulsed. We all knew that the day had gone against us, but the full extent of the disaster was only known in high quarters. The carnage of the day was generally understood to have been frightful, yet our army was not in retreat, and it was surmised in camp that with to-morrow's dawn would come a renewal of the struggle. All felt and appreciated the momentous consequences to the cause of Southern independence of final defeat or victory on that great field.

It was a warm summer's night; there were few camp-fires, and the weary soldiers were lying in groups on the luxuriant grass of the beautiful meadows, discussing the events of the day, speculating on the morrow, or watching that our horses did not straggle off while browsing. About 11 o'clock a horseman came to summon me to General Lee. I promptly mounted and, accompanied by Lieutenant George W. McPhail, an aide on my staff, and guided by the courier who brought the message, rode about two miles toward Gettysburg to where half a dozen small tents were pointed out, a little way from the roadside to our left, as General Lee's headquarters for the night. On inquiry I found that he was not there, but had gone to the headquarters of General A. P. Hill, about half a mile nearer to Gettysburg. When we reached the place indicated, a single flickering candle, visible from the road through the open front of a common wall-tent, exposed to view Generals Lee and Hill seated on camp-stools with a map spread upon their knees. Dismounting, I approached on foot. After exchanging the ordinary salutations General Lee directed me to go back to his headquarters and wait for him. I did so, but he did not make his appearance until about 1 o'clock, when he came riding alone, at a slow walk, and evidently wrapped in profound thought.

When he arrived there was not even a sentinel on duty at his tent, and no one of his staff was awake. The moon was high in the clear sky and the silent scene was unusually vivid. As he approached and saw us lying on the grass under a tree, he spoke, reined in his jaded horse, and essayed to dismount. The effort to do so betrayed so much physical exhaustion that I hurriedly rose and stepped forward to assist him, but before I reached his side he had succeeded in alighting, and threw his arm across the saddle to rest, and fixing his eyes upon the ground leaned in silence and almost motionless upon his equally weary horse,— the two forming a striking and never-to-be-forgotten group. The moon shone full upon his massive features and revealed an expression of sadness that I had never before seen upon his face. Awed by his appearance I waited for him to speak until the silence became

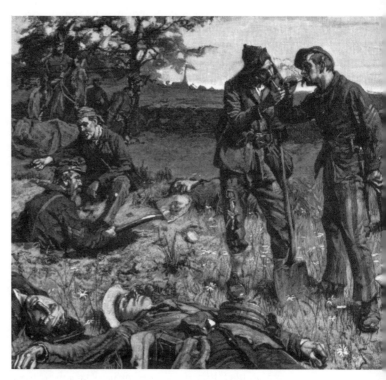

Yankee and Confederate troops inter a fallen comrade in the cold soil.

In their haste to retreat from the field of battle, the Confederates failed to bury most of their dead properly. This shallow grave was abandoned before the grave diggers had the time to spread any earth over the bodies.

embarrassing, when, to break it and change the silent current of his thoughts, I ventured to remark, in a sympathetic tone, and in allusion to his great fatigue:

"General, this has been a hard day on you."

He looked up, and replied mournfully:

"Yes, it has been a sad, sad day to us," and immediately relapsed into his thoughtful mood and attitude. Being unwilling again to intrude upon his reflections, I said no more. After perhaps a minute or two, he suddenly straightened up to his full height, and turning to me with more animation and excitement of manner than I had ever seen in him before, for he was a man of wonderful equanimity, he said in a voice tremulous with emotion:

"I never saw troops behave more magnificently than Pickett's division of Virginians did to-day in that grand charge upon the enemy. And if they had been supported as they were to have been,—but, for some reason not yet fully explained to me, were not,—we would have held the position and the day would have been ours." After a moment's pause he added in a loud voice, in a tone almost of agony, "Too bad! *Too bad!* Oh! Too bad!"

I shall never forget his language, his manner, and his appearance of mental suffering. In a few moments all emotion was suppressed, and he spoke feelingly of several of his fallen and trusted officers; among others of Brigadier-Generals Armistead, Garnett, and Kemper of Pickett's division. He invited me into his tent, and as soon as we were seated he remarked:

"We must now return to Virginia. As many of our poor wounded as possible must be taken home. I have sent for you, because your men and horses are fresh and in good condition, to guard and conduct our train back to Virginia. The duty will be arduous, responsible, and dangerous, for I am afraid you will be harassed by the enemy's cavalry. How many men have you?"

"About 2100 effective present, and all well mounted, including McClanahan's six-gun battery of horse artillery."

"I can spare you as much artillery as you require," he said, "but no other troops, as I shall need all I have to return safely by a different and shorter route than yours. The batteries are generally short of ammunition, but you will probably meet a supply I have ordered from Winchester to Williamsport. Nearly all the transportation and the care of all the wounded will be intrusted to you. You will recross the mountain by the Chambersburg road, and then proceed to Williamsport by any route you deem best, and without a halt till you reach the river. Rest there long enough to feed your animals; then ford the river, and do not halt again till you reach Winchester, where I will again communicate with you."

After a good deal of conversation about roads, and the best disposition of my forces to cover and protect the vast train, he directed that the chiefs of his staff departments should be waked up to receive, in my presence, his orders to collect as early next day as possible all the wagons and ambulances which I was to convoy, and have them in readiness for me to take command of them. His medical director [Dr. Lafayette Guild] was charged to see that all the wounded who could bear the rough journey should be placed in the empty wagons and ambulances. He then remarked to me that his general instructions would be sent to me in writing the following morning. As I was about leaving to return to my camp, as late, I think, as 2 A.M., he came out of his tent to where I was about to mount, and said in an undertone: "I will place in your hands by a staff-officer, to-morrow morning, a sealed package for President Davis, which you will retain in your possession till you are across the Potomac, when you will detail a reliable commissioned officer to take it to Richmond with all possible dispatch and deliver it into the President's own hands. And I impress it on you that, whatever happens, this package must not fall into the hands of the enemy. If unfortunately you should be captured, destroy it at the first opportunity."

On the morning of July 4th my written instructions, and a large official envelope addressed to President Davis, were handed to me by a staff-officer.

It was apparent by 9 o'clock that the wagons, ambulances, and wounded could not be collected and made ready to move till late in the afternoon. General Lee sent to me eight Napoleon guns of the famous Washington Artillery of New Orleans, under the immediate command of Major Eshleman, one of the best artillery officers in the army, a four-gun battery under Captain Tanner, and a Whitworth under Lieutenant Pegram. Hampton's cavalry brigade, then under command of Colonel P. M. B. Young, with Captain James F. Hart's four-gun battery of horse artillery, was ordered to cover the rear of all trains moving under my convoy on the Chambersburg road. These 17 guns and McClanahan's 6 guns gave us 23 pieces in all for the defense of the trains.

Alfred R. Waud, one of the most prolific sketch artists during the Civil War is captured in film drawing a picture of the Gettysburg battlefield.

Lee's escape route across the Potomac near Falling Waters, Virginia. With the Army of the Potomac badly mauled from the confrontation at Gettysburg, Meade opted to allow the Army of Northern Virginia to escape to the safety of the old Dominion rather than attempt to bring on another battle.

Murderous rabble put a orphanage for black children to the torch during the massive draft riot in New York in July of 1863. Resentment against the draft laws created unrest that exploded on 13 July into an orgy of violence, destruction and murder. Blacks were often singled out by mobs as scapegoats for the draft and the war. All told hundreds of citizens were killed and wounded while property damage amounted to hundreds of thousands of dollars.

Shortly after noon of the 4th the very windows of heaven seemed to have opened. The rain fell in blinding sheets; the meadows were soon overflowed, and fences gave way before the raging streams. During the storm, wagons, ambulances, and artillery carriages by hundreds—nay, by thousands, were assembling in the fields along the road from Gettysburg to Cashtown, in one confused and apparently inextricable mass. As the afternoon wore on there was no abatement in the storm. Canvas was no protection against its fury, and the wounded men lying upon the naked boards of the wagon-bodies were drenched. Horses and mules were blinded and maddened by the wind and water, and became almost unmanageable. The deafening roar of the mingled sounds of heaven and earth all around us made it almost impossible to communicate orders, and equally difficult to execute them.

About 4 P.M. the head of the column was put in motion near Cashtown, and began the ascent of the mountain in the direction of Chambersburg. I remained at Cashtown giving directions and putting in detachments of guns and troops at what I estimated to be intervals of a quarter or a third of a mile. It was found from the position of the head of the column west of the mountain at dawn of the 5th—the hour at which Young's cavalry and Hart's battery began the

Johnny Reb on the retreat.

Meade's army crossing the golden waters of the Potomac in a slow passive pursuit of Lee into Virginia.

ascent of the mountain near Cashtown—that the entire column was seventeen miles long when drawn out on the road and put in motion. As an advance-guard I had placed the 18th Virginia Cavalry, Colonel George W. Imboden, in front with a section of McClanahan's battery. Next to them, by request, was placed an ambulance carrying, stretched side by side, two of North Carolina's most distinguished soldiers, Generals Pender and Scales, both badly wounded, but resolved to bear the tortures of the journey rather than become prisoners. I shared a little bread and meat with them at noon, and they waited patiently for hours for the head of the column to move. The trip cost poor Pender his life. General Scales appeared to be worse hurt, but stopped at Winchester, recovered, and fought through the war.

After dark I set out from Cashtown to gain the head of the column during the night. My orders had been peremptory that there should be no halt for any cause whatever. If an accident should happen to any vehicle, it was immediately to be put out of the road and abandoned. The column moved rapidly, considering the rough roads and the darkness, and from almost every wagon for many miles issued heart-rending wails of agony. For four hours I hurried forward on my way to the front, and in all that time I was never out of hearing of the groans and cries of the wounded and dying. Scarcely one in a hundred had received adequate surgical aid, owing to the demands on the hard-working surgeons from still worse cases that had to be left behind. Many of the wounded in the wagons had been without food for thirty-six hours. Their torn and bloody clothing, matted and hardened, was rasping the tender, inflamed, and still oozing wounds. Very few of the wagons had even a layer of straw in them, and all were without springs. The road was rough and rocky from the heavy washings of the preceding day. The jolting was enough to have killed strong men, if long exposed to it. From nearly every wagon as the teams trotted on, urged by whip and shout, came such cries and shrieks as these:

"O God! why can't I die?"

"My God! will no one have mercy and kill me?"

"Stop! Oh! for God's sake, stop just for one minute; take me out and leave me to die on the roadside."

"I am dying! I am dying! My poor wife, my dear children, what will become of you?"

Some were simply moaning; some were praying,

A son of the South bids farewell to a wounded comrade.

and others uttering the most fearful oaths and execrations that despair and agony could wring from them; while a majority, with a stoicism sustained by sublime devotion to the cause they fought for, endured without complaint unspeakable tortures, and even spoke words of cheer and comfort to their unhappy comrades of less will or more acute nerves. Occasionally a wagon would be passed from which only low, deep moans could be heard. No help could be rendered to any of the sufferers. No heed could be given to any of their appeals. Mercy and duty to the many forbade the loss of a moment in the vain effort then and there to comply with the prayers of the few. On! On! we *must* move on. The storm continued, and the darkness was appalling. There was no time even to fill a canteen with water for a dying man; for, except the drivers and the guards, all were wounded and utterly helpless in that vast procession of misery. During this one night I realized more of the horrors of war than I had in all the two preceding years.

And yet in the darkness was our safety, for no enemy would dare attack where he could not distinguish friend from foe. We knew that when day broke upon us we should be harassed by bands of cavalry hanging on our flanks. Therefore our aim was to go as far as possible under cover of the night. Instead of going through Chambersburg, I decided to leave the main road near Fairfield after crossing the mountains, and take "a near cut" across the country to Greencastle, where daybreak on the morning of the 5th of July found the head of our column. We were now twelve or fifteen miles from the Potomac at Williamsport, our point of crossing into Virginia.

Here our apprehended troubles began. After the advance—the 18th Virginia Cavalry—had passed perhaps a mile beyond the town, the citizens to the

President Abraham Lincoln reads with his son Tad. Lincoln had much reason to be disappointed over the events in the East in 1863 with Hooker's defeat and Meade's failure to follow up the victory of his army at Gettysburg.

number of thirty or forty attacked the train with axes, cutting the spokes out of ten or a dozen wheels and dropping the wagons in the streets. The moment I heard of it I sent back a detachment of cavalry to capture every citizen who had been engaged in this work, and treat them as prisoners of war. This stopped the trouble there, but the Union cavalry began to swarm down upon us from the fields and cross-roads, making their attacks in small bodies, and striking the column where there were few or no guards, and thus creating great confusion. I had a narrow escape from capture by one of these parties—of perhaps fifty men that I tried to drive off with canister from two of McClanahan's guns that were close at hand. They would perhaps have been too much for me, had not Colonel Imboden, hearing the firing turned back with his regiment at a gallop, and by the suddenness of his movement surrounded and caught the entire party.

To add to our perplexities still further, a report reached me a little after sunrise, that the Federals in large force held Williamsport. I did not fully credit this, and decided to push on. Fortunately the report was untrue. After a great deal of desultory fighting and harassments along the road during the day, nearly the whole of the immense train reached Williamsport on the afternoon of the 5th. A part of it, with Hart's battery, came in next day, General Young having halted and turned his attention to guarding the road from the west with his cavalry. We took possession of the town to convert it into a great hospital for the thousands of wounded we had brought from Gettysburg. I required all the families in the place to go to cooking for the sick and wounded, on pain of having their kitchens occupied for that purpose by my men. They readily complied. A large number of surgeons had accompanied the train, and these at once pulled off their coats and went to work, and soon a vast amount of suffering was mitigated. The bodies of a few who had died on the march were buried. All this became necessary because the tremendous rains had raised the river more than ten feet above the fording stage of water, and we could not possibly cross them. There were two small ferry-boats or "flats" there, which I immediately put into requisition to carry across those of the wounded, who, after being fed and having their wounds dressed, thought they could walk to Winchester. Quite a large number were able to do this, so that the "flats" were kept running all the time.

A dejected group of soldiers in butternut captured during the desperate struggle at Gettysburg.

Our situation was frightful. We had probably ten thousand animals and nearly all the wagons of General Lee's army under our charge, and all the wounded, to the number of several thousand, that could be brought from Gettysburg. Our supply of provisions consisted of a few wagon-loads of flour in my own brigade train, a small lot of fine fat cattle which I had collected in Pennsylvania on my way to Gettysburg, and some sugar and coffee procured in the same way at Mercersburg.

The town of Williamsport is located in the lower angle formed by the Potomac with Conococheague Creek. These streams inclose the town on two sides, and back of it about one mile there is a low range of hills that is crossed by four roads converging at the town. The first is the Greencastle road leading down the creek valley; next the Hagerstown road; then the Boonsboro' road; and lastly the River road.

Early on the morning of the 6th I received intelligence of the approach from Frederick of a large body of cavalry with three full batteries of six rifled guns. These were the divisions of Generals Buford and Kilpatrick, and Huey's brigade of Gregg's division, consisting, as I afterward learned, of 23 regiments of cavalry, and 18 guns, a total force of about 7000 men.

"Four score and seven years ago...," Lincoln delivers his immortal address at Gettysburg.

Soldiers and civilians gather for the dedication of the National Cemetery at Gettysburg on 19 November 1863, several months after the battle had been fought and most of the dead had been interred.

I immediately posted my guns on the hills that concealed the town, and dismounted my own command to support them—and ordered as many of the wagoners to be formed as could be armed with the guns of the wounded that we had brought from Gettysburg. In this I was greatly aided by Colonel J. L. Black of South Carolina, Captain J. F. Hart commanding a battery from the same State, Colonel William R. Aylett of Virginia, and other wounded officers. By noon about 700 wagoners were organized into companies of 100 each and officered by wounded line-officers and commissaries and quartermasters,—about 250 of these were given to Colonel Aylett on the right next the river,—about as many under Colonel Black on the left, and the residue were used as skirmishers. My own command proper was held well in hand in the center.

The enemy appeared in our front about half-past one o'clock on both the Hagerstown and Boonsboro' roads, and the fight began. Every man under my command understood that if we did not repulse the enemy we should all be captured and General Lee's army be ruined by the loss of its transportation, which at that period could not have been replaced in the Confederacy. The fight began with artillery on both sides. The firing from our side was very rapid, and seemed to make the enemy hesitate about advancing. In a half hour J. D. Moore's battery ran out of ammunition, but as an ordnance train had arrived from Winchester, two wagon-loads of ammunition were ferried across the river and run upon the field behind the guns, and the boxes tumbled out, to be broken open with axes. With this fresh supply our guns were all soon in full play again. As the enemy could not see the supports of our batteries from the hill-tops, I moved the whole line forward to his full view, in single ranks, to show a long front on the Hagerstown approach. My line passed our guns fifty or one hundred yards, where they were halted awhile, and then were withdrawn behind the hill-top again, slowly and steadily.

Confederate prisoners from Gettysburg being taken to the Federal rear.

Leaving Black's wagoners and the Marylanders on the left to support Hart's and Moore's batteries, Captain Hart having been put in command by Colonel Black when he was obliged to be elsewhere, I moved the 18th Virginia Cavalry and 62d Virginia Mounted Infantry rapidly to the right, to meet and repel five advancing regiments (dismounted) of the enemy. My three regiments, with Captain John H. McNeill's Partisan Rangers and Aylett's wagoners, had to sustain a very severe contest. Hart, seeing how hard we were pressed on the right, charged the enemy's right with his little command, and at the same time Eshleman with his eight Napoleons advanced four hundred yards to the front, and got an enfilading position, from which, with the aid of McClanahan's battery, he poured a furious fire into the enemy's line. The 62d and Aylett, supported by the 18th Cavalry, and McNeill, charged the enemy who fell back sullenly to their horses.

Night was now rapidly approaching, when a messenger from Fitzhugh Lee arrived to urge me to "hold my own," as he would be up in a half hour with three thousand fresh men. The news was sent along our whole line, and was received with a wild and exultant yell. We knew then that the field was won, and slowly pressed forward. Almost at the same moment we heard distant guns on the enemy's rear and right on the Hagerstown road. They were Stuart's, who was approaching on that road, while Fitzhugh Lee was coming on the Greencastle road. That settled the contest. The enemy broke to the left and fled by the Boonsboro' road. It was too dark to follow. When General Fitzhugh Lee joined me with his staff on the field, one of parted from the general that morning. He had left with his staff to ride toward Hagerstown, where a heavy artillery fire indicated an attack by the enemy in considerable force. When I overtook him he said that he understood I was familiar with the fords of the Potomac from Williamsport to Cumberland, and with the roads to them. I replied that I was. He then called up one of his staff, either General Long or General Alexander, I think, and directed him to write down my answers to his questions, and required me to name and describe ford after ford all the way up to Cumberland, and to describe minutely their character, and the roads and surrounding country on both sides of the river, and directed me, after I had given him all the information I could, to send to him my brother and his regiment, the 18th Virginia Cavalry, to act as an advance and guide if he should require it. He did not say so, but I felt that his situation was precarious in the extreme. When about to dismiss me, referring to the freshet in the river he laughingly said: "You know this country well enough to tell me whether it ever quits raining about here? If so, I should like to see a clear day soon." I did not see him again till he left the Shenandoah Valley for the east side of the Blue Ridge.

Lee's Army of Northern Virginia on the retreat after their defeat on the soil of Pennsylvania.

★★★

SAMUEL LOVER

"The Girl I Left Behind"

A tearful song lamenting the pains of leaving a lover to face possible death on the fields of battle, "The Girl I Left Behind Me" enjoyed a great deal of popularity among Union troops. Yankee bands played the song as Hooker led the Army of the Potomac out of the encampment at Falmouth to move on Chancellorsville and the Iron Brigade went into the fight at Gettysburg to the same tune.

The hour was sad I left the maid, a lingering
    farewell taking,
Her sighs and tears my steps delay'd, I thought
    her heart was breaking;
In hurried words her name I bless'd, I breathed
    the vows that bind me,
And to my heart in anguish press'd the girl I left
    behind me.

Then to the East we bore away, to win a name
    in story,
And there where dawns the sun of day, there
    dawns our sun of glory;
Both blazed in noon on Alma's height, where in
    the post assign'd me,
I shar'd the glory of that fight, Sweet Girl I left
    Behind Me.

Love in a time of bloodshed, cruelty, and warfare; a soldier marries his beloved.

★ ★ ★

CHARLES C. SAWYER

"When this Cruel War Is Over"

One of the greatest "hits" of the Civil War was Charles Sawyer's "When This Cruel War Is Over." It eventually sold over a million copies. Soldiers on both sides played the tune and sang the word "gray" or "blue" depending on their allegiance. The lyrics were so sentimental that troops were often moved to tears.

Dearest love, do you remember,
When we last did meet,
How you told me that you loved me,
Kneeling at my feet?
Oh, how proud you stood before me,
In your suit of blue,
When you vowed to me and country
Ever to be true.

Chorus—
Weeping, sad and lonely,
Hopes and fears how vain!
Yet praying, when this cruel war is over,
Praying that we meet again!

Consecration ceremonies of the National Cemetery in honor of the thousands of men that had fought and died there.